REVISED EDITION

MARKET SEGMENTATION

■ Using
Demographics,
Psychographics
and
Other Niche
Marketing
Techniques
to Predict
and
Model
Customer
Behavior

ART WEINSTEIN

PROBUS PUBLISHING COMPANY
Chicago, Illinois
Cambridge, England

ISBN 1-55738-492-4

Printed in the United States of America

BB

1 2 3 4 5 6 7 8 9 0

With Love to Sandee, My Number One Fan

CONTENTS

v

vi

PART II. SEGMENTING MARKETS

PART III. SEGMENTATION STRATEGY AND CONTROL

PART IV. SEGMENTATION STRATEGY CASES

ix

PREFACE

This book was written to provide marketing/business practitioners and scholars (professors and students) with an informative, state-of-the-art guide to strategically segmenting markets. While top executives advocate being marketing-oriented and carving market niches, I have found that few companies use target marketing to its fullest potential. In spite of the many advances made in segmentation methodology and technology, a majority of firms base their marketing plans on cursory, incomplete, or intuitive analyses of their potential markets. However, used effectively, segmentation techniques are valuable for increasing sales and improving overall marketing performance.

Does your company suffer from the following marketing deficiencies: a "fuzzy" business mission, unclear objectives, information that is not decision-oriented, lack of agreement as to segmentation's role in the firm, a production-driven focus (products reflect corporate desires rather than customer needs), an unfocused promotional strategy, or failure to attack niche markets? If you answered "yes" to any of these questions, you're not alone. Cognizant of such problems faced by successful *Fortune* 500 companies as well as struggling start-ups, this book develops a systematic process for introducing and improving segmentation planning and execution in your firm. If you responded "no" to all of these queries, my hat's off to you. Keep up the great work! Perhaps you can maintain your competitive edge by adopting some of the ideas suggested in this book.

If you're a marketer, manager/executive, or entrepreneur, I am confident that you will find *Market Segmentation*, Revised Edition, to be a valuable resource to assist you in your business endeavors. It is also a thought-provoking reading and case book for advanced/graduate students who want to go beyond theory and learn how to make "real world" decisions in changing and competitive markets.

The book offers a balanced coverage of information relevant to consumer and business marketers. This edition also has an increased focus on international and high technology markets. Realizing your need for practical information, a theoretical and quantitative approach has been avoided. Instead, this book is a "how-to" guide to the effective use of market segmentation planning, techniques, and strategies.

Market Segmentation is built on the latest thinking from the business and academic communities. Much of the material appearing in this book has been discussed at length in the classroom and in executive seminars, or is based on important research in leading marketing publications. In addition to many useful exhibits, each chapter features a Segmentation Action List (a series of questions related to key topics) and a Segmentation Skillbuilder (exercises to help you improve your working knowledge of crucial segmentation topics). Many boxed items also offer tips and personal experiences that have worked for me.

Market Segmentation is organized into five major parts. Part 1, "Segmentation Planning," provides a blueprint for conducting effective, cost-efficient, and profitable segmentation studies. An overview of market segmentation, segmentation's role in the marketing plan, how to use primary, secondary, syndicated and single-source data, and the 10 critical elements of designing the segmentation analysis are discussed.

Part 2, "Segmenting Markets," details the major segmentation dimensions (geographics, demographics, psychographics, usage, benefits, and behavioral bases), highlights the procedures and mechanics of segmenting markets, offers insights from the 1990 Census (including the new TIGER system), provides expanded coverage of the latest lifestyle and cluster-based segmentation services such as VALS 2 and PRIZM, notes special considerations for the industrial and international marketer, and explains two important models for segmenting markets—the 8-S formula and the nested approach.

Part 3, "Segmentation Strategy and Control," discusses target market selection, positioning, nichemanship, strategy formulation, implementation and control, managerial guidelines for enhancing segmentation's value in your company, and a view of segmentation in the year 2000.

Part 4, "Segmentation Strategy Cases," presents five all-new, in-depth case studies demonstrating how segmentation strategy has been used successfully by a diverse group of organizations in highly competitive markets. End-of-case questions for analysis and suggestions for further reading are also included.

Part 5, "Segmentation Resources," serves as a "hands-on" reference for further segmentation information needs. These appendixes feature an updated directory of low-cost consumer and industrial demographics and secondary information, research firms specializing in providing segmentation services, and a list of 30 related books for your marketing library.

ACKNOWLEDGEMENTS

Many individuals provided important illustrative examples, insights, and ideas that helped shape the second edition of *Market Segmentation*. In alphabetical order, I would like to thank Domenica Barbuto, Thomas Bonoma, Lynn Brown, Eric Cohen, Doran Levy, Bruce MacEvoy, Gary Madison, Stephanie Major, Laurie Mahoney, Bill McDonald, Carol Morgan, Marvin Nesbit, Mike Reinemer, and Benson Shapiro.

Also, an expression of gratitude goes out to Art Boudin, Steve Morris, Ed Oswald, Jim Paris, Joan Perrell, and Lois Steinberg for assistance in the first edition of the book. A special mention of appreciation is extended to Marvin Nesbit and Bruce Seaton for their advice and helpful comments on the ground-breaking edition.

Last, but not least, I want to thank J. Michael Jeffers, Marlene Chamberlain, and Probus Publishing; and my business clients, seminar participants, colleagues, and students for making this exhilarating book possible. And of course, I especially thank you for reading it!

—Art Weinstein

PART ONE

PLANNING

1 MARKET SEGMENTATION: AN OVERVIEW

He who pays the piper can call the tune.
—John Ray, 1670

The 1990s have been called the "era of super-segmentation or micromarketing."[1] Consumer and business markets are rapidly changing and increasingly competitive. Having top-quality goods and services is no longer sufficient. Companies must satisfy discriminating customers who can choose from a multitude of product offerings in a global marketplace. Mass marketing is now a distant memory; today's marketers must attack niche markets that exhibit unique needs and wants. STP (segmentation, targeting, and positioning) marketing has replaced LGD (lunch, golf, and dinner) marketing as the primary strategy for surviving and thriving in volatile business environments.[2]

Micromarketing means *knowing your customers*, giving them what they want, targeted promotion (such as using special interest magazines or event sponsorship), and building strong channel relationships. Warner-Lambert (the producer of Listerine, Trident, and Schick) has experimented with everything from direct mail to cable TV to advertising on blood pressure monitors in pharmacies.[3] *Farm Journal* has more than 1 million readers whose interests vary widely by acreage, crop, and geography; it publishes more than 1,000 different versions of each issue![4]

Increased specialization does not necessarily require an extreme degree of market fragmentation. Technological innovation and diversification are highly desirable. As an example, the video rental giant, Blockbuster Entertainment, recently began an aggressive corporate expansion program featuring music retailing ventures and the test marketing of family entertainment centers (mini-amusement parks) and a movie and music on demand service.[5]

SEGMENTATION: THE KEY TO MARKETING SUCCESS

A marketing orientation is based on a customer-driven focus. During the past decade marketers have seen the renaissance of market segmentation. First recognized by the late Wendell R. Smith in the mid-1950s, segmentation has evolved from an academic concept into a viable, "real-world" planning strategy.[6] Everyone has jumped on the segmentation/target marketing bandwagon, from large multinational companies to mom-and-pop small businesses. Marketing newcomers such as healthcare organizations (hospitals, physicians, health maintenance organizations, and so forth), professional service firms (accounting, legal, and computer consultants), and nonprofit organizations (universities, museums, and associations) have embraced the benefits of building marketing muscle.

Consider the tiny Dutch retailer called de Witte Tanden Winkel (the White Tooth Shop). This Amsterdam neighborhood merchant found its niche by selling only toothbrushes, floss, and related products. Viewing the other end of the spectrum, segmenters are also some of the world's largest companies. Coca-Cola has been the market leader in the turbulent soft drink industry for more than a century by developing a product line appealing to varied consumer tastes. Using a "multilocal" system involving rapid adaptation to foreign markets, this quintessential American company now earns 80% of its profits from outside of the United States.[7]

The Segmentation Imperative

Segmentation is the process of partitioning markets into groups of potential customers with similar needs and/or characteristics who are likely to exhibit similar purchase behavior. It has emerged as a key marketing planning tool and the foundation for effective strategy formulation in many U.S. and international companies. The objective of segmentation research is to analyze markets, find niche opportunities, and capitalize on a superior competitive position. This can be accomplished by selecting one or more groups of users as targets for marketing activity and developing unique marketing programs to reach these prime prospects (market segments).

From a practical perspective, segmentation efforts must be managed to be effective. It is impossible to pursue every market opportunity so you must make strategic choices:

1. *Recognize that everyone is not a prospect for every good or service offered.* As evidenced by the great successes of computer industry challengers such as Apple, Compaq, Dell, and others, everybody does not own or want to own an IBM PC. Excluding President Bill Clinton, of course, many people choose not to patronize McDonald's restaurants.

2. *Control your firm's product mix for maximum efficiency.* Recently, business costs have escalated in all areas (personnel, technology, equipment, materials, and insurance). Ideally, production runs should reflect customers' needs and wants for optimal use of resources. Hence, the marketing challenge is to efficiently match your products to customers' desires and stay one step ahead of your competitors.

Segmentation in Action

Marketing professionals recognize that segmentation is both a science and an art. You can learn about market segmentation analysis through the guidelines and techniques discussed in this book and other valuable references (see Appendix C: Your Segmentation Bookshelf and the chapter notes). Also, segmentation is a marketing discipline that can be acquired and enhanced through experience, training (such as executive seminars), observation, and strategic thinking.

There are many alternative methods for segmenting markets. Many of these approaches are derived from the consumer behavior field. Consumer decision making is impacted by rational and emotional factors (demographics, psychographics, motivations/needs, perceptions, purchasing habits, and so forth). Assume that a major oil company wants to segment its market. A geographic sales analysis of its dealers is a logical starting point. Consumer demographic and socioeconomic measures (age, sex, income, and so forth) could be studied. Product consumption levels (types of unleaded or diesel grade gasoline) can be evaluated. Additionally, credit card usage, brand loyalty/switching patterns, and price sensitivity issues may be insightful for segmenting this market. As you can see, the options are many; therefore, further research is necessary to determine the best approach(es). The following mini-examples illustrate five common segmentation dimensions in action:

- *Geographic.* A medical instrumentation firm can obtain data from American Hospital Association directories to target hospitals by region and number of beds. This approach can be valuable for defining markets for a new blood gas analyzer.

- *Socioeconomic.* Department stores evaluate consumer income levels and social class. It is no secret that the Nordstrom customer differs from the Wal-Mart shopper, socioeconomically.

- *Psychographic.* Progressive banks attempt to differentiate their services by appealing to customers' needs, personality traits, and lifestyles. Financial institutions have developed credit cards related to consumer activities and interests (favorite sports team, college alma mater, civic organization memberships, and so on).

- *Product Usage.* Markets can be segmented according to consumption levels of various user groups (heavy, medium, light, or nonusers). For example, Hertz and American Airlines are key accounts for GTE's Mobile Communications and Airfone business units, respectively.[8]

- *Benefits.* What factors does a firm weigh in selecting an office copying machine? Are they price, service, special features (enlargement or reduction capabilities, color availability, high volume, speed), and/or reputation of the seller (Xerox or brand X)? A benefit to one customer (enhanced features) may be a drawback to another (higher price).

SEGMENTATION OPTIONS

A company has two basic strategic choices: to segment the market or to treat the entire market as potential customers for its goods or services. This latter option means that the firm uses an undifferentiated marketing strategy. Few (if any) companies can benefit from this approach. One can argue that utilities can employ this strategy, because you must have their service in an essentially monopolistic environment. But even that's not true anymore. In today's free market, you do not have to use the electricity provided by your local power company (some people opt to use solar panels, windmills, and other environmentally friendly energy sources). In the once uncontested telecommunications industry, AT&T and the Baby Bells now face formidable competition from MCI and Sprint.

Despite the fact that undifferentiation is for virtually no one, many companies still treat their marketing as if everyone is a likely customer, rather than targeting those who are the *most likely* prospects for their products. Recognizing the great diversity in the marketplace, it is clearly desirable to segment markets to improve marketing performance. Thus, segmentation is the development of differentiated marketing strategies for the different needs of the marketplace. Segmentation options include differentiation, ✳ concentration, and atomization.

Differentiation

If a firm identifies and actively markets its products or services to two or more segments of the market based on varied customer needs, a differentiation strategy is being used. The computer retailer that separately targets the home user, business professional, and small business is employing a differentiation approach to marketing PCs, peripherals, software, and supplies.

Mark the distinction between market and product differentiation. *Market differentiation* (a segmentation strategy) is customer-oriented and depends on market demand; *product differentiation* (which is not a segmentation strategy) is supply-side-oriented. Product differentiation is desirable for commodity-type products such as bars of soap. Because brands of soap are viewed by consumers as basically the same and the product is used for a single purpose (cleanliness), creating product variations is important. Product differences such as branding, size, color, scent, and packaging assist the marketer in distinguishing the product from the competition. Hence, based on primarily physical characteristics, alternatives within a designated product class are not perceived equally.[9]

On the other hand, market differentiation is a much broader functional area. It includes product differences, as well as unique promotional, price, and distribution strategies earmarked for specific market segments. For example, the Snapple Natural Beverage Company has successfully carved its niche in the highly competitive soft drink market by offering good tasting, healthy products with no artificial flavors, colors, or ingredients (the Snapple product line is illustrated in Exhibit 1-1). Segmentation Skillbuilder 1 examines segmentation and product differentiation for the soft drink industry.

EXHIBIT 1-1: THE SNAPPLE PRODUCT LINE

The Average Tongue has 10,000 Taste Buds. We Didn't Want to Take Any Chances

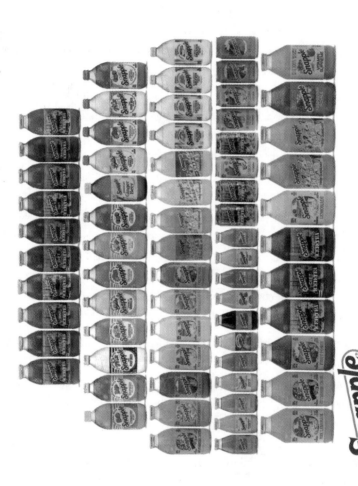

Snapple

52 All-Natural Iced Teas, Sodas, Drinks and Juices to suit everyone's taste.

Natural Beverages. Made from the best stuff on earth.™

A major advertising theme by Coca-Cola in the not too distant past stressed that "Coke Is It." Under the visionary leadership of Roberto C. Goizueta, the company introduced several highly successful new products and aggressively attacked niche markets in the 1980s. This product proliferation strategy meant that Coke was no longer *it*, but rather *them*.

As an example, Diet Coke filled a void in the market for a quality adult diet cola for men as well as women (Tab was targeted to loyal female consumers who were weight conscious). Diet Coke's internationally known name, superior taste, and big-budget promotional campaigns catapulted the product to a position of prominence within two years of its introduction. Other successful spin-offs such as Cherry Coke and the Classic Coke/New Coke products (and controversy) created crowded supermarket shelves and provided new profit centers for the Atlanta-based company.

The 1990s presents new challenges: global expansion and threats from natural beverages (such as Snapple), bottled water producers, and Pepsi's clear colas (Crystal Pepsi and Diet Crystal Pepsi).

7

1. Critique Coca-Cola's segmentation strategy in the 1980s.

    a. Assess the Diet Coke and Cherry Coke product introductions.

    b. Was introducing New Coke a sound strategic move?

    c. How about bringing back the original product as Coke Classic?

2. Segmentation and product differentiation are both important in the soft drink industry.

    a. What are some methods used to differentiate such products?

    b. How are segmentation and differentiation similar/different?

    c. What are the implications of product proliferation?

3. How should Coca-Cola compete in the 1990s?

Suggested Reading: Oliver, Thomas. *The Real Coke, The Real Story.* (New York: Penguin Books, 1986).

Concentration

A *concentration strategy* means that the firm decides to serve one of several potential segments of the market. Under a concentration segmentation approach, a computer dealer may direct its products and services to small businesses only, ignoring potential opportunities in the home user or business professional segments. Concentrated marketing is less expensive than differentiated marketing and is the appropriate choice for a new business with limited resources or a firm diversifying in a market outside of its core business.

Atomization

The least used segmentation option, *atomization*, breaks down the market to the finest detail—the individual customer level. This strategy might be appropriate for manufacturers of high-priced and specialized equipment (such as multimillion dollar supercomputers or luxury sports cars).

Other applications for an atomization strategy may include designing a marketing program for government markets (remember $600 toilet seats?) or selling real estate to Palm Beach socialites. A customized marketing program to your few, but key, prospects would be designed in these instances.

THE BENEFITS OF SEGMENTATION

The overall objective of using a market segmentation strategy is to improve your company's competitive position and better serve the needs of your customers. Some specific objectives may include increased sales (in units and dollars), improved market share, and enhanced image/reputation. It's not impossible to accomplish these goals using mass marketing tactics, but by focusing on areas that your firm can best serve, it is more likely to prosper. An undifferentiated strategy is the shotgun approach to marketing, whereas segmentation is the high-powered rifle.

There are four major benefits of market segmentation analysis and strategy:

- *Designing responsive products to meet the needs of the marketplace.* Through researching customer preferences—an essential component of segmentation analysis—the company moves toward accomplishing the marketing concept (customer satisfaction at a profit). The firm places the customer first and designs and refines its product/service mix to satisfy the needs of the market.

- *Determining effective and cost efficient promotional strategies.* As a planning tool, segmentation identification and analysis is extremely valuable in developing the firm's communications mix. Appropriate advertising campaigns can be designed and targeted to the right media vehicles. This marketing investment can be supplemented by public relations initiatives and sales promotion methods. In addition to mass promotional thrusts, the personal sales process can be greatly improved by providing sales representatives with background customer research, recommended sales appeals, and ongoing support.

- *Evaluating market competition, in particular the company's market position.* The 1990s are characterized by intense domestic and global competition. A segmentation study explores the firm's market position— how the company is perceived by its customers and potential customers relative to the competition. Segmentation research provides a competitive intelligence mechanism to assess how well your company compares to industry standards. Additionally, this analysis is useful for detecting trends in changing and volatile markets.

- *Providing insight on present marketing strategies.* It is important to periodically reevaluate your present marketing strategies to try to capitalize on new opportunities and circumvent potential threats. Market segmentation research is useful in exploring new markets (such as secondary smaller or fringe markets). Furthermore, effective segmentation provides a systematic approach for controlled market coverage, as opposed to the hit-or-miss effectiveness of mass marketing efforts.

In summary, segmentation analysis provides that necessary research base on which all other marketing strategies can be successfully formulated and implemented. Is your company using market segmentation techniques effectively? Segmentation Action List 1 identifies 15 key issues to explore further to help you answer this question.

Segmentation Action List 1:
How Well Is Your Company Using Segmentation Techniques?

1. Does your company segment the market? If not, why not?

2. What strategy is used—differentiation, concentration, or atomization?

3. What segment(s) of the market are you trying to serve?

4. How successful are you at meeting this objective?

5. What is your typical customer profile?

6. Are target market definitions based on research?

7. What dimensions (methods) are used to segment markets?

8. When was your last segmentation analysis conducted?

9. How frequently are updates obtained?

10. What is your budget for segmentation analysis?

11. Are product decisions based on segmentation research?

12. Are promotional decisions based on segmentation research?

13. Are pricing and distribution decisions based on segmentation?

14. Is segmentation analysis used in assessing competition, trends, and changes in the marketplace?

15. Is segmentation analysis used to evaluate your present marketing efforts (such as markets to pursue)?

LIMITATIONS OF SEGMENTATION

The picture isn't totally rosy however, and the marketer must be cognizant of the following potential shortcomings of segmentation analysis:

- *Increased costs.* A segmentation-based strategy generally costs more than does a mass marketing approach. For example, differentiation implies two or more promotional campaigns, possible new product offerings, channel development/expansion, and additional resources for implementation and control. On the plus side, target marketing means limited waste (advertising reaches prospects, not suspects) and increased marketing performance.

- *Requires a major corporate commitment.* Segmentation analysis is limited by management's ability to *implement* strategies based on the research. A marketing orientation requires a strong commitment by the firm—support in personnel, resources to hire marketing consultants, time investment of management, and the willingness to follow the prescribed recommendations. This transition from mass marketing may take months. Segmentation research is not a remedy for other marketing or organizational deficiencies. The best segmentation information is worthless unless it is supported by consistent product, promotional, pricing, and distribution strategies that are regularly evaluated and revised as situations dictate. Market segmentation strategies are not a panacea for other potential organizational shortcomings (managerial, financial, and research and development).

- *Provides composite, not individual, profiles.* Although segmentation research provides meaningful marketing information, it explains expected segment-wide (not individual) purchasing behavior. Whereas customers may appear to be similar based on demographic, psychographic, and/or usage profiles, marketers must still appeal to specific buyers through personal selling initiatives.

  As an example, two men may both be 40 years old, college educated, and earn $50,000 annually. By using demographic analysis only, the marketer may erroneously stereotype these consumers as similar prospects. In reality, they may have different interests, attitudes, and perspectives on life. Psychographic research can assist the marketer by presenting a more complete picture of a market situation.

In addition, the great diversity of consumer lifestyles in the 1990s has made segmentation more difficult (but more necessary) in many markets. In the past, a "typical" American family consisted of a husband, stay-at-home wife, two children, and a dog. Segmenting markets given this scenario was

11

relatively easy. This is not true anymore because of the rise of women in the labor force, increases in single-person and nontraditional households, the explosive growth of minority markets, and changing lifestyles (convenience-seeking, health and fitness consciousness, environmental awareness, and so on). These changes have created a plethora of opportunities and problems for marketers.

SEGMENTATION: SOME MISUNDERSTANDINGS RESOLVED

There are three major misconceptions about market segmentation held by many business professionals. This brief section explores and clarifies these issues.

Myth 1: Market Segmentation Is a Partitioning Process

The overall effect of segmentation is to divide markets into two or more manageable submarkets. However, in reality, segmentation is a gathering process, because potential customers are assembled by commonalities in specific characteristics to form segments.

Myth 2: Segmentation Is Only a Process or Technique

Although segmentation is research-based, its real impact comes from its role as a strategic marketing variable. Market segmentation is the primary strategic element in a company's marketing plan. It is the foundation on which all other marketing actions can be based.

Myth 3: Everyone Is Part of a Market Segment

Although an assumption that everyone fits some subgroup might be an ideal for the marketer, all customers do not fit neatly into a market segment. It is likely that a small percentage of the population will be unclassifiable based on the specified segment formation criteria. This aberrant "other" group has one or more inconsistencies in key segmentation decision characteristics; hence, they are not good prospects for concentrated marketing activity.

One cautionary note: The "other" group should be limited in size (less than 10% of the market). One study yielded an "other" category of 40%; this segment was larger than the three identified segments! Such categorization was inadequate and indicated that further subsegmentation was necessary.

INTEGRATING MARKET SEGMENTATION INTO YOUR ORGANIZATION

A successful customer-based marketing program can be initiated using a four-stage process: 1) plan the segmentation analysis (Chapters 2 through 4), 2) conduct the study (Chapters 5 through 11), 3) develop a segmentation-based strategy (Chapter 12 and case studies), and 4) assess marketing performance and revise as necessary (Chapter 13). A framework for introducing/improving market segmentation in your organization is presented in Exhibit 1-2.

EXHIBIT 1-2: A SEGMENTATION FRAMEWORK

Segmentation Planning

1. Commit to segmentation-based marketing strategy.
2. Incorporate segmentation into the marketing plan.
3. Use segmentation planning guidelines.
4. Use segmentation research guidelines.

+ Segmenting Markets

5. Define the market geographically.
6. Use consumer demographics, as applicable.
7. Use consumer psychographics, as applicable.
8. Apply benefits, product usage, and behavioral bases.
9. Use business segmentation dimensions, as applicable.
10. Add international segmentation bases, as applicable.
11. Conduct the study: use segmentation models.

+ Segmentation Strategy

12. Develop a segmentation-based marketing strategy.
13. Monitor segmentation results: note managerial tips.

= SEGMENTATION RESULTS!!!

Improved business performance (market share, image, profits)

SUMMARY

To compete successfully in the volatile and challenging global markets of the 1990s, companies (large and small) can use segmentation techniques and strategies to find their niche and competitive advantage. Three market selection options are differentiation, concentration, and atomization. Market differentiation means that the firm designs two or more marketing strategies to serve designated segments based on differing customer characteristics and needs. Concentrated marketers recognize the diversity of the marketplace but choose to attack a single target market opportunity (this is generally cost efficient and enables management to focus on what they do best). An atomization approach develops custom marketing programs for each key prospect (this strategy is costly and used appropriately only for high-cost products or services).

Segmentation-driven marketing strategy helps companies design responsive products, develop effective promotional tactics and campaigns, gauge competitive positions, and fine-tune current marketing initiatives. Despite numerous benefits, marketers must also recognize that segmentation strategy is generally more costly than mass marketing and necessitates a major commitment by management to customer-oriented planning, research, implementation, and control.

NOTES

1. Aimee L. Stern, "In Search of Micro Niches," *Business Month,* July 1989, pp. 19-20.

2. Philip Kotler, *Marketing Management: Analysis, Planning, Implementation, and Control,* Seventh Edition (Englewood Cliffs, N.J.: Prentice Hall, 1991), p. 262.

3. Zachary Schiller, "Stalking the New Consumer," *Business Week,* August 28, 1989, pp. 54-62.

4. David Jacobson, "Magazines Being Customized to Individual Readers," *Miami Herald,* January 7, 1990, p. 2F.

5. Steve Halpern, "Blockbuster Explores New Paths to Growth," *Miami Herald Business Monday,* November 23, 1992, p. 32.

6. Wendell R. Smith, "Product Differentiation and Market Segmentation as Alternative Marketing Strategies," *Journal of Marketing,* July 1956, pp. 3-8.

7. Roger Cohen, "For Coke, World Is Its Oyster," *New York Times,* November 21, 1991, pp. D1, D5.

8. *GTE Annual Report,* (Stamford, Conn.: GTE Corporation, 1991), pp. 21, 23.

✳ 9. Peter R. Dickson, and James L. Ginter, "Market Segmentation, Product Differentiation, and Marketing Strategy," *Journal of Marketing,* April 1987, pp. 1-10.

10. Art Weinstein, "Market Selection in Technology-Based Industry: Insights from Executives." In Rajan Varadarajan and Bernard Jaworski (eds.), *American Marketing Association Winter Educators' Conference Proceedings,* Newport Beach, Calif., February 20-23, 1993, pp. 1-2.

Segmentation's Role in the Marketing Plan

The development of an annual marketing plan is one of those things like going to the dentist—everyone knows that it should be done on a regular basis, but somehow it just keeps getting put off.

—Michael MacInnis and Louise A. Heslop, 1990

For segmentation strategy to work effectively, it must be an integrated part of a company's marketing plan. The marketing plan is a systematic approach to coordinating all marketing activities—a blueprint for action. This custom document, developed specifically for a particular firm's needs, should be part of an overall business plan and long-range strategy. A well-developed marketing plan is a dynamic tool capable of anticipating change and reflecting the future.

The marketing plan should be prepared for a specified time frame. Typically, the working or operational marketing plan is developed annually, with frequent periodic updates and revisions as circumstances dictate. For example, if a major competitor enters or leaves the market, industry regulations change, or a new product or technology comes on the scene, the marketing plan should be modified to reflect the latest situation. Often a master (longer-term) marketing plan will also be advisable for a business.

Exhibit 2-1 illustrates one of General Electric's marketing plans. This company uses a variety of different plans for various divisions. As you will note from the detail in this diagram, marketing planning is taken seriously at G.E. Recently, the company's annual report stated that G.E. was in the business of "creating businesses." Your firm can also benefit greatly by carefully planning all marketing activities.

EXHIBIT 2-1: A GENERAL ELECTRIC MARKETING PLAN

18

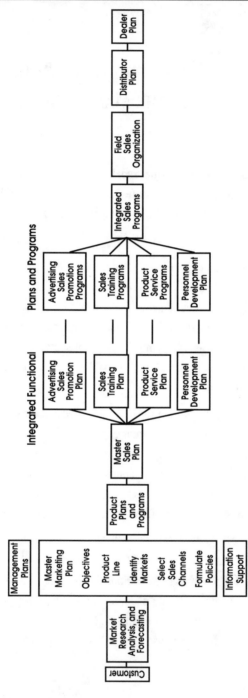

BENEFITS OF A MARKETING PLAN

According to the Bank of America, California, failing to plan and inattention to marketing are two of the four major business pitfalls (the others are insufficient leadership and unsound financial management). The formal, written marketing plan helps alleviate this potential lack of a marketing planning focus. The advantages to your firm in having a marketing plan are these:

- It helps to produce desired results by giving your business direction and organization.

- It is an excellent planning and control tool. Results can easily be compared to your forecast.

- A marketing plan is a useful management aid. A wealth of marketing information is at your fingertips.

ELEMENTS OF THE MARKETING PLAN

Proper segmentation requires sound marketing planning. The marketing plan is that framework on which effective marketing decisions can be built. The five required components of a good marketing plan are depicted in Exhibit 2-2. Take a moment to explore these major elements of the marketing plan.

EXHIBIT 2-2: THE FIVE STEPS TO SUCCESSFUL MARKETING PLANNING

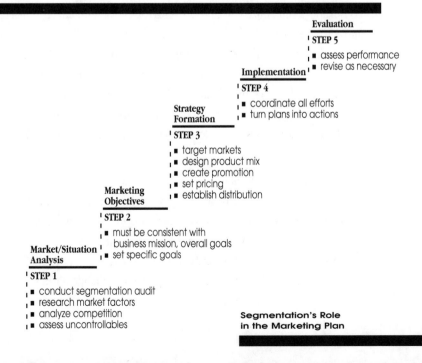

Evaluation
STEP 5
- assess performance
- revise as necessary

Implementation
STEP 4
- coordinate all efforts
- turn plans into actions

Strategy Formation
STEP 3
- target markets
- design product mix
- create promotion
- set pricing
- establish distribution

Marketing Objectives
STEP 2
- must be consistent with business mission, overall goals
- set specific goals

Market/Situation Analysis
STEP 1
- conduct segmentation audit
- research market factors
- analyze competition
- assess uncontrollables

Segmentation's Role in the Marketing Plan

Step 1: Market and Situation Analysis

Fact finding is the purpose of the *market and situation analysis*, which is also commonly called environmental analysis. A company has two environments to research—its own (the internal environment), and the industry in which it competes (the external environment). The marketing background is the most difficult section of the marketing plan to prepare. To do it right, expect to invest 50 to 100 hours (or more) in compiling this necessary fact base.[1]

The Segmentation Audit. Every firm should periodically place itself under the microscope. One of the best ways of assessing your current marketing situation is to conduct a marketing audit. This is not an easy task, however. As Hal W. Goetsch, former director of marketing for the American Marketing Association points out, marketing audits can present problems for a company when it attempts to administer them internally. He states,

> Even when a conscientious effort is made to see the situation objectively, the focus can be blurred by tradition, unquestioned procedures, personalities, manipulated programs, corporate politics, indifference, or laziness. Too often the picture is faulty because facts are missing, guesses are not reliable, or important elements of the marketing environment have been ignored or overlooked.[2]

To resolve this problem, the audit can be administered by outside marketing consultants to minimize bias and maximize objectivity. An effective marketing audit will gather information about your current marketing efforts, but more importantly, analyze the marketing health of your firm (similar to the ways a medical checkup assesses one's physical well being). Strengths and weaknesses of the company are readily identified; the aim is to capitalize on the former while rectifying the latter. Goetsch's overall marketing audit questions for a business provide a good starting point for undertaking such an analysis.

The audit must be modified, however, to meet the information-gathering needs of a particular firm or industry. For example, an adapted audit consisting of 31 key segmentation issues in 6 marketing functional areas is presented in Segmentation Action List 2. This instrument was personally administered to several marketing executives at Intel's OEM Systems Division. The output of this planning and diagnostic tool was the identification of some significant marketing problems/issues, proposed solutions, and ideas for pursuing viable niche opportunities.

Segmentation Action List 2: The Segmentation Audit*

I. Sales History

1. How do sales break down within the product line?
2. Do you know where sales are coming from—segments and customer classification?
3. Which products/markets/segments are not meeting potential? Why?

II. Marketing Commitment

1. Is formal marketing planning ingrained with all marketing management?
2. Do you implement a marketing plan, set objectives, measure performance, and adjust for deviation?
3. Is the marketing plan largely based on segmentation findings?

III. Marketing Environment

1. What major developments and trends pose opportunities or threats to the company?
2. What actions have been taken in response to these developments and trends?
3. What major changes are occurring in technology? What is the company's position in these technologies?
4. What are the competitor's positions in the market (strengths and weaknesses, strategies, and so on)?
5. What is happening to market size, growth rates, profits, and related market considerations?

IV. Market Segments

1. In your view, what are the major market segments?
2. How do different customer segments make their buying decisions?
3. Who are potential customers for your product?
4. Are segments identified, measured, and monitored?
5. Are any small but profitable segments overlooked?
6. How do you presently segment the market?

7. Is the present segmentation approach effective?
8. Have you developed detailed customer profiles for major market segments?
9. Should the company contract or withdraw from any business segment? What would be the short- and long-run consequences of this decision?
10. Are market segment definitions based on research?

V. Product

1. What are product line objectives?
2. Is the company well-organized to gather, generate, and screen new product ideas?
3. Does the company carry out adequate product and market research before launching new products?
4. Is there a well-defined program to weed out unprofitable products and add new ones?
5. Is there a systematic liaison with R&D, and other key departments in the company?

*Adapted based on ideas from Hal W. Goetsch, "Conduct a Comprehensive Marketing Audit to Improve Marketing Planning," *Marketing News*, March 18, 1983, Section 2, p. 14; and from Philip Kotler, *Marketing Management: Analysis, Planning, Implementation, and Control*, Seventh Edition (Englewood Cliffs, N.J.: Prentice-Hall, 1991), pp. 726-728.

What types of organizations can benefit most from a marketing/segmentation audit? Although this planning review should be periodically conducted for all firms, it is particularly helpful for production and technically oriented companies, troubled divisions, high performing business units, young companies, and nonprofit organizations.[3]

The External Environment. This is actually a compilation of several subenvironments: market factors, the competitive situation, and other marketing uncontrollables. Market factors include such considerations as identification and description of consumer needs and wants, research on market size/potential, possible business affiliates, and so forth. A competitive analysis is required to determine direct and indirect competition, as well as to develop sound counterpositioning strategies. Marketing uncontrollables complete the market analysis by examining such areas as the economic environment, regulatory rulings/agencies, technological forces, media impact, and social and lifestyle considerations. The result of a comprehensive environmental analysis will be a concise profile for a given market situation.

The Environmental Scorecard, a blank copy of which is given for your use in Exhibit 2-3, can serve as a comparative measure of strength or weakness for major internal and external marketing factors. An expert industry analyst provides further insights on the preparation of a good market profile in Exhibit 2-4.

EXHIBIT 2-3: THE ENVIRONMENTAL SCORECARD

Rate the following items as a Strength (+), Weakness (—), or Neutral factor (0)

Internal Situation	External Situation
Resources:	*The industry:*
People	Size of the market
Financial	Industry structure
Facilities	Homogeneity of market
Equipment	Market potential
Computers	Growth trends
Other (list)	Opportunities/problems
Past performance:	*Competition:*
Company	Number of competitors
Division	Strength of competitors
SBU	
Product line	*Environmental factors:*
Product	Economic conditions
Constraints:	Technology
Objectives	Political environment
Commitment	Legal environment
Policies (list)	
Present marketing mix:	
Product	
Promotion	
Pricing	
Distribution	

EXHIBIT 2-4: COMPILING A MARKET/INDUSTRY OVERVIEW*

The problem: produce an "overview" of an industry, market, or service sector—something that can be compiled and comprehended quickly, yet covers all the essential aspects of the subject; something that can stand on its own and serve as the framework for further, more focused research. A researcher with good knowledge of secondary sources can plunge right in and start collecting information; no special preparation is necessary. However, without a model or outline as a guide, it will be difficult to decide whether or not certain details ought to be included, and to be certain that there are no significant gaps. The task is not impracticable, but a haphazard methodology makes the research comparatively less rapid and less efficient.

Most overviews are put together in this fashion, without an underlying structure to focus and guide the research. While such a method is adequate, it leaves too much to chance. Moreover, when the same researcher is asked to provide similar information for a completely different market or industry, he or she will have to return to square one, "reinventing the wheel" each time an overview is required. But there is a better way.

In learning to meet the demands of our clients, we have derived an outline for conducting overviews. It may seem disarmingly simple but, as in most problem-solving tasks, simplicity is a virtue. While the same results might be obtained using a less-directed, more random approach, more time would be required and thoroughness could not be guaranteed. Furthermore, if you ever found yourself in a position of having to complete five very different overviews in the same day, you would be grateful for such an outline. Without it, your task would be nearly impossible; with it, you could succeed and, perhaps more importantly, be certain that your results were thorough and useful.

The first step is to determine the size of the market. Ideally, market size will be represented both in dollars and units, but finding one or the other will suffice for a quick overview. Next, identify the "major players," the top three or four companies (manufacturers, suppliers, etc.) in the industry. And as a complement—frequently this is difficult, but nonetheless essential—determine the leading companies' market share. (Knowing that Campbell's is the leader in the soup category takes on a different cast when you realize its market share is 80%!)

In all likelihood, older versions of the sources already employed can be accessed in order to supply information for the next step in the outline: historical trends. Growth of the market, shifts in composition or rank of the leaders, new technologies, legislation, lawsuits, mergers, and acquisitions—details of this type should be noted for a period of at least two to three years and as far back as five years when the emergence of influential factors would be missed otherwise.

To be complete, an overview must contain information on the market situation for the past, present, and future. Therefore, you will need to supply projections, but nothing too elaborate or involved; while everyone would like to see year-by-year projections out to the year 2000 and beyond, three to five years is adequate at this juncture.

The overview now contains information on how large the market is, who's in it, how it got to where it is, and where it's going. These are the absolute essentials and no overview can be complete if it omits any of them. The rest of the overview involves looking for information that is often not readily available, and the particulars of the market being studied may necessitate substituting other factors for those given here.

User demographics and psychographics can help round out the picture and explain some of the market behavior seen in the past or anticipated in the future. The projections should also be augmented by a look at what's new. Products, promotions, techniques, strategies, and so forth—a sketch of the new and emerging developments that may have an impact on a market.

For a well-documented market, this outline is useful because it helps focus and direct the research. For a small, new, or poorly documented market, the outline is essential. It enables you to be certain that the inevitable "gaps" remain unfilled only because information is unavailable, and never as a result of slipshod research. Knowing, with certainty, what is not available (and why) often can be just as useful as the information that actually is available.

Following this outline, sifting and sorting through the available information, a researcher will be able to gain significant insight into the market in question. The time invested can be minimal. Yet, this insight will enable the researcher to draw informed conclusions and make appropriate recommendations; for example, abandoning or pursuing further research. In this way, the outline extends its usefulness. Thus, in addition to serving as a functional model for gathering information, it provides a perspective from which to study and evaluate the material gathered.

*Peter Beck, "Compiling a Market/Industry Overview? Follow This Outline," *Marketing News*, January 6, 1984, Section 2, p. 1. Reprinted with permission of the American Marketing Association.

Step 2: Marketing Objectives

Objectives are the marketing results sought by management. As the foundation for marketing strategy, goal setting is useful in these ways:

- Providing direction for the marketing plan (determining what you want to accomplish)

- Motivating the staff (identifying what you should be accomplishing)

- Providing a timetable for implementing the marketing plan (noting if you are on schedule)

- Measuring marketing performance (evaluating whether you are meeting your goals)

Goals are objectives made specific, measurable, and time-oriented. Furthermore, goals should be realistic, objective, clear, and concise. Some typical marketing goals include sales (in units, dollars, and/or percentage change increases), market share, prospect visits, inquiries, and awareness/recognition for your company or product. Examples of some specific goal statements organized into major marketing functional areas are listed in Exhibit 2-5. These are provided as guidelines only and should be adapted and expanded where necessary to meet the needs of your firm's marketing plan.

EXHIBIT 2-5: TYPICAL MARKETING GOAL STATEMENTS*

1. Sales Productivity/Volume Goals

- Increase the number of customers __ % by December 31, 19__.
- Increase penetration into a specific market with existing products by __ % by December 31, 19__.
- Increase sales volume of product X by __ % in selected regions, districts, and territories by specific dates.
- Attain sales performance goals on calls per rep, orders per call, calls per day, and so on, by given amounts by specific dates.

2. Profitability and Market Share Goals

- Increase overall return on investment by __% for the next fiscal year.
- Increase profit rate for key regions, districts, and territories by __%, by a specific date.
- Increase by __ %, market share in "X" market by December 31, 19__.
- Attain market share sub-goals for regions, districts, and territories by June 30, 19__.

3. Marketing Mix Goals

- Establish new distributors in specific geographic regions by December 31, 19__.
- Increase awareness of company products among key purchase influences in specific new markets by __% by December 31, 19__.
- Develop high quality inquiries at $__/inquiry for company products.
- Introduce new products to fill out product-line offering by specific dates.
- Prices should be competitive (within 5% of primary competitors) and yield a minimum unit contribution to profit of __%.

4. Other Objectives

Other objectives must also be set for personnel development and training, budget adherence, customer relations, and your service program.

*Adapted with permission of the Chilton Book Company, Radnor, Penn. This material was originally published in Cochrane Chase and Kenneth L. Barasch's *Marketing Problem Solver*, Second Edition, 1977, p. 78.

Step 3: Strategy Formulation

Once the environment has been carefully researched and analyzed, and objectives set, it is then possible to formulate appropriate marketing strategies for the business. Strategies need to be developed for two major areas—target markets and marketing mix elements (product, promotion, pricing, and distribution).

TARGET MARKET SELECTION—THE PRIMARY STRATEGIC ELEMENT

Ideally, target market identification, evaluation, and selection should be undertaken prior to determining specific strategies in the other marketing areas. If you know who your likely customers are, you are in a much better position to provide desired products and services to this market segment. Similarly, promotion, pricing, and distribution strategies can be tailored to segment needs. As strategic element number one, segmentation techniques act as a bridge to effectively link customers' needs and desires to a company's offerings.

Although segmentation findings should be the heart of the marketing plan, many companies neglect this central area and focus on product offerings and intended promotional strategy. However, progressive marketing-driven companies put the cart (customer) in front of the horse (means for satisfaction); and strategic issues naturally follow, based on careful analysis.

Exhibit 2-6 summarizes the segment profiles for Dollars for Scholars, Inc., a private-sector provider of financial-aid services for college students.

EXHIBIT 2-6: SEGMENT PROFILES FOR DOLLARS FOR SCHOLARS, INC.

Background and Objective

Dollars for Scholars, Inc., a South Florida-based company, is a computerized financial-aid researcher that assists college students in locating funds for higher education. Corporations, foundations, philanthropic organizations, and professional associations provide millions of dollars annually to students throughout the country through scholarships, grants, and loans. Management is interested in determining the potential for this service in Florida.

The Approach

1. Expected customer profile:

    a. young—sixteen to twenty-nine (there are undergraduate and graduate services)
    b. lower-middle to middle income households
    c. educated consumer or from an educated household
    d. enrolled or likely to enroll in a private college
    e. liberal thinker, non-traditionalist or product innovator

2. Market segments by education level:

    a. college students and parents (undergraduate)
    b. college students or parents (graduate)
    c. high school seniors and parents

3. Florida college market potential:

Type of college	Total students	Targeted students
State Universities	150,177 (9)	150,177 (9)
Jr./Community Colleges	235,261 (28)	206,705 (17)
Private Institutions	67,023 (50)	56,390 (9)
TOTALS	**452,461 (87)**	**413,272 (35)**

By targeting 35 of the 87 colleges and universities in Florida (40%), it is possible to reach 413,272 students (91%). A similar volume approach toward high schools is recommended. The above data is from the 1990 Florida *Statistical Abstract.*[4]

4. Target markets: further segmentation research needed

This example is based on a segmentation project conducted for a small business client. The company name has been disguised.

MARKETING STRATEGY AND THE 4 Ps—THE OTHER PLAYERS

Product, promotion, price, and place (distribution) strategies—the 4 Ps—are the "meat" of a company's marketing plan. For maximum effectiveness they should be broadly based on segmentation findings, as well as other strategic variables (such as company resources, management's values and policies, and potential risk and return). Strategies are the way in which marketing operations will be conducted prior to actual implementation. Unlike the external environment, the firm has complete control over the marketing methods it can employ to meet its objectives.

Strategies should not be developed in isolation from one another (strive for synergy). Rather, you should seek consistency and compatibility among all of the strategic elements. Tactics, the short-term strategies (often viewed as lasting less than a year), are the nuts and bolts portion of the plan. Tactics consist of such marketing initiatives as advertising budgets, media schedules, sales force organization, and pricing lists, to name a few.

Chapter 12 examines the development of strategies and tactics from market segmentation research. Additionally, several in-depth strategy profiles are featured in Part 4 of the book, "Segmentation Strategy Cases." Exhibit 2-7 illustrates the interrelationship between research, goal setting, strategic planning, and implementation and control.

EXHIBIT 2-7: THE MARKETING PLANNING CYCLE

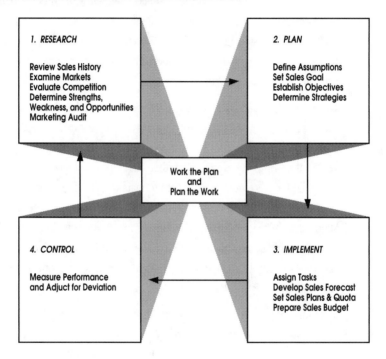

Reprinted with permission. H.W. Goetsch, *How to Prepare and Use Marketing Plans for Profit,* (Marketing for Profit, Inc., 1979.) p. 12.

Effective marketing strategy combines sound marketing decision making with a sprinkling of business creativity. Miller Brewing Company's Lite beer was a classic example of successful marketing strategy and execution. Now, the Philip Morris subsidiary and the nation's second largest brewer has found another taste-oriented niche opportunity—full-flavored ales. Its recent rollout of Miller Reserve Amber Ale in major U.S. markets is in direct response to double-digit sales growth evidenced in the microbrew category (that is, brewers such as Anchor Brewing, Boston Beer Company, and Brooklyn

Brewery that produce small quantities of beer for primarily local consumption). Miller's new ale competes head-to-head with Bass English Ale, Samuel Adams beers, and other quality ales.[5]

Steps 4 and 5: Implementation and Evaluation

At this point, the overall marketing plan is laid out. Will it work? To check the success of your marketing program, the plan must be executed and evaluated. Practicality is of the essence. A lengthy marketing plan can be a hindrance to its use by management. One business writer recommends limiting the master marketing plan to no more than 20 pages (although many more pages of detailed supporting plans for product lines, advertising schedules, sales force management, and so on, are likely needed).[6]

Implementation. In this phase, strategies are translated into action. Tactics, the company's short-term marketing plans, are featured. Specific timetables, budgets, and assignment responsibilities are carried forth. Communication within the company is critical in this stage, as employees at different levels are called on to get the marketing machinery rolling. At this point, the marketing plan progresses from a report to a working document. The "coffee stain test" provides one indicator of the value of the marketing plan. Is it clean, fresh, and never used? Or does the document have smudge marks, coffee stains, and dog-eared edges? The latter case often means that a good marketing plan is in place—and working.

Evaluation. Just as the implementation phase is the *how it will be done* part of the plan, evaluation determines *how well you are actually doing*. Control measures are maintained to check whether specific objectives are being met, variances in performance have occurred, efforts are on schedule, and changes may be required. Advertising budget/media planning models are one type of marketing tool you can use for implementation and evaluation purposes.

The key to a marketing plan is its practicality. Marketing planning is not a one-shot process, but a recurring business activity. As such, it requires regular reviews and monitoring by management. Revisions and updates should be expected—the goal is a workable plan that will improve your marketing performance.

To conclude this chapter on segmentation and marketing planning, a market profile for the personal computer industry is provided in Segmentation Skillbuilder 2. Given this market situation, how would you meet the challenge of the computer wars?

SEGMENTATION SKILLBUILDER 2: THE PORTABLE COMPUTER INDUSTRY

Assume that you were just hired as the North American Marketing Manager for a major personal computer (PC) manufacturer. It is your second day at work, and your boss, the Vice President of Marketing, has called an unexpected meeting to discusss niche marketing opportunities in the U.S. portable computer market. Impressed with your consumer goods background, your boss invites you (the rookie) to say a "few words" about how you view the PC market and how you propose the company could segment the portable computer sector. (Note: various types of portables comprise about 20% of the PC market, desktops account for the balance—80%.)

Immediately you ask your secretary for any background information on the PC market. She hands you the accompanying executive summary of a recent market analysis (left in your predecessor's desk drawer). You start to review the document and then glance at your watch; the meeting is less than 10 minutes away.

1. How would you respond?
2. What are some segmentation alternatives and your reasoning behind these options?
3. What is your next move?

The 1992 U.S. Portable Computer Market*

Market Overview. Dataquest expects the portable computer market to grow by 42.8%, to almost $7 billion, from 1991 to 1992. This number includes transportables, laptops, notebooks, and palmtops. The market growth for portables varied across the product line. Transportables and laptops, which require AC power, have had the slowest growth. A sales decline was expected in 1991. In contrast, battery-based systems had rapid growth. Portables, with 1 to 3 hours of battery life and weighing an average of 10 pounds, are estimated to grow around 20% per year from 1990 through 1994. This segment, maybe more than any other, felt the impact of fully PC-functional notebooks. Dataquest estimates that the notebook and handheld categories will grow an extraordinary 90% during the same period.

Pen-Based Systems. A portable device that continues in development is the pen-based "electronic tablet." The market for pen-based systems continues to expand, largely due to the creative sales efforts of vendors that offer them as replacements for paper order forms. Users of these pen-based computers have their choice of operating systems designed to maximize the inherent advantages of this technology. However, there is a lack of applications software.

**Segmentation's Role
In The Marketing Plan**

Distribution Methods. Portables are available through all the same channels in which desktop computers are sold, and some where desktops are not available. Recently, consumers saw the opening of several stores that specialize in portable computing. Mass merchandisers and the popular electronics super stores are also expanding their inventories to include the latest in laptops and notebooks. Direct sales, which have the best margins for the manufacturers, are still available for large purchases and special orders.

International Competitiveness. In international trade, two separate decisions by the U.S. government had a strong effect on the sourcing and manufacturing decisions of portable computer makers: (1) the removal of 100% duties on certain personal computers from Japan, and (2) the imposition of duties on certain flat-panel displays.

Outlook for 1992. By the end of 1991, virtually all computer vendors were offering notebook or laptop products. Product cycles will continue to shorten for these products, placing pressure on suppliers and perhaps leading to a market shakeout. Manufacturers and dealers agree that profit margins in the portable sector are some of the thinnest ever seen on a personal computer product. Companies that have the latest component technologies in their systems should have a competitive advantage over their rivals.

Long-Term Prospects. In the long-term, portable computers will continue to see strong demand, outpacing all other types of computers. Sales of notebook and handheld computers will lead the way as prices drop and their capabilities increase. Demand for pen-based systems will also rise as these systems become an accepted productivity tool for business, home, and school. Portables will share in the demand stimulated by advances in multimedia. These systems include telecommunications functions, advanced color video screens, and CD-ROM storage, and they will have wireless access to all types of peripherals.

*Adapted from "Computer Equipment and Software—Portables," *U.S. Industrial Outlook 1992* (Washington, D.C.: U.S. Department of Commerce, January 1992), pp. 27-16—27-18.

Suggested Reading: "Computer Equipment and Software," *U.S. Industrial Outlook* (most recent year).

SUMMARY

Customer-oriented companies understand their markets. The marketing plan is the tool used for assessing and responding to the firm's marketing challenges. Additionally, the plan helps managers to anticipate change and react to future business conditions. Benefits of the marketing plan are (1) helping produce desired results, (2) planning and control, and (3) providing a wealth of on-call market information.

A five-step marketing planning process is advocated. This process consists of market and situation analysis (an examination of the internal and external marketing environments), setting objectives, strategy formulation, implementation, and evaluation. A segmentation-based marketing plan is recommended. The segmentation audit provides a good starting point. The marketing plan should be practical and workable, as well as frequently revised to reflect changing market conditions.

NOTES

1. Roman G. Hiebing, Jr., and Scott W. Cooper, *The Successful Marketing Plan: A Disciplined and Comprehensive Approach* (Lincolnwood, Ill.: NTC Business Books, 1990), p. 4.

2. Hal W. Goetsch, "Conduct a Comprehensive Marketing Audit to Improve Marketing Planning," *Marketing News*, March 18, 1983, Section 2, p. 14.

3. Philip Kotler, William T. Gregor, and William H. Rodgers III, "The Marketing Audit Comes of Age," *Sloan Management Review*, Winter 1989, pp. 49-62.

4. *Florida Statistical Abstract*, 24th Edition, Anne H. Sherman (ed.) (Gainesville: The University Presses of Florida, 1990), pp. 91-92.

5. Alan J. Wax, "Miller Goes for the Refined Taste," *New York Newsday*, March 11, 1993, p. 35.

6. David H. Bangs, Jr., *The Market Planning Guide: Gaining and Maintaining the Competitive Edge*, (Portsmouth, N.H.: Upstart Publishing Company, Inc., 1987), p. 89.

THE SEGMENTATION ANALYSIS: PLANNING GUIDELINES

It was not the possibility of planning as such which has been questioned . . . but the possibility of successful planning.

—F. A. Hayek, 1935

Small and large companies have made great strides toward adopting the marketing concept and becoming market-oriented in the past decade or so.[1] As the key ingredient in this transformation, segmentation analysis has emerged as a viable "real world" marketing strategy tool. However, in too many cases, segmentation studies are not practical enough to have a major impact on overall marketing performance. This has, at times, prevented targeted marketing from assisting management in increasing sales, attracting new customers, maintaining existing customer relationships, and/or expanding market share.

THE NEED FOR PRACTICAL SEGMENTATION ANALYSIS

There are three primary reasons why market segmentation has not lived up to its much heralded expectations in the business world. First, although marketers acknowledge that segmentation is critical to marketing success, relatively few individuals have the understanding, expertise, and authority to incorporate this technique into a company's marketing plan. (After reading this book you will not be one of them!) Therefore, a majority of firms—market leaders as well as market challengers—base their marketing strategies and tactics on informal, inadequate, or limited analyses of potential target markets. Occasionally, companies overanalyze their markets. Here's an example: A leading statewide healthcare insurance provider commissioned 18 different segmentation studies over a five-year period. Not surprising, none of them were implemented. (Is it any wonder why the U.S. healthcare industry is in crisis?)

Second, traditional approaches to segmentation analysis often emphasize methodology and multivariate statistics over substantive issues. The product of such a study is a complex segmentation model understood only by the researcher and seldom implemented by management (the classic "report on the executive's shelf" syndrome). And third, marketing research can be expensive, and management may not perceive the benefits of market segmentation analysis relative to its cost.

THE REMEDY: DESIGN A PRACTICAL SEGMENTATION STUDY

To enhance the value of market segmentation and provide "hands-on" decision-oriented information that can solve today's crucial marketing problems, practicality is of the essence. Four features typify the practical approach:

- Systematic planning frameworks are stressed.
- Management is actively involved in the study.
- Appropriate analytical techniques are used.
- Findings can be readily translated into marketing strategy.

A 10-point program for systematically and efficiently conducting segmentation studies is the major topic addressed in this chapter and in Chapter 4. This managerial framework emphasizes essential planning and research guidelines. In addition, other practical segmentation models—the 8-S Formula and the nested approach (an industrial segmentation framework) are discussed in Chapter 11, "Segmentation Models and Procedural Guidelines."

Coordination, cooperation, and a close working relationship among the entire marketing team (top management, such as vice presidents and division managers; marketing and product managers; researchers, support staff, consultants, and so on) are vital to the success of a practical segmentation study.

HELPING MANAGEMENT OWN THE MARKETING INVESTMENT

In my segmentation consulting engagements, I encourage active involvement from all levels of marketing management, not just the professionals in the company I am working with directly. Management then "buys in," recognizing that the project is a worthwhile marketing investment rather than an expense. Frequent meetings and two-way communication ensure that the project is on schedule and meeting corporate research objectives.

Complex segmentation analysis is not necessarily better than sound, simpler analysis.[2] This is especially true for initial studies or analyses using new segmentation bases and variables. Once an in-depth understanding of a market situation exists, advanced methodologies and analysis may be appropriate. This is not to imply that there is no place for factor and cluster analysis, multidimensional scaling, and other multivariate statistical techniques. When used in the right situations by skilled researchers, these approaches can be insightful. However, be careful that you don't lose sight of the customer via too much number crunching (creating information overload). Sometimes, the details can be mastered, but the big picture may be blurred. Provide only the data that is absolutely necessary for solving the problem and dispense with complex methodologies that contribute little to the study except added confusion. The research challenge is to focus on customers as people rather than numbers—explore their characteristics, needs, and wants—and design marketing mixes that best satisfy your designated target markets.

The incorporation of these three basic principles—systematic planning, management involvement, and realistic data analysis—leads to the production of segmentation findings that can be readily translated into marketing strategy. In today's dynamic and globally competitive markets, companies must improve their analyses of potential target markets. The product (actionable marketing information) of a well-planned and executed segmentation study will be used to improve and fine-tune a company's marketing operations.

THE 10-POINT PROGRAM FOR EFFECTIVE SEGMENTATION ANALYSIS: PLANNING GUIDELINES

The most important determinant in whether a segmentation study will deliver the desired results is the framework in which the information will be gathered and evaluated. A segmentation research design is a blueprint for action and lays out a systematic approach to data collection and analysis. The two-part "game plan"—consisting of planning and research guidelines—outlined here helps marketers to conduct effective, cost efficient segmentation studies.

There is no "best" plan for designing a segmentation analysis; market and situational factors must carefully be assessed. Because no standard package suffices, segmentation analyses must be customized. There are 10 necessary components that you should specify, however, before you launch the study.[3] Exhibit 3-1 lists elements of a good segmentation plan. *Segmentation planning guidelines* (points 1 through 5) are discussed in this chapter. *Segmentation research guidelines* (points 6 through 10) are addressed in Chapter 4.

EXHIBIT 3-1: THE 10-POINT PROGRAM TO CUSTOMIZE SEGMENTATION STUDIES

I. Segmentation Planning Guidelines

1. Establish research objectives
2. Specify target population measurement units
3. State relevant definitions
4. Recognize segmentation viability/segment formation criteria
5. Select segmentation bases

II. Segmentation Research Guidelines

6. Choose appropriate data collection methods
7. Employ sampling procedures
8. Analyze the data
9. Consider budgetary constraints
10. Know how the information will be used

Point 1: Research Objectives

The first step in conducting a segmentation analysis is to establish appropriate objectives for the study. The goal is to be able to answer the question "What are you trying to accomplish in the research project?"

Objectives provide a checklist of information needs useful for strategy development. A two-stage *Research Objective/Research Question (RO/RQ)* approach to problem definition can be effective.[4] The RO/RQ uses a single-sentence research objective statement to guide the segmentation research effort.

Research objectives may focus on market segment identification (possible through techniques such as benefit segmentation), description of segments (establishing demographic and psychographic profiles), understanding levels of product usage (profiles of heavy versus light users), segment validation, target market strategy formation, and so on.

A series of research questions that relate to the focal problem statement is then developed. Some typical research objective questions appropriate for a segmentation study deal with target market options, user categories for the product, and competitive/marketing mix strategies. A sample (but not exhaustive) list of 20 key questions relevant for segmentation analysis is provided in Segmentation Action List 3. Exhibit 3-2 illustrates the RO/RQ process for an automobile dealership. Segmentation SkillBuilder 3 gives you an opportunity to relate the objective-setting challenge to your business situation.

Segmentation Action List 3: Research Objective Questions

1. What are some of the possible market segments for your product or service?

2. How do these segments compare with your present customer profile(s)?

3. How large are these potential target markets?

4. What is the expected profitability of serving these submarkets?

5. How are these segments defined (names, sizes, and key variables)?

6. What is unique about the specific groups?

7. Where are the potential customers located?

8. How much effort and resources should be allocated to the various market segments now? In the future?

9. What segments are competitors pursuing?

10. What unique niche (competitive advantage) does your company have compared to others in the market?

11. What past segmentation studies have been employed?

12. How useful were past segmentation findings/strategies?

13. Who are the heavy users for your goods or services?

14. What features or benefits are sought by customers?

15. What alternative marketing strategies and tactics are available?

16. Does your product or service meet segment needs? Are any changes required?

17. What promotional appeals can best be used toward the target markets?

18. How price-sensitive are the markets?

19. What role do distribution channels play in the market?

20. How will customer purchase behavior be measured and monitored to evaluate marketing effectiveness?

Exhibit 3-2: A Segmentation Research Objective and Research Questions for an Automotive Services Study

RO:* To determine the feasibility of WH Motors sponsoring an automobile membership club for Volvo owners, particularly the postwarranty segment. The program would include various discounted automotive services/benefits sought by consumers.

RQ1: What are consumer perceptions (reaction) and levels of interest, by segment, toward the club?

RQ2: What specific features of the program are most and least attractive to new and existing Volvo owners?

RQ3: What is an acceptable price for the membership club? Considerations include consumer price expectations, price-level thresholds, cost-benefit tradeoffs to WH Motors, and competitive offerings.

RQ4: Who is the "typical customer" for this program based on demographic, lifestyle, and automobile ownership factors?

RQ5: What are present purchasing habits of Volvo owners for parts/accessories, maintenance, and repairs?

*RO = research objective; RQ = research question.

Segmentation Skillbuilder 3: Setting Research Objectives

Assume that you are the Director of Marketing Research for your company and your input is solicited for developing next year's marketing plan. Reviewing your research needs, you note the need for a major segmentation analysis for an important product or product line.

1. Explain the background situation and need for this study to your company's Vice President of Marketing. (Note: It is likely that you will have to "sell" this project to the VP.)

2. How would you explain your research needs to an outside marketing research firm? List one or two (or more, if applicable) specific objectives of such a study and develop associated research questions based on objectives.

Suggested Reading: Pope, Jeffrey L. *Practical Marketing Research*. (New York: AMACOM, 1981), p. 48 is particularly insightful.

Point 2: Target Population Measurement Units

Market segments are groups of individuals or organizations with similar characteristics. In analyzing markets, you must specify a unit of measure to quantify the size and scope of the target customer segments. In consumer marketing, common descriptors include customers, shoppers, prospects, and patients. In industrial applications, purchasing agents, decision makers, managers, users, influencers, and clients are typically targeted individuals. Once the basic descriptor has been identified, additional modifiers (segmentation bases and variables) can be used to better understand and explain market segments.

Sometimes the targeted prospect is not the obvious prospect. For example, research has shown that women purchase approximately 70% of men's underwear. Recognizing this statistic, Jockey's strategy to use Jim Palmer as its "pitchman" was a sound one. Would women react as favorably to Yogi Berra in his undershorts?

Additionally, in some consumer markets there is a dual decision-maker. Breakfast cereals generally must appeal to both the child and the parent. Multiple buying influences and buying centers dominate industrial purchase decisions. Strategies for coping with this challenge and reaching the right buyer are discussed further in Chapter 9.

Point 3: Relevant Definitions

In addition to customer specification, other definitions are important in segmentation planning. The market service area is a critical one. The population of prospects for a company must have a definite geographical limitation. Although the 1990s means increased global marketing, few companies can effectively serve the needs of the world. (Chapter 10 discusses international segmentation strategies.) Factors that affect the market definition include the nature of the business (retailers will attract most of their customers from within a certain-mile radius or so-many minute drive), the goods or services offered (the uniqueness and availability of products), competition, and physical boundaries (expressways, access roads, topography, and so on).

Other definitions needed in a segmentation study often include the demographic and socioeconomic classifications to be evaluated, criteria for determining benefits or lifestyles, and consumptive measures (what constitutes a heavy versus light user in a given product class). In a recent study, a marketing analyst for USAir struggled with the best operationalization of a frequent flyer. Options considered included air miles flown, number of flights taken annually, business versus personal travel, as well as membership in its (and competitive) frequent flyer programs.

Point 4: Segmentation Criteria

Segmentation Viability. Not every market can be segmented. Other markets that can be segmented may not be feasible to pursue from a marketing perspective. There are four key issues that must be assessed. Positive responses to these questions indicate that market segmentation is worth undertaking. These pivotal criteria are called the 4 Rs of the market decision, and are explored next (see Exhibit 3-3).[5]

Exhibit 3-3: The 4 Rs

Can you *rank* your target markets by their importance to your overall marketing program?
Are your target markets of *realistic size*, large enough to profitably pursue?
Can you *reach* your customers easily?
Will your targeted customers *respond* to marketing strategies and tactics?

R1: Ranking Your Target Markets. By ranking a market, the marketer objectively and subjectively evaluates its potential relative to other market opportunities. The goal is to quantify the size of the aggregate market and possible submarkets. If segmentation is to be viable, the market must be identifiable and measurable.

One dentist was interested in specializing in cosmetic dentistry (bonding, implants, and related aesthetic services) and wanted to know the relative size of this potential market in his service area. Research indicated that only 10% of the potential dental patients were prime candidates for cosmetic dentistry. This segment consisted of professionals, managers, and administrators near their earnings peak with high discretionary income. On the other hand, two other segments, emphasizing preventive and preventive/remedial dentistry, accounted for more than 44% of the market potential. Based on the segmentation study, the dentist adopted a dual marketing program. He primarily concentrated on "traditional" dentistry while slowly building a practice geared to cosmetic procedures and services. (A detailed account of this analysis was presented in the first edition of this book.)[6]

R2: Markets Realistic in Size. Most segmentation studies identify two or more segments for the company to consider targeting. The market(s) considered must be large enough to support the cost of the marketing effort. The segments identified must be of sufficient magnitude so that distinct marketing programs can be developed for the target markets. For example, if a retail rare coin dealer were interested in selling Civil War currency to collectors, given the limited number of potential customers for the product, segmentation into two or more submarkets would not be prudent.

Also, avoid the temptation to oversegment (divide the market into a multitude of minimarkets); this is extremely costly and generally an ineffective marketing strategy. In some instances, combining two or more small markets is advisable. It is then possible to form a segment of sufficient size to efficiently market goods or services to a targeted population. Are there 100 prospects or 100,000 for your goods or service?

R3: Reaching Your Customers Easily. Are potential segments readily accessible? The increased costs of reaching distinct markets can be justified by higher sales to those markets. For segmentation to work effectively, groups have to be reached easily to minimize marketing investment and maximize performance. The widespread availability of trade journals such as *Advertising Age* or *Progressive Grocer* and directories such as *The Electronics Buyer's Guide* or *The Aviation Buyer's Directory* provide excellent opportunities to reach desired target markets. Additionally, tens of thousands of highly targeted mailing lists can be purchased or rented. Once a profile of your customers has been established, comparisons to media kits, *Standard Rate and Data Service (SRDS)* media summaries, and other media references can be made for effective advertising planning.

In a project conducted for a minority-owned Goodyear automotive franchisee, a low-cost promotional plan was designed based on a demographic market analysis. It was recommended that the target market could be reached by using discount coupons, special offers, premiums, and contests; supporting school sporting events and neighborhood activities; and employing media vehicles targeted to the predominantly African-American population (radio stations and community newspapers).

R4: Response by Your Targeted Customers. Identifying a potential market segment that can be reached is of little value if customers will not respond to your marketing initiatives. Thorough market research, including surveys of noncustomers as well as customers, can help determine whether there is a genuine need for your product before you allocate expensive promotional dollars.

A retail office supply business illustrates this point. Research indicated that the firm's merchandise mix, store hours, and promotional strategy were inappropriate for its suburban location. By gearing products to home users and small business owners (as prospects for computer-related supplies and custom office products) rather than the corporate segment, extending store hours to meet the needs of two-income working professionals, and revising advertising and selling tactics (such as offering back-to-school promotions), revenues increased dramatically within a three-month period.

Segment Formation. If your marketing situation fulfills all of the criteria for the 4 Rs, segmentation analysis is worth pursuing. The next issue to consider is how to form good market segments. The following general criteria can be used as a benchmark. Specific segment formation standards must also be developed and adapted to your business situation.

- *Homogeneity within the segment.* This is the test for commonalties among group members. Individuals within each segment should fit a typical profile. Given the similarities in specific characteristics, it is likely that members will exhibit similarities in purchase behavior. For example, the Trivial Pursuit "Baby Boomers Edition" has been successfully marketed to those born between 1946 and 1964.

- *Heterogeneity between segments.* This is the test for differences among the various market segments. Segments should be distinctive from one another and have their own identity. It should be clear which group an individual/organization belongs to based on key attributes. Different segments generally have different needs and buying motives that the marketer can target. Toyota has captured a global leadership position with its full line of vehicles, each appealing to different market segments and desires.

- *Meaningful segment data.* The "acid test" for the effectiveness of segmentation analysis is the value of the marketing information generated. Good segmentation research provides decision-makers with operational data that is practical, usable, and readily translatable into marketing strategy.

Point 5: Bases for Segmentation

Markets can be segmented in a variety of ways. There is no clear, best method. Planning for segmentation all depends on a company's marketing situation and the type of information needed by management. A segmentation base is a dimension for segmenting a market, and in most cases, several bases need to be considered simultaneously to provide a complete customer profile. One dichotomy for classifying segmentation dimensions is physical versus behavioral attributes.

Physical attributes regularly used in segmenting markets include geography, demography, and socioeconomic factors (see Chapters 5 and 6). Behavioral attributes often used as segmentation bases include psychographics, product usage, benefits, perceptions, media exposure, and the marketing mix factors (see Chapters 7 and 8). Industrial and international segmentation bases are the scope of Chapters 9 and 10, respectively.

SUMMARY

The success of your market segmentation program depends on the planning process employed in designing, collecting, and analyzing relevant customer information. Segmentation analysis must be practical to be effective. This can be accomplished by using systematic planning frameworks, soliciting the involvement of management at all levels within the company, and using appropriate analytical methods. The result of such efforts will be segmentation findings that are readily translated into marketing strategy; ultimately, this will improve business performance.

This chapter introduced a 10-point program for designing a good market segmentation study. The five planning guidelines—setting research objectives, identifying target population measurement units, stating relevant definitions, establishing segmentation criteria (recognizing segmentation viability and segment formation), and selecting segmentation bases—were discussed in this chapter. The next chapter considers the five segmentation research guidelines in detail.

NOTES

1. J. David Lichtenthal and David T. Wilson, "Becoming Market Oriented," *Journal of Business Research* 24 (1992), pp. 191-207.

2. Subhash Jain, *Marketing Planning and Strategy*, Third Edition, (Cincinnati: South-western Publishing, 1990), p. 133.

3. Art Weinstein, "Ten-Point Program Customizes Segmentation Analysis," *Marketing News*, May 23, 1986, p. 22.

4. Randall G. Chapman, "Problem Definition in Marketing Research Studies," *The Journal of Consumer Marketing*, Spring 1989, pp. 51-59.

5. Marvin Nesbit and Art Weinstein, "How to Size Up Your Customers," *American Demographics*, July 1986, pp. 34-37.

6. Art Weinstein, *Market Segmentation: Using Demographics, Psychographics, and Other Segmentation Methods to Explore and Exploit New Markets*, (Chicago: Probus Publishing Company, 1987), pp. 162-173.

4

THE SEGMENTATION ANALYSIS: RESEARCH GUIDELINES

Knowledge is power.

—*Sir Francis Bacon, 1597*

A good segmentation study is built on objective, workable marketing information. The American Marketing Association defines marketing research as follows:

> Marketing research is the function which links the consumer, customer, and public to the marketer through information—information used to identify and define marketing opportunities and problems; generate, refine, and evaluate marketing actions; monitor marketing performance; and improve the understanding of marketing as a process.[1]

Via systematic data collection and analysis, marketing research is the business activity that assists marketers in making sound business decisions. Just as gasoline powers an automobile, marketing information is the energy source that guides the segmentation study. The higher the grade of fuel (information), the better the performance of the vehicle (the segmentation study).

The results of segmentation analysis may indicate that your company should make some planning changes or undertake a new marketing approach for particular market segments. This corporate refocus may require strategic or tactical adjustments in the various aspects of the marketing mix. Mistakes in the marketing controllables can span from costly to disastrous. Marketing research helps to minimize risk (confirms some expectations and dispels others) and is the solid foundation on which effective segmentation decisions should be based.

Additionally, research improves the odds of an anticipated occurrence actually happening. Put yourself in the shoes of a high-rolling racetrack bettor for a moment. Imagine how valuable it would be to you knowing that three of the eight horses running in a big race definitely would not win. Although this wouldn't guarantee that your horse *would* win, your chances would have increased substantially given this scenario. The same is true of segmentation research. You may not have all the facts about the marketplace, but the knowledge that you now possess about the "field" can greatly enhance your market position.

THE 10-POINT PROGRAM FOR EFFECTIVE SEGMENTATION ANALYSIS: RESEARCH GUIDELINES

The five planning guidelines discussed in the last chapter—establish research objectives, specify target market measurement units, state relevant definitions, recognize segmentation viability/formation criteria, and select segmentation bases—provide a foundation for designing an effective segmentation study. The second set of guidelines—choose appropriate data collection methods, use sampling techniques, analyze the data, consider budgetary constraints, and know how the information will be used—are research-based and are explored in this chapter.

Point 6: Data Collection

Primary Versus Secondary Data. The market analyst has basically two sources to tap in assembling marketing information: primary and secondary data. *Primary research* is information collected for a specific purpose/project; *secondary research* relates to data that was previously gathered (for a purpose other than your project at hand). In a sense, primary data is a misnomer, because secondary data should generally be sought first.

Secondary data offers tremendous cost and time savings over primary research, so it should be incorporated into your segmentation project wherever feasible. Although data manipulation may be required, and publication lags and inappropriate measurement or classification units may be encountered, secondary research is a logical starting point for a segmentation study. As an example, trade associations and reference sources such as the *U.S. Industrial Outlook or Standard and Poor's Industry Surveys* can be helpful as you determine the size of the market, major competitors, and other basic industry information.

Consider this example. Secondary information was used as one determinant of the feasibility of establishing a battery (automobile, truck, and industrial) assembling plant in South Florida. Data supplied by the Independent Battery Manufacturers Association and the Battery Council International included such valuable references as statistics annuals, convention proceedings, and *The Battery Man* (a trade journal).

Exhibit 4-1 summarizes the major sources of secondary information. You are also urged to carefully review Appendix A, "Major Sources of Demographic/Marketing Information" (Part III), for further details on these references.

EXHIBIT 4-1: SECONDARY SOURCES OF MARKETING INFORMATION

Category	References
Trade Journals	Ulrich's International Periodicals Directory, Standard Rate and Data Service-Business Publications Rates and Data, Bacon's Publicity Checker, Writer's Market, and Gale Directory of Publications and Broadcast Media
Trade Journals (Special Issues)	Harfax Guide to Industry Special Issues, Special Issues Index, Ulrich's Irregular Serials and Annual
Business Indexes	Predicasts' F&S Index, Business Periodicals Index, Wall Street Journal Index, New York Times Index
Directories	Encyclopedia of Associations, National Trade and Professional Associations of the U.S., Findex Directory of Marketing Research Reports, Thomas Register, MacRAE's Blue Book, State Industrial Directories, Ward's Business Directory of U.S. Firms, Standard and Poor's Directories, Dun & Bradstreet Directories, Directory of Directories
Statistical Sources	U.S. Industrial Outlook, Standard and Poor's Industry Surveys, Predicasts' Forecasts, Department of Commerce publications
Computer Databases	Predicasts' series, Dialog, ABI Inform, Trade and Industry, UMI's Newspaper Abstracts, Nexis/Lexis (see Gale Directory of Databases)
Other	Note demographic sources discussed in Appendix A (Parts I and II)

Although this exhibit lists specific sources for marketing information, in many cases additional legwork is required. For example, you could consult trade journal references to determine the publications in your industry. Then you would obtain these sources. Similarly, business indexes are helpful for locating citations or abstracts, but you then must research specific articles to collect the needed information.

Although secondary sources are important for solving "pieces of the puzzle," you also need primary data to provide the balance of the marketing information that management requires. If you were seeking information on customers' perceptions about your product, a primary research approach would be required. Secondary data would not help to answer such a specific question.

For most segmentation studies, primary research will be your major source of information. Behavioral segmentation dimensions such as psychographics, product usage, and benefits are all customized projects demanding specific research for a given situation. Even demographics that are readily available from secondary data require updated market measures, projections, and detailed analysis to maximize their value.

You can view data as raw facts, statistics, or numbers. The goal of the marketing research process is to translate data into meaningful marketing information. Information is knowledge or intelligence that assists management in making business decisions in changing markets. To obtain the requisite primary information for strategic planning and control, follow a systematic research process. A general framework for conducting a segmentation-based research project is detailed in Segmentation Action List 4.

Segmentation Action List 4: The Marketing Research Process

1. What are the objectives of your study?

2. What information is known and what information is needed? Have you formulated possible hypotheses and considered the impact of alternative courses of action?

3. What type of research instrument (personal or telephone interview surveys, mail or self-administered questionnaires, focus group topic guide, observation forms, and so forth) will be used?

4. Can you describe the appropriate sample for the project?

5. How will the data be collected? (This is the fieldwork.)

6. How will the data be analyzed? (These are the statistical procedures.)

7. What type of report is required by management? (This should be a written document that provides direction in using the segmentation information.)

The basic primary data collection options include face-to-face and telephone interviews, direct mail, focus groups, and observation methods. The data collection form is the research instrument used to collect the marketing information needed (questionnaires, surveys, observation forms, and so on). They should be customized to fit the situation at hand. In many segmentation studies, a combination of primary, secondary, and syndicated data (to be discussed momentarily) is used, with multiple data collection methods and forms used for information gathering.

Syndicated Sources: The Hybrid Approach. Secondary sources generally will solve part of the problem, and primary research is complex and costly. Is there an alternative or middle ground? Yes! At times, syndicated or standardized information services can be of great value in meeting a firm's research needs. This hybrid approach is a cross between primary and secondary sources, at fees considerably below custom research projects. Essentially, syndicated research is cooperative information. Two or more companies are purchasing related information from a common research supplier.

51

One of the best known marketing research firms offering syndicated services is Nielsen Marketing Research. Nielsen is the largest marketing research company in the world based on revenues, and part of the Dun and Bradstreet Corporation. Nielsen provides standardized services through several of its divisions, including ScanTrack and its media research services. Other examples of syndicated research providers include Dataquest (for the computer and electronics industry), Biomedical Business International (for medical devices), and J. D. Power and Associates (for automobiles). Low-cost syndicated research reports—generally in the $500 to $3,000 price range—are available for hundreds of industry sectors from such companies as FIND/SVP (New York), Off-the-Shelf (Northport, NY), and Market Search (Evanston, IL). *Findex*, a directory published by the Cambridge Information Group (Bethesda, MD), lists 13,000 syndicated studies, reports, and surveys, a total that increases by several thousand every year.[2]

Several research firms specialize in syndicated segmentation services. Examples of some of the leading companies are listed in Exhibit 4-2.

Exhibit 4-2: Syndicated Segmentation Services

Company	Service Name	Description
Claritas	PRIZM	40 neighborhood lifestyle clusters through geodemographic targeting
Donnelley Marketing Information Services	ClusterPlus	47 geodemographic lifestyle clusters
SRI International	VALS 2	8 values and lifestyle segments
Simmons Market Research Bureau	Study of Media and Markets	Surveys media habits, product consumption, and lifestyles relating to 800+ product categories, 4,000 brands, and 7 media

Although these and other companies/services (CACI's ACORN, Dun and Bradstreet's Market Identifiers, and the Yankelovich Monitor) provide valuable information that can enhance segmentation findings, when used in isolation the information provided is generally insufficient for adequate segmentation analysis. Additional primary and secondary data is needed to present the total picture. An additional shortcoming of the syndicated services (in particular, the lifestyle services) is that they are market-driven, as opposed to product-driven (recognize consumer characteristics only, and don't consider key attributes about specific product categories or individual product items). This is addressed further in Chapter 7, in the psychographics and lifestyle discussion. For additional information on the services provided by the syndicated services and other marketing research firms specializing in market segmentation, see Appendix B, "Companies Providing Market Segmentation Services," and the examples in Part 2 of this book.

Segmentation Research: An Assessment. The research approach a firm uses depends greatly on the stage of segmentation analysis through which your firm is passing. For example, if your company has never formally analyzed the marketplace to derive potential target segments, exploratory research is recommended. The purpose of this research is to obtain as much market information that may be relevant to the situation as possible. Because precise information needs are indeterminable at this stage, secondary sources will play a prominent role in the research. As you sift through the market information and obtain a better understanding of basic relationships, you become ready to undertake primary research projects.

At the other extreme, say that yours is a well-versed company that has defined and described the market in terms of segment profiles (perhaps through demographics, psychographics, product usage criteria, or a combination of bases). You need a higher-level segmentation analysis. A causality design can be introduced, whereby you link purchase behavior to isolated variables. Benefit segmentation or perceptual research often tries to establish this cause-and-effect relationship. Although this latter approach may seem to be ideal, it has some drawbacks. The research is much more complex; because it uses sophisticated multivariate analytical techniques, it is more costly; and identified segments may be more difficult to reach than through traditional segment profiles (a descriptive approach).

Segmentation research can take many forms. It can vary from an initial full-blown or baseline study to an investigation into one or more aspects of a market. Some compromises may often be necessary, recognizing the company's research needs and budgetary constraints. You should also plan ongoing or periodic studies, given the dynamic nature of markets.

The bottom line is that your company should use whatever source of information that can best meet its needs at a cost it can afford. Typically, this means a combination of primary and secondary sources. This research can either be conducted in-house through your marketing research department or contracted to a commercial marketing research firm or marketing consultant. Syndicated services should also be considered, subject to the scope of your information needs. The newest form of segmentation research is known as *single-source data (SSD) systems* or *database marketing*. SSD systems are explored in the end-of-chapter appendix.

Additionally, universities can be of great value in designing and/or implementing segmentation studies. Many universities have research bureaus, specialized business centers, or Small Business Institutes that can provide advice and technical assistance for such projects. And of course, marketing faculty can be an excellent source for obtaining consultants specializing in segmentation analysis.

Although at times it can be costly, research should be a high priority in your firm's marketing budget. The alternative to research is trial and error. Can your company afford the cost of failure through guesswork? The cost of "missing the boat" is often much greater than the cost of obtaining solid information. Marketing research can be thought of as a high-yielding cash value insurance policy. It can protect the company from marketing mistakes but also return great dividends through identifying potential new opportunities. Market research facilitates executive decision making. Raphael and Parket offer five solid recommendations for marketing managers:

1. Market research should be proactive, not reactive.

2. Bring in market research early in the decision process.

3. Product teams should include a representative from market research.

4. Develop corporate policies requiring managers to use market research.

5. Give market research a direct line to upper management.[3]

Despite the inherent value of research, there is still a place for "gut feel" in the business environment. Intuition through years of experience can provide a stimulus for the creative implementation of basic findings. Although Japanese companies use surveys, they trust their instincts first. Their "soft research" often includes observing customers in their natural environment and in-depth talks with channel members.

Sony's primary research indicated that consumers wouldn't buy a tape recorder that didn't record. Chairman Akio Morita introduced the Walkman anyway, and it was a huge success.[4] This "judgment call" may at times be the difference between what works and what doesn't.

In addition, management insight may provide the 2% solution. About 98% of the time, research-based answers are possible. Sometimes, however, research is not the way to go—it is too costly to solve the problem, or research cannot effectively solve the problem.

> The "hit list" approach is also useful for conducting segmentation research. Develop a list of the 6 to 10 issues that come to mind immediately as research needs. Ask a key associate or two to add to this list and let the right (creative) side of your brain take over this task for a couple of days. The revised list may now contain 12 to 20 items. It is likely that you can find 70% to 80% of your answers from secondary or syndicated sources. Primary research should account for the balance (18% to 28%)—exclusive of that elusive 2%, of course.

Point 7: Sampling Procedures

It is seldom feasible to attempt to collect data from all prospects in a market. Although the census approach is occasionally desirable (such as in a small, specialized industrial sector), invariably marketers opt for researching representative subgroups within larger markets. The use of carefully designed samples provides a most efficient and effective means of obtaining information from a given population. By using a sampling approach, data can be projected to provide a realistic profile of a market at a minimal cost. The objective of sampling is to minimize research errors, provide data reliability, and produce representative findings. Major considerations involved in designing the research sample include the sampling frame, alternative sampling techniques, and the sample size.

The *sampling frame* is the master listing of population elements to be evaluated. It is presumed that the sampling frame is similar to the total population under study. For example, the annual *Corporate Technology Directory* published by Corporate Technology Information Services, Inc. (Corptech), provides detailed information on more than 35,000 U.S.-based, high-tech manufacturers representing more than 3,000 product categories and 18 industries.[5] This database/mailing list was found to be an excellent source for reaching top-ranking marketing executives in industrial high-technology markets.

The next decision is the selection of a sampling process. There are two broad categories to choose from: nonprobability or probability samples. *Nonprobabilistic samples* are the simplest and least expensive to use. These include convenience, judgment, and quota samples. The second group, *probabilistic samples*, are more objective, difficult to administer, and costly than the former group. Random, stratified, cluster, and systematic samples are some of the most frequently used probability-based samples. Exhibit 4-3 provides a brief description of the sampling options.

EXHIBIT 4-3: TYPES OF SAMPLES

I. Nonprobabilistic Samples

Convenience samples	Participation based on being near the study—such as the man/woman on the street interview.
Judgment samples	Expert opinions used—for example, AP and UPI college football ratings.
Quota samples	Key characteristics of the sample match those of the population—such as important demographic or socioeconomic variables.

II. Probabilistic Samples

Random samples	Every population element has an equal chance of participating in the study—state lotteries are one example.
Stratified samples	The population is grouped into two or more subsets, and all subsets are then randomly sampled—for example, small versus medium versus large businesses.
Cluster samples	The population is again grouped into subsets, but whole subsets are sampled separately—as in sampling by industry sectors.
Systematic samples	This is one of the easiest and best approaches to probability sampling. After a random start, every nth element (such as every 5th, 20th, or appropriate number) is systematically selected for sample inclusion.

The size of the ideal sample is difficult to specify and depends on several factors. Among these include the type of sampling techniques selected; the data analysis approach used; the population characteristics; the importance of the decision; and the time, budget, and marketing researchers available for the study. A review of past research studies found that the following sample sizes (the number of completed and usable surveys) were frequently used:

- Regional analyses of households with few data analysis breakouts (200 to 500)

- National analyses of households with few data analysis breakouts (1,000 to 1,500)

- National analyses of households with considerable data analysis breakouts (2,500)[6]

Point 8: Data Analysis

Once you have gathered the data, it must be analyzed to provide meaningful information. However, data analysis begins before you collect the data. To maximize the value of your findings, you should have a clear understanding of what information is being sought. You can develop blank data or "dummy" tables to provide a research model for the segmentation analysis. Exhibit 4-4 illustrates a simplified view of the educational computer market.

Exhibit 4-4: Data Table for the Educational Computer Market

Company Market/	Apple	Compaq	Dell	IBM	Other—Specify
Private Universities					
Public Universities					
Junior/Community Colleges					
Technical/Trade Schools					
High Schools					
Junior High Schools					
Elementary Schools					
Other					

For primary research, data analysis consists of three major procedures: coding, tabulating, and statistical analysis. Coding simplifies further analysis by classifying responses into predetermined categories. Tabulating, a basic data analysis procedure, provides the researcher with a mechanism to assess general relationships for key marketing variables. One of the most important data analysis techniques available, cross-tabulation, extends the value of tabulation by studying interrelationships among groups of marketing variables. Statistical computations can span the gamut from simple analysis (such as computing means, variances, or percentages) to advanced analyses (the multivariate techniques). Exhibit 4-5 provides a nontechnical summary of the major multivariate techniques used in segmentation analysis. In data analysis, practicality is of the essence. A complex segmentation model is not advisable if a simpler design adequately provides the required information.

EXHIBIT 4-5: MULTIVARIATE STATISTICAL TECHNIQUES

This synopsis provides a nontechnical overview of analytical techniques frequently employed in segmentation studies. These techniques are valuable when they are used in the right situation by experienced researchers. However, they will generally only be used after managers have a basic understanding of a market. In this capacity, they can enhance and complement prior segmentation findings. The objective of this summary is not to explain how to use multivariate analysis (that is a book in itself) but rather to acquaint the marketing planner with potential applications for these procedures. Just as carpenters carry many tools in their toolbox, the segmentation researcher should be knowledgeable about various analytical procedures. You are advised to consult marketing research or statistics texts for further information on multivariate statistical techniques. Two good sources are by Churchill[7] and Hair et al.[8]

Following are the major multivariate options:

Factor Analysis. Factor analysis is a marketing research technique that analyzes a large number of variables and reduces them to a smaller number of key factors to better explain a given marketing situation. Factor analysis is useful in psychographic and benefit research segmentation. There are two major types of factor analysis used in market segmentation studies. R-factor analysis reduces the amount of data by finding similarities in responses to particular variables. Q-factor analysis (the more important customer segmenting means) finds groupings of people who respond similarly to selected questions.

Cluster Analysis. Under this procedure, a set of related objects or variables (for example, demographic, socioeconomic, and/or psychographic) are analyzed, and through grouping techniques, segments are formed that have similarities in the overall statistical measure, and are therefore likely to exhibit similar purchasing behavior.

Multidimensional Scaling. Also referred to as *perceptual mapping*, this analytical technique graphically represents product attributes based on consumers' perceptions and preferences for brands, product or service categories, and/or ideal products. The objective of multidimensional scaling is to identify market segments of consumers with similar needs or attitudes toward products. Because more than two attributes cannot be visually depicted in two-dimensional space, variables are computer-reduced to portray appropriate market measures. This technique is frequently used in benefit and perceptual segmentation studies.

Conjoint Analysis. Also called *multiple trade-off analysis*, this analytical method measures the impact of varying product attribute mixes on the purchase decision. It models customer preferences or reactions to product concepts in terms of bundles of attributes.

This statistical approach ranks customer perceptions and preferences toward products. These are then evaluated and grouped for segment homogeneity. Conjoint measurement is frequently used for new product design, pricing-value studies, vendor/competitor evaluation, and media selection.

Multiple Regression. This versatile research technique is useful in analyzing associations among marketing variables. A mathematical equation is derived measuring a single dependent (criterion) variable based on two or more independent (predictor or explanatory) variables.

Predicting product usage as a function of age and household income is one example of multiple regression.

Discriminant Analysis. This technique is useful for comparing differences between segments or predicting group membership. Discriminant analysis is performed through computer-generated equations (Discriminant functions). This technique is effective in profiling Japanese versus American car buyers, heavy versus light users, loyal versus nonloyal customers, or adopters versus nonadopters for a new product concept, to show a few applications.

For secondary research, analysis often means updating and verifying information, manipulating figures, and adapting the data to appropriate units of measure for a given study. Statistical software packages such as SPSS and SAS are being used frequently by marketers to analyze a wide range of research problems.

Point 9: Cost Factors

In designing the research plan for the segmentation analysis, management's primary concern is minimizing costs. A decision has to be made on whether the research will be conducted in-house (are the requisite skills and time available for the project?) or through an outside agency (for example, a marketing research or consulting firm). A project conducted in-house is generally less expensive, because labor and related project expenses can be better controlled. A cost/benefit trade-off often exists in this situation. Management must ascertain the opportunities and risks in the marketplace, as well as the impact of a potentially wrong decision. In many cases, a hybrid approach may be desirable. The company may have the resources to assist in the segmentation analysis, but experienced advisers can be consulted to design the research plan, supervise the data collection process, and/or analyze the research data.

The expected value of the information must also be considered. A $50,000 research project should not be authorized if it is likely that the study will provide only $40,000 worth of answers. In many cases, the value of the information is difficult to assess. However, if a precedent exists, you can select those projects that appear most promising. Good-quality information is preferable to perfect information in most business situations, when cost factors are recognized. Although small firms have limited research budgets, a study found that 84% of small business owners felt that formal marketing research information was worth its cost. Nearly 60% of the entrepreneuers were able to substantially incorporate the findings into their business decisions.[9]

Point 10: Know How the Information Will Be Used

This final research element relates directly to the first planning guideline—establishing research objectives. Carefully prepared objectives provide you with clues for many of the answers to questions asked by management. In the course of the segmentation analysis, it is likely that the researcher will uncover other interesting findings. The key however, is the value of this information. New knowledge, serendipity, or surprising statistics are not important unless they are useful for marketing planning, strategy, or control. Written reports are seldom sufficient. A short research presentation is a great way of conveying technical information and segmentation recommendations to an interested audience. An informative briefing (use visuals!) can present complicated marketing research material to nontechnical listeners.[10]

Another consideration is the "real" purpose of the study. Research is sometimes authorized in order to justify a preconceived opinion, attitude, or position held on a subject by management. In such an instance, unless the findings agree with the established notion, the results of the research project will be downplayed or ignored.

Marketing information serves a definite purpose in the business world. It reduces uncertainty and provides a knowledge base on which you can make marketing decisions. The bottom line is that the information must be practical, workable, and used. Skillbuilder 4 gives you a chance to demonstrate your knowledge of segmentation research procedures.

SEGMENTATION SKILLBUILDER 4: DESIGNING AND IMPLEMENTING THE SEGMENTATION STUDY

The Vice President of Marketing liked your research concept (see Segmentation Skillbuilder 3: Setting Research Objectives) and wants to move forward with this project within 30 days. She asks you to "flesh out" a few details regarding the segmentation project as soon as possible. How would you address these ten important research issues?

1. Research design—exploratory, descriptive, or causal

2. Types of segmentation bases to be used

3. Source of data—primary, secondary, or syndicated

4. Type of survey instrument to be used

5. Sampling plan—type of sample and size

6. Field procedures and controls

7. Analytical and statistical methods

8. Projected value of the information

9. Personnel and timeframe

10. Required budget

✳ Suggested Reading: Wind, Yoram. "Issues and Advances in Segmentation Research," *Journal of Marketing Research*, August 1978, pp. 317-337.

SUMMARY

The 10 points discussed in this and the previous chapter are the key planning and research guidelines for successfully conducting a market segmentation analysis. However, segmentation projects require more than just following a series of steps. Every project is unique; sound planning and research procedures are critical. Other factors also can play a significant role in the analysis and must be scrutinized. These variables include the personnel employed, management's values, past marketing efforts, competitive actions, and perceived opportunities and threats.

Part 2 of the book (Chapters 5 through 11) builds on this information base and begins the segmentation process. The focus will be choosing the best consumer, industrial, and international segmentation bases and variables. In addition, that part looks at some important segmentation models and offers tips on how to maximize the value of segmentation research.

APPENDIX: SINGLE-SOURCE DATA SYSTEMS

Single-source data (SSD) systems are the latest information-based research method used to segment consumer and business markets. Developed during the 1980s, SSD technologies have come into their own in the 1990s. Also known as *relationship, integrated,* and *database marketing,* this powerhouse technology is defined (in great detail) by the National Center for Database Marketing as:

> Managing a computerized relational database system, in real time, of comprehensive, up-to-date, relevant data on customers, inquiries, prospects, and suspects, to identify your most responsive customers for the purpose of developing a high-quality, long-standing relationship of repeat business, by developing predictive models which enable us to send desired messages at the right time in the right form to the right people—all with the result of pleasing our customers, increasing our response rate per marketing dollar, lowering our cost per order, building our business, and increasing our profits.[11]

This high-tech, computer-driven approach measures marketing performance (sales, product usage, advertising effectiveness, and so forth) via the following forms: bar code scanners, television meters, databases, and electronic applications (advertising, couponing, or identification cards). Major players in the single-source field include giant marketing research firms such as Arbitron, Information Resources Inc. (IRI), Nielsen, NPD Group, and SAMI/Burke.

The retail grocery industry illustrates various applications of scanner information. Vons uses electronic couponing via a frequent shopping card, Lucky Stores employs zoned direct mail, and Ukrop's Super Markets generates targeted coupons for a frequent-shopper mailing.[12]

Marketing channel levels are useful for conceptualizing the diversity of SSD systems. Factory shipments are assessed at the manufacturer and wholesaler levels. In-store point-of-sale information is captured by retailers. Consumer information is provided by in-home SSD systems (such as TV audimeters).

Pros and Cons of SSD Systems

There are three major advantages of SSD systems: the behavioral variables employed, the wealth of information generated, and longitudinal analysis capabilities. Single-source data emphasizes action-oriented measures such as actual purchase behavior or television viewing patterns. This focus enables marketers to pinpoint relationships between independent variables (such as demographic or psychographic characteristics) and relevant behavioral dependent measures (for example, unit sales). Although correlations among variables may be evident, causality is difficult to infer. Nevertheless, market segments based on product/brand loyalty may be identified. The development of frequent buyer programs is a logical strategic outcome from this data.

SSD systems generate a tremendous amount of customer data. Improvements in computer technology enable marketers to create and sort ever-expanding databases. (Note: this data explosion can lead to information overload.) The key is to properly manage customer records and use this information effectively. Tracking changing customer patterns over time—longitudinal analysis—is an important benefit of SSD technology. This application has key implications for customer retention, customer upgrading, promotional activity, and competitive strategy.

Four limitations of SSD systems must also be recognized by potential users:

- Customer behavior is not explained. Single-source data is quantitative-based and does not qualitatively probe why customers act as they do.

- SSD systems are only useful in limited segmentation applications. Although database marketing opportunities are widespread, promotional-based applications are useful only for selected media. Although television and direct mail are well suited for this technology, to date, similar approaches cannot assess the effectiveness of radio, newspaper, or outdoor media vehicles.

- Many customers are concerned about the invasion of privacy issue that is omnipresent with this new technology.

- Costs for developing, implementing, and monitoring SSD systems are high. They must be carefully weighed against potential benefits.

Should You Enter the SSD Arena?

Companies thinking about initiating a SSD system can take one of three routes. They can develop a database system from scratch which often provides the best information at a reasonable cost. Drawbacks to this approach include a major investment in time and personnel resources and a lack of in-house expertise. Hence, this option is often not viable for the small firm. At the other extreme, a company can go with an established vendor and an existing system. This is an expensive proposition and may not be tailored enough to meet your firm's precise information needs. The third option, a hybrid system, is frequently the best alternative. Here, a firm buys a basic SSD system and customizes it to meet the firm's segmentation/information needs.

Following are five key questions to ask before you opt for single-source technology:

1. What behavioral variables will you measure?

2. What segment descriptors (demographic/psychographic variables) will you use?

3. Is your product/service category considered high involvement to customers?

4. How will the information generated be used to make segmentation and marketing strategy decisions?

5. What funds are available to invest in this technology?

Can you justify the cost of this investment?

Suggested Readings on SSD Systems

※ Curry, David J. "Single-Source Systems: Retail Management Present and Future." *Journal of Retailing,* Spring 1989, pp. 1-20.

※ Harrison, Randolph. "High-Tech Market Research." *Sky Magazine* (Delta Airlines), September 1987, pp. 24-37.

Mayer, Martin. "Scanning the Future." *Forbes,* October 15, 1990, pp. 114-117.

Schwartz, Joe. "Back to the Source." *American Demographics,* January 1989, pp. 22-26.

Winski, Joseph M. "Research Business Report: Gentle Rain Turns to Torrent." *Advertising Age,* June 3, 1991, p. 34.

Wolfe, Michael J. "'90s Will See 'Great Leap Forward' in Sales Tracking." *Marketing News,* September 3, 1990, p. 2.

NOTES

1. "Definition of Marketing Research," Chicago: American Marketing Association.

2. David A. Weiss, "Syndicated Studies Appeal to Marketers in a Hurry," *Marketing News*, September 11, 1989, p. 46.

3. Joel Raphael and I. Robert Parket, "The Need for Market Research in Executive Decision Making," *The Journal of Business and Industrial Marketing*, Winter/Spring 1991, pp. 15-21.

4. Johny K. Johansson and Ikujiro Nonaka, "Market Research the Japanese Way," *Harvard Business Review*, May/June 1987, pp. 16-18, 22.

5. *Corporate Technology Directory*, 7th U.S. Edition (Woburn, Mass.: Corporate Technology Information Services, Inc., 1992), Volumes 1-4.

6. Douglas J. Lincoln and Nina Ray, "Conducting Your Own Survey Research—Do's and Don'ts," *Nebraska Business Development Center Report*, January 1988, pp. 1-4.

7. Gilbert A. Churchill, Jr., *Marketing Research: Methodological Foundations*, Fourth Edition (Chicago: Dryden Press, 1987).

8. Joseph F. Hair, Jr., Ralph E. Anderson, and Ronald L. Tatham, *Multivariate Data Analysis with Readings*, Second Edition (New York: Macmillan, 1987).

9. Stephen W. McDaniel and A. Parasuraman, "Practical Guidelines for Small Business Marketing Research," *Journal of Small Business Management*, January 1986, pp. 1-8.

10. N. Carroll Mohn, "How to Effectively Present Marketing Research Results," *Quirk's Marketing Research Review*, January 1989, pp. 14, 16-17, 22-23.

11. Skip Andrew, The National Center for Database Marketing, 916-292-3000.

12. Bradley Johnson, "Grocers Learn to Nibble, Not Gulp: After Expensive Lessons, Chains Target More Carefully," *Advertising Age*, January 13, 1992, pp. 28-29.

MARKETS

GEOGRAPHIC SEGMENTATION

Where you live determines how you live.

—Michael J. Weiss, 1988

In identifying and selecting market segments, marketers evaluate consumers' residence, neighborhood, age, income, occupation, education, and myriad other descriptive characteristics. These critical issues can be understood by analyzing the geodemographic or physical attributes of a population. Geographic, demographic, and socioeconomic segmentation bases provide important decision-oriented insights about consumer and business markets.

Geodemographic segmentation is a logical starting point because

- The data is relatively easy to obtain through secondary sources or demographic vendors.

- It is less expensive than other forms of segmentation research.

- It provides a quick snapshot of a market—an understanding of market structure and potential customer segments.

- Populations can be sampled and accurately projected to represent characteristics of the entire market.

Physical attribute segmentation begins with geographic factors. Geographic analysis is one of the simplest methods for dividing markets into possible target segments. Therefore, this approach is the first step to consider when segmenting markets. Where people live, work, and play has a great impact on their purchasing behavior (see Exhibit 5-1). Regional differences can greatly impact product consumption in the United States. Consider these examples:

- Participation in jogging, aerobics, and health clubs is concentrated among young adults living in large coastal cities.[1]

- Coca-Cola's Mello Yello brand is popular in the south but not in the northeast.

- Campbell's markets a spicy nacho cheese soup for those west of the Mississippi but a milder version for easterners.

- General Foods found that coffee tastes vary locally, but breakfast cereal choices have wide appeal on a nationwide basis.

EXHIBIT 5-1: WHO'S NUMBER ONE? THE TOP U.S. MARKETS (PER CAPITA) FOR SELECTED PRODUCTS

Market	Product Class
Atlanta	Antacids and Aspirin
Dallas/Fort Worth	Popcorn
Denver	Vitamins
Grand Rapids	Rat Poison
Indianapolis	Shoe Polish
Miami	Prune Juice
New York	Laundry Soap
New Orleans	Ketchup
Oklahoma	Motor Oil Additives
Philadelphia	Iced Tea
Pittsburgh	Coffee
Portland, Oregon	Dry Cat Food
Salt Lake City	Candy Bars and Marshmallows
Savannah	MSG and Meat Tenderizers
Seattle	Toothbrushes

Source: SAMI (Selling Areas-Marketing Inc.), *Fortune Magazine,* © 1985 Time Inc. All rights reserved.

Geographic segmentation bases, market area definition, and mapping via the Census Bureau's TIGER system are the key topics discussed in this chapter. Consumer demographics and socioeconomics are the focus of the next chapter (business demographics are discussed in Chapter 9).

GEOGRAPHIC SEGMENTATION BASES

There is no single, best method for geographically segmenting the market. Factors to consider include the market you're competing in, available corporate resources (assets, capital, and personnel), competitors' strategies, flexibility in the manipulation of the marketing mix variables, and the firm's operating philosophy. Major geographic segmentation dimensions can be grouped into two categories: market scope factors and geographic market measures. Specific geographic bases (subgroupings) and variables (subgroup elements) to consider are summarized here as part of market scope and geographic market measures.

Market Scope

Global Scope. The global scope comprises worldwide, international regional markets (the European Community, Latin America, or Asia), selected countries, or domestic market only (a nonglobal outlook). One interesting view of North America stated that there were nine "nations" rather than three. These nations (and their capital cities) were: Islands (Miami), Empty Quarter (Denver), Breadbasket (Kansas City), Quebec (Quebec City), New England (Boston), Dixie (Atlanta), Ecotopia (San Francisco), Mexamerica (Los Angeles), and Foundry (Detroit).[2]

National/Regional Scope. The national and regional scope comprises the entire U.S. market, regional (Southeast or Pacific Northwest), selected states, or selected metropolitan areas. A one-state (Florida) strategy worked successfully for Publix Super Markets, Inc. for more than 60 years.

Local Scope. Local is, of course, just a county, city, township, ZIP code, or a neighborhood focus. This is of particular interest to many small retailers and service firms.

Geographic Market Measures

Census Classifications. Metropolitan Statistical Areas (MSAs), Primary Metropolitan Statistical Areas (PMSAs), Consolidated Metropolitan Statistical Areas (CMSAs), census tracts, and census blocks are some of the more important geographic breakdowns the marketer needs to be familiar with (Exhibit 5-2 discusses the census classifications). From 1980 to 1990, most of the U.S. population growth was in the Sunbelt. It is interesting to note that 37 of the 50 fastest growing metropolitan areas were in Florida, California, or Texas.[3]

EXHIBIT 5-2: CENSUS GEOGRAPHY

According to the Bureau of the Census, an area qualifies for recognition as a Metropolitan Statistical Area (MSA) in one of two ways: if it is a city/place with least 50,000 inhabitants, or an urbanized area with a total metropolitan population of at least 100,000 (75,000 in New England). In addition to the county containing the main city, an MSA also includes additional counties having strong economic and social ties to the central county, determined chiefly by the extent of the urbanized area and census data on commuting to work. An MSA may contain more than one city of 50,000 population and may cross state lines.

If an area has more than 1 million population and meets certain other specified requirements, it is termed a Consolidated Metropolitan Statistical Area (CMSA). A CMSA consists of major components called Primary Metropolitan Statistical Areas (PMSAs). As of December 31, 1992, there were 19 CMSAs consisting of 62 PMSAs, and 253 defined MSAs.

Blocks/block groups, census tracts, and minor civil divisions are some other important measures of localized census geography. Aggregating data at these levels provides the neighborhood business (the retailer, bank, or shopping center developer) with precise information to make market/site decisions.

For further information contact:

Customer Services Branch
Data User Services Division
Bureau of the Census
Washington, D.C. 20233-0001
(301) 763-4100 (telephone)
(301) 763-4794 (fax)

Standardized Market Area Measures. Leading marketing research companies have designated geographic market areas for television coverage and other studies. Arbitron's Areas of Dominant Influence (ADIs) and A.C. Nielsen's Designated Market Areas (DMAs) are two such examples.

Population Density and Climate-Related Factors. Urban, suburban, or rural markets reveal population density levels and lifestyle, and relate to purchase behavior. Car alarms and security devices are popular in inner cities. Barbecue grills sell well in suburban areas, whereas rural consumers are likely to own a riding lawnmower. The product's usage can determine natural geographic markets. For example, suntan lotion can be sold year round in Florida or California, whereas ice scrapers require frigid, northern weather conditions.

Summary of Geographic Bases

The market scope and geographic market measures provide a basic framework of the most common dimensions on which geographic market decisions can be based. The categories are not mutually exclusive, however. Within some classifications, you should examine more than one variable, and explore and analyze several forms of geographic bases to maximize the value of the marketing information. How do you define your market geographically? Segmentation Skillbuilder 5 raises pertinent issues in the geographic market definition.

SEGMENTATION SKILLBUILDER 5: DEFINING GEOGRAPHIC MARKETS

A critical task facing marketers is market definition. A market is people (actual and potential customers), purchasing power, needs, and products. Geographic issues also play a large role in this formula. A market defined too narrowly limits opportunities; one defined too broadly may lead to mass marketing mentality. Using the geographic segmentation insights described in this chapter, how do you presently define your market? Are there other geographic approaches that you are not but should be using? Here are a dozen issues to ponder:

1. Do you compete internationally? (If not, go to question 3.)
2. Are your products marketed worldwide or to selected nations/regions? Specify current and proposed markets. (Stop here—be sure to read Chapter 10, "Segmenting International Markets.")
3. Are your products sold in two or more U.S. states? Specify current and proposed regions/states. (If you do business locally or in a single state, go to question 9.)
4. What CMSAs, PMSAs, and MSAs are you targeting now? Which are you thinking about targeting?
5. Are you using ADIs or DMAs to define markets?
6. Does population density (urban, suburban, or rural) impact your geographic market definition?
7. Does climate impact your geographic market definition?
8. Do regional factors impact your market?
9. Are your products sold locally? Specify current and proposed counties, cities, townships, ZIP codes, and/or neighborhoods.
10. Are you using minor civil divisions (county subunits), census tracts, block groups, or blocks to understand localized geography?
11. Is your market defined via rings, bands, sectors, or polygons? Describe your market geometrically.
12. Have you identified a primary, secondary, and/or tertiary trade area?

✳   Suggested Reading: McKenna, Shawn. *The Complete Guide to Regional Marketing.* (Homewood, Ill.: Business One Irwin, 1992.)

Geographic Segmentation

DEFINING MARKET AREAS

A major strategic decision that all companies face is how to define and best serve their geographic market areas. Many options are possible, ranging from the global view (the multinational company) to the local view (the small business merchant). To better understand their markets, retailers and service firms can benefit by identifying a primary trade area (PTA) and secondary trade area (STA). Sometimes, even a tertiary trade area (TTA) is desirable. Based on research conducted by Donnelley Marketing Information Services, Exhibit 5-3 presents localized guidelines for trade area definition.

Although distance measures are typically used to define markets, Arby's found that drive time was more important. Seventy-five percent of their customers traveled eleven minutes or less from their home or workplace to the restaurant.[4]

Geographic areas based on postal ZIP codes, census classifications, or standardized market area measures, as well as customized geometric market areas such as rings, bands, sectors, or polygons are also typically used to define markets (see Exhibit 5-4). Although circles are popular, they cannot accurately represent trade barriers because of natural barriers (for example, rivers), transportation networks, the irregular shopping patterns of consumers, and competitive store locations.[5]

EXHIBIT 5-3: A RETAILER'S GUIDE TO DEFINING TRADE AREAS

- *Primary Trade Area:* The trade area from which the store receives approximately 75% of its customers; the area immediately surrounding the store.

- *Secondary Trade Area:* The trade area from which the store receives an additional 15-25% of its customers; an area more distant from the store than the primary trade area.

- *Tertiary Trade Area:* The remaining area from which the store may draw customers (generally less than 10% of its customers).

Convenience Goods	Radius	Shopping Goods	Radius
Urban Area		**Urban Area**	
Primary	1 Mile	Primary	3 Miles
Secondary	2 Miles	Secondary	5 Miles
Tertiary	3 Miles	Tertiary	10 Miles
Suburban Area		**Suburban Area**	
Primary	1 Mile	Primary	10 Miles
Secondary	3 Miles	Secondary	15 Miles
Tertiary	5 Miles	Tertiary	20 Miles
Rural Area		**Rural Area**	
Primary	2 Miles	Not Applicable	
Secondary	5 Miles	N/A	
Tertiary	8 Miles	N/A	

75

- *Convenience Goods:* Products/services that consumers purchase on a regular/repeat basis. Consumers will not normally travel great distances for convenience goods. Examples include grocery stores, fast food restaurants, drug stores, banks, and hair salons.

- *Shopping Goods:* These are usually products/services that are higher ticket items, purchased on an irregular basis. Consumers will normally travel greater distances for such products or services. Examples are furniture stores, department stores, catalog showrooms, and elegant restaurants.

Source: Donnelley Marketing Information Services, Inc., a company of the Dun and Bradstreet Corporation.

Exhibit 5-4: Geographic and Geometric Market Areas

GEOGRAPHIC STUDY AREAS

Data can be requested for any of the following types. If they do not overlap, it is possible to aggregate data for different area types.

United States Summary

The 50 states and the District of Columbia.

States

The District of Columbia is counted as a state. Data is not available for Puerto Rico, Guam, Virgin Islands, American Samoa, or other outlying U.S. territories.

Counties

Also includes Independent Cities, such as Baltimore, MD; St. Louis, MO; Carson City, NV; and more than 40 cities in Virginia. In Alaska, boroughs and census tract areas act as county equivalents. In Louisiana, parishes act as county equivalents.

Metropolitan Areas

These areas are determined by the Office of Management and Budget (OMB) and include: Consolidated Metropolitan Areas (CMSAs), Primary Metropolitan Statistical Areas (PMSAs), and Metropolitan Statistical Areas (MSAs).

Areas of Dominant Influence (ADIs)

These are media areas defined by the Arbitron Company, usually consisting of one or more whole counties.

Designated Market Areas (DMAs)

These are media areas defined by A.C. Nielsen, usually consisting of one or more whole counties.

County Subdivisions

(Townships, New England Towns, etc.)

When you specify a township, New England town, or other legally constituted county subdivision, please provide the county in which the area resides.

Zip Code Areas

Specify only those five-digit Zip Codes that have residential population associated with them.

Census Tracts

Specify the state and county for each group of census tracts.

Block Groups

A cluster of blocks having the same first digit of their three-digit identifying numbers within a census tract or block numbering area.

Other standard area types (such as school districts or wards) may be simulated by polygons.

©1993 UDS, Los Angeles, CA (800) 633-9568.

GEOMETRIC STUDY AREAS

Rings are determined by specifying the radius—the distance from a site to the periphery of the ring. There is no limit to the number of concentric radii around a site.

Bands are like rings in every respect, except that they are mutually exclusive. A 5-10 mile band includes only the area that falls within the 5-10 mile band from your specified site.

Sectors divide your study area into segments—like a pie that has been cut into pieces.

Polygons are areas defined by a series of line segments. Polygons may have as few as three points or as many as several thousand. Polygons are best accomplished by your providing a map of your study area.

Other geometric study areas are also available, including corridors (equal band widths on both sides of a line) or cuts (lines that subdivide a ring or polygon based on proximity to nearby competitor sites). Call for details.

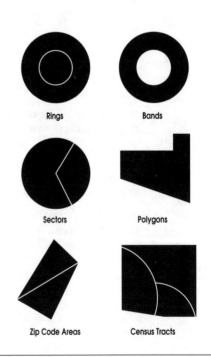

Rings	Bands
Sectors	Polygons
Zip Code Areas	Census Tracts

GEOGRAPHIC MAPPING: PUT A TIGER ON YOUR TEAM?

It has been said that the business world is a jungle. Perhaps that means that you need to add a TIGER to your side. The TIGER (Topologically Integrated Geographic Encoding and Referencing) system is the Census Bureau's newest, most innovative service, which provides computer-readable mapping and a geographic database for the entire United States. Plotting geographic coordinates, TIGER serves as the underlay for address/area data (demographic, economic, and so on) that users provide that results in high-quality, digital maps for a variety of geographic areas. An example of a TIGER map for the Washington, D.C. area is shown in Exhibit 5-5.

EXHIBIT 5-5: A TIGER MAP

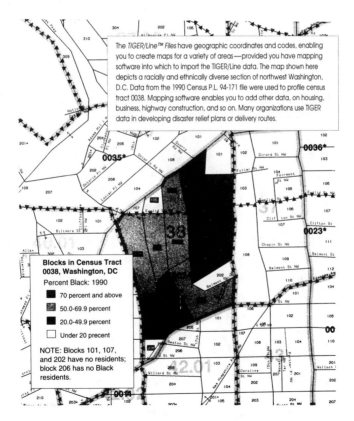

Source: U.S. Department of Commerce, Bureau of the Census

Geographic Segmentation

There are many marketing and geographic information system (GIS) applications for the TIGER system. Direct marketers and delivery-intensive businesses can greatly benefit from TIGER. For example, pizza delivery drivers can easily locate their targeted destinations, whereas pizzerias can accurately track who their customers are and where they live.[6] Banks can use TIGER to better place ATMs, automakers can put car owners in touch with nearby dealers, and Federal Express trucks can deliver faster.[7] TIGER is also valuable for site selection decisions, analyzing trade areas, setting up distribution routes, tracking subscriber services, and targeted promotion (direct mailings, couponing, product sampling, and so forth). Future enhancements through the incorporation of demographics, psychographics, and product usage data can make TIGER ideal for market segmentation.

TIGER/Line files can be purchased on a statewide or national basis on computer tape or CD-ROM. (Each compact disk is equivalent to 1,600 360K floppy diskettes.) Currently, the price of TIGER files varies from as little as $100 for a single CD (there are 44 disks for the United States) to $38,000 for the whole country on computer tape. Because this information requires further data processing, you might want to consider using a "TIGER trainer" (specialist) to generate your maps. As of April 1993, more than 140 vendors have notified the Census Bureau that they have the capacity to process TIGER files. These include demographic leaders CACI and Claritas; geographic product specialists such as DATAMap, Geographic Data Technology, Sammamish Data Systems, Urban Science Applications, and Western Economic Research; as well as dozens of other companies that provide specialized TIGER-related services.

For further information on the TIGER resource list, contact the Bureau of the Census at (301) 763-4100 or via modem at (301) 763-7554.

Segmentation Action List 5: Computer Mapping: Key Questions

1. What type of system is appropriate? PC-based, mini, or mainframe?

2. What type of software is provided?

3. How good is the quality of the finished maps?

4. Are zooming (the ability to blow up the picture) capabilities provided?

5. Can you add your own data to the system?

6. How flexible is the output?

7. How easy is the system to use?

8. Can you "test drive" the system?

9. How much support is provided by the vendor?

10. How much does it cost?

Note: Several questions are adapted from the list developed by Marci L. Belcher in Martha Farnsworth Riche's article, "Computer Mapping Takes Center Stage," *American Demographics,* June 1986, p. 30.

SUMMARY

Geographic analysis is the logical starting point for market segmentation. This information is low cost and readily available. Regional marketing is on the rise in the 1990s. Often, geographic insights can tell you a great deal about customer purchase patterns.

Geographic bases for segmentation include market scope (global, national/regional, or local) and geographic market measures (census classifications, standardized market area measures, and population density and climate-related factors). It is a good idea to use various geographic bases to define markets. Retailers and service firms can use standard geographic areas, custom geometric areas, and drive time to identify their market trade or service areas.

The Census Bureau's TIGER (Topologically Integrated Geographic Encoding and Reference) system offers promise for enterprising marketers. Computer mapping is an emerging field in the 1990s. The next chapter extends this discussion by integrating demographic analysis into your market profiles.

NOTES

1. Paul Hall, "The Real America," *American Demographics,* December 1989, pp. 22-27.

2. Joel Garreau, *The Nine Nations of North America* (Boston: Houghton Mifflin, 1981).

3. Joe Schwartz and Thomas Exter, "This World Is Flat," *American Demographics*, April 1991, pp. 34-39.

4. John Freeling, "Use Drive Times to Build Trading Areas and Market Segments," *Marketing News*, May 10, 1993, p. 2.

5. Stephen J. Tordella, "How to Relate to Centroids," *American Demographics,* May 1987, pp. 46, 50.

6. Howard Schlossberg, "Census Bureau's TIGER Seen as a Roaring Success," *Marketing News,* April 30, 1990, p. 2.

7. Len Strazewski, "Mega Map," *The Marketer*, May 1990, p. 52, 54.

8. Martha Farnsworth Riche, "Computer Mapping Takes Center Stage," *American Demographics,* June 1986, pp. 26-31.

DEMOGRAPHIC AND
SOCIOECONOMIC SEGMENTATION

**Nowadays people can be divided into three classes—the Haves,
the Have-Nots, and the Have-Not-Paid-For-What-They-Haves.**

—Earl Wilson, 1964

Demography is the statistical study of human populations and their vital
characteristics. Socioeconomic factors, which are closely linked to demographics,
are used to analyze a population in terms of economic and social classes.
The broad definition of demographics as used in market analysis includes
both demographic and socioeconomic variables (as well as geographics). For
illustrative purposes, this chapter examines these areas separately (see Exhibit
6-1). Later in this chapter, these segmentation bases will be combined for the
discussion of geodemographic clustering. The chapter concludes with a
discussion of where to find demographics and managerial guidelines for the
purchase and use of this information.

EXHIBIT 6-1: DEMOGRAPHICS VERSUS SOCIOECONOMICS

Demographics	Socioeconomics
Population	Education
Number of Households/Families	Occupation
Household Size/Family Size	Income
Age Distribution	Home Ownership Factors:
Family Life Cycle	*Homeowner versus renter
Marital Status	*Type of dwelling
Gender	*Mobility/stability
Race*	Social Class
Nationality*	
Religion*	

*Note: Although race, nationality, and religion are inherent attributes like age
and marital status, many demographers feel that in actual practice they are used
as if they were related to economics and social class (socioeconomic variables).

DEMOGRAPHIC BASES

Many of the common demographic dimensions are interrelated, or similar, from an analytical perspective. Recognizing this, it is possible to group these variables into four major categories. Because demographic analysis has been the traditional approach to market segmentation and these dimensions are understood by most managers, comments about these bases will be kept brief. It should be noted, however, that prior to conducting demographic or socioeconomic analysis, a geographic market area (as discussed in Chapter 5) must be specified.

Group 1: Market Size Factors

This group consists of population, the number of households or families, and household or family size. The key variable that must be gathered in a demographic study is the total population of the market in question. Although total population is not a segmenting variable (rarely is it feasible to go after the whole market), it acts as a yardstick against which other dimensions can be measured. For example, by knowing the total population in a market, it is possible to state that 15% of the individuals within that market are under 18 years old.

The number of households or families in an area provides a similar measure. However, instead of determining how many individuals are within a given market, the number of "buying centers" are identified. A doctor looking to expand his or her practice would find this statistic helpful. If one family member used the physician's services, it is likely that the others would follow suit when they needed medical attention.

The third variable within this group—household or family size—is a derivation of the other two. By dividing the number of households or families into the total population, the average household or family size for an area can easily be calculated. For example, most Florida counties have below average household sizes (due to the high percentage of senior citizens); in contrast, Salt Lake City, Utah, has large households due to high birth rates. Such information is of great value in assessing market potential, particularly for a company offering goods or services with widespread market appeal.

Group 2: Age and Stage

The underlying premise behind the factors in group two, age distribution and family life cycle, is that individuals classified by certain age groups (18-24, 25-34, 35-44, and so on) or stages in their family life cycle (unmarried; married—no children, young children, or teenagers; or empty nest) will exhibit certain similarities in purchasing behavior. New parents—whether 21 or 39—have the same need for diapers and related products for their babies.

Age impacts many product categories. Teenagers purchase a large share of the compact disks and cassettes, middle-age consumers buy most of the life insurance, and senior citizens account for a disproportionate share of health care expenditures.

By the year 2000, half of all Americans will be more than 38 years of age.[1] The graying of America presents many opportunities (as well as challenges) to marketers. Promising niches for the mature market include these product categories: home-based goods and services, healthcare, leisure products, personal and business counseling, educational services, financial products and services, and products that combat aging.[2]

Group 3: Men and Women

This grouping looks at marital status and gender categories. Changing lifestyles—including the high divorce rate, increases in one-parent families, cohabitation, increasing number of singles, and more visible gay population—necessitates research on marital status to understand consumer markets. A comparison of 1991 census data to 1970 information revealed that:

- 30% of American households were married couples without children at home (no change from the 1970 level).

- 30% were single person households (an increase from 20%).

- Only 26% of U.S. households were traditional married couples with at least one child living at home (decline from 40%).

- Single-parent families have increased from 3.8 million to 10.1 million (90% of the these households were headed by mothers).

- POSSLQs (persons of opposite sex sharing living quarters) or unmarried couples increased from 0.5 million to 3 million.[3] These statistics show that the "Leave it to Beaver" nuclear family has declined dramatically in number.

As a result, many companies are targeting "nontraditional" households. Health club owners, home builders, restaurants, travel agents, and telecommunications services are among those who have recently pursued the significant purchasing power of the expanding singles market.

The second half of this grouping looks at the number of males and females in a market. Although there still are many male- or female-oriented products (Right Guard versus Secret deodorant) or services (barber shops or nail care) in the marketplace, many changes have occurred in purchasing behavior. A lot of this is due to the redefinition of traditional male-female roles that has taken place as women have entered the labor force. Although it is typically reported that about two-thirds of women work, a recent study found that about 90% of females, aged 18 to 49, can be considered working women.[4]

Group 4: Race, Nationality, and Religion

A local advertising slogan proclaimed the message, "We're all different; we're all the same." This theme relates well to the variables in group four. America embodies a great diversity of people, with different ethnic backgrounds, countries of national origin, and religious preferences. These differences can greatly affect individuals' values, beliefs, and needs—and at times, purchasing behavior. Minority marketing is the rage for the 1990s. Projections show that minorities will represent the majority of all growth for the foreseeable future, accounting for as much as 80%.[5]

Research shows that New York City's Hispanics have a highly concentrated purchasing influence on grocery products, which can increase a brand's overall market share dramatically in that area. Consider these examples by Hispanic, non-Hispanic, and total usage: Libby's canned fruit (40%, 8%, 14%), Mazola salad oil (67%, 19%, 25%), and Hawaiian Punch (72%, 22%, 32%).[6] Although Spanish language advertising is common in leading Hispanic markets such as Miami, New York, Los Angeles, and San Antonio, a new trend is the creation of products geared specifically for ethnic groups. General Mills recently introduced Bunuelitos, a sweetened corn puff cereal in five Southwestern states that account for 60% of the nation's Hispanic population.[7]

In addition to Hispanics, Asian-Americans are the fastest growing and most affluent group, and African-Americans are still the largest in number (Hispanics are projected to become the largest American minority group in the early twenty-first century). Metropolitan Life Insurance has found that Asian-Americans are a hard working, well educated, loyal and good paying market segment. Specially designed promotional literature reflects further subsegmentation for their Chinese, Japanese, Korean, and Vietnamese customers.

McDonald's, Maybelline, and Mattel are some of the many companies actively targeting African-Americans in their print and broadcast advertising. Research found that the three groups—African-Americans (30 million), Hispanic Americans (22.3 million), and Asian-Americans (7.3 million) value a positive role for minorities in advertising. The marketer's challenge is to hit the subculture's "hot button" while avoiding stereotypical images that might offend the targeted minority market. Exhibit 6-2 summarizes background and geodemographic issues relevant to the three major minority markets.

EXHIBIT 6-2: MINORITY MARKETS IN THE UNITED STATES

Issue	African-Americans	Asian-Americans	Hispanic-Americans
Market Size and Growth	Largest racial minority	Fastest-growing minority	Projected largest minority by 2015?
Regional Stronghold	South, MSAs, central cities	West coast (CA)	CA, FL, TX, and NY
Demographic Sketch	Young families, many female head of household	Family-oriented	High birth rates, male dominant, extended families
Socioeconomic Sketch	Lower income, less education (generally)	High income, well-educated, entrepreneurs	Income varies by subgroup
Marketing Implications	Strong middle class emerging, twofold media (general and black)	Influenced by Eastern cultures, savers, loyal customers	Spanish-language media, quality seekers

Yet, for other product categories, ethnic differences have little bearing on consumption patterns. Recently there have been more interracial marriages than ever before, religion has been deemphasized by many people, and cultures and nationalities are assimilating into American society. These forces serve to "blend" America and minimize differences among people.

**Demographic and
Socioeconomic Segmentation**

SOCIOECONOMIC BASES

Just as demographic measures can be combined for discussion purposes into smaller groups, socioeconomic factors also can be viewed as clusters.

Group 1: The Monetary Factors

It is no secret that a person's educational background, occupation, and income are interrelated. There is a direct relationship among these three variables. Generally, the more education a person has, the greater the likelihood of a better position and increased earnings. However, people have varying propensities to buy, and income alone cannot always accurately predict purchasing behavior. One certified financial planner acknowledged that some of his clients get by on $30,000 a year, whereas others "struggle" on $300,000 annually.

One market segment in particular has gained notoriety during the past few years: the young affluent professional sector. As numerous companies have targeted the dual-income baby-boomer generation, such acronyms as Yuppies (young urban professionals), Yaps (young aspiring professionals), and Yummies (young upwardly mobile mommies) have become part of the marketer's jargon. However, if you are not careful, this media publicity can backfire on you. A large number of companies have focused their efforts on Yuppies. With so many goods and services chasing this limited customer submarket, the saturation point can often be quickly reached. Additionally, other potentially profitable market opportunities may be neglected or even missed. The Sears Financial Network (Allstate Insurance, Dean Witter Securities, and Coldwell-Banker Real Estate companies) have recognized that most financial concerns are targeting consumers in the upper 10% income bracket. They have responded by going after middle America, a lucrative market largely ignored by major competitors.

A major reason for the increased attention on baby boomers—those born between 1946 and 1964—was the election of the all-boomer ticket of Bill and Hillary Clinton (and Al Gore?) to the highest political offices. Aging Yuppies have spawned a new acronym: Grumpies (grown-up mature professionals). Marketers have responded to the "old youth" with such products as miniature Oreos and Haagen-Daz ice cream bars, lineless bifocals, and jeans that accommodate those with expanding behinds. [9]

Other generations have recently burst onto the marketing scene. Waiting in the wings are the post-boomers, Generation X or the Thirteenth Generation (disgruntled teens and twenty-somethings often reported by the media to be worse off financially than their parents) and the Millennial Generation (preteens) who represent the hope for the world's future.[10]

Group 2: Homeownership Factors

Among the variables composing this group are the issues of homeowner versus renter, the type of dwelling that households reside in, and household mobility and stability measures. Homeowners are better prospects than renters for a number of products and services. Examples include furniture, major appliances, and wall coverings (products), and lawn care, exterminating, and insurance (services). On the other hand, renters are preferable choices for rental furniture and roommate referral services. The type of dwelling also influences purchasing behavior. The owner of a single family home has different (and similar) needs for goods and services than the owner of a multifamily dwelling, townhouse, condominium, or the apartment resident.

Household mobility and stability are other interesting marketing statistics. The former measures the population turnover (influx and exodus) for an area within a designated time frame. The latter examines the length of time households reside in a given area. If a metropolitan area has an average household mobility factor of 0.25, one out of every four residences have changed over (households have either moved in or out) within the past year. Donnelley's *Market Profile Analysis* is a good source for finding this information. Stability indicates the percentage or numbers of households that have resided in an area for a given period; for example, less than a year, one to three years, three to five years, or more than five years.

These statistics arm the marketer with valuable knowledge. Some of this information can be critical in decision making. Here are some marketing implications:

- A stable community may be difficult to penetrate for a new company. Because the residents tend to be older, they are more likely to be set in their ways.

- In an area with a high turnover ratio, it may be easier for a company to attract new customers, but developing long-term customer relationships is more difficult.

- New homeowners are an excellent segment to target. They need furniture, wall coverings, dry cleaners, dentists, and a whole lot more. New homeowners spend substantially more than established residents and are seeking businesses to patronize.

Group 3: Social Class and Geodemographic Clustering

Social class is a reflection and compilation of many of the aforementioned demographic and socioeconomic bases. Space doesn't permit a detailed review, but a couple of key points need to be made about this variable. Traditionally, the lower-lower to upper-upper social class pyramid was the most common method of categorizing individuals by caste, although this method was somewhat simplistic. Today more advanced cluster-based geodemographic systems are frequently used by major companies throughout the United States. Services such as Donnelley's Cluster-Plus, Claritas' PRIZM, and CACI's ACORN are census-based and useful for understanding neighborhood types. An adaptation of Cluster-Plus is Donnelley's Hispanic Clusters (Exhibit 6-3). A profile of Cluster M1 in the Mexican-American submarket is shown in Exhibit 6-4. According to Donnelley, knowing in which cluster a consumer lives provides a reasonable means of understanding how that consumer will behave in the marketplace. The product potential index (penetration index average = 100) can be compared by Cluster-Plus segments. An index of 50 means that the cluster purchases only half of the norm, while an index of 250 means that cluster consumes 2.5 times what is expected on a national basis.

EXHIBIT 6-3: HISPANIC CLUSTERS

		% of U.S. Hispanic Households
Mexican Submarket		**63.5%**
M1	Higher income, middle aged, large families, single family homes	10.7%
M2	High income, older, established, large families, single family homes	2.0%
M3	Young, upwardly mobile, average income, average size families	17.0%
M4	Young, low income, few children, newcomers, singles, apartment dwellers	17.8%
M5	Lowest income, younger, low mobility, Hispanic neighborhoods	16.0%
Cuban Submarket		**6.6%**
C1	Higher income, professionals, families, single family homes	2.3%
C2	Older, established, above average income, Hispanic neighborhoods	0.8%
C3	Middle aged to older, low income, small families, apartment dwellers	2.8%
C4	Older, lowest income, Spanish speaking, Hispanic neighborhoods	0.7%
Puerto Rican Submarket		**11.3%**
P1	High income, younger, established, single/multifamily homes	3.3%
P2	Below-average income, singles and small families, apartment dwellers	3.7%
P3	Very low income, younger, Spanish speaking, apartments and low value housing	3.1%
P4	Lowest income, very young, small families, Spanish speaking, large apartment buildings	1.2%
Other Hispanic Submarket		**18.8%**
H1	Higher income, younger to middle aged, professionals, high value homes	1.6%
H2	High income, middle aged to older, established, large families, single family homes	2.8%
H3	Average income, young, low value homes, mixed Hispanic neighborhoods	7.6%
H4	Average income, young, newcomers, small families, large apartment buildings	2.4%
H5	Very low income, young, families, female head of households, Spanish speaking, mixed Hispanic neighborhoods	4.4%

©1991 DMIS, Stanford, CT 12/91.

Exhibit 6-4: A Mexican-American Cluster

Mexican Submarket

Cluster M1.   **10.7% of the U.S. Hispanic Market**

Higher income, many lines of credit, middle aged (40 and above) head of household, large families, single-family homes.

Household Description	
Median Income:	35.5K
Length of Residence:	8 years
Credit:	Many lines of credit
Car:	Two cars, one car new; high value; Japanese and American (Toyotas, Fords); hatchbacks, Jeeps, Pick-ups.
Mail Responsiveness:	High
Contributions:	Health, Religious

Neighborhood Description		
Mostly White and Mexican, medium to high income, single-family home.		
Blue Collar:	33%	
White Collar:	52%	
Public Assistance	7%	
Ethnic Composition:	Mexican	22%
	Other Hispanic	3%
Foreign Born:	10%	
Foreign Language spoken at home:	17%	
Speak only Spanish:	3%	

Cluster PLUS Hispanic Portraits ©DMIS, Stanford, CT.

The PRIZM (Potential Rating Index for Zip Markets) system was founded in 1974. Jonathan Robbin created a new way of looking at the United States— not as fifty states but rather forty neighborhood types, each with distinctive boundaries, values, and consuming habits. In a nation that prides itself on being classless and egalitarian, cluster systems reflect the marketing reality of how different consumers live.[11] Today, the PRIZM service is widely used by advertisers, banks, direct mailers, healthcare providers, insurance companies, retailers, and many other target marketers.

This powerful marketing system integrates geodemographic data with neighborhood lifestyle information and is well suited for segmenting markets, understanding customers' product preferences, choosing sites, and designing advertising and promotional strategies. PRIZM's forty clusters (which are easily grouped into 12 broader social groups) are listed in Exhibit 6-5. A comparison of two distinct PRIZM clusters, "Pools & Patios" and "Heavy Industry" is shown in Exhibit 6-6. PRIZM output is available in a variety of formats, such as magnetic tape, desktop PC files, on-line access, and hard-copy reports. PRIZM Canada classifies every Canadian neighborhood in terms of 24 clusters that are compatible with its American counterparts.

At the time of publication, Claritas was completing the next generation of PRIZM, which includes the ability to integrate household data for customized microsegmentation. The new and improved PRIZM system combines 1990 census data with annual demographic updates and behavioral information. To maximize its value, clients can also add their own industry-specific data to the basic PRIZM structure.

EXHIBIT 6-5: AMERICA'S 40 NEIGHBORHOOD TYPES: PRIZM R

PRIZM Cluster	Thumbnail Description	% of U.S.Households
Blue Blood Estates	America's wealthiest neighborhoods, including suburban homes, and 1 in 10 millionaires	1.1
Money and Brains	Posh big-city enclaves of townhouses, houses, condos and apartments	0.9
Furs and Station Wagons	New money in metropolitan bedroom suburbs	3.8
Urban Gold Coast	Upscale urban high-rise districts	0.4
Pools and Patios	Older, upper-middle class, suburban communities	3.3

Demographic and
Socioeconomic Segmentation

PRIZM Cluster	Thumbnail Description	% of U.S.Households
Two More Rungs	Comfortable multiethnic suburbs	0.7
Young Influentials	Yuppie, fringe-city condo and apartment developments	3.0
Young Suburbia	Child-rearing, outlying suburbs	6.3
God's Country	Upscale frontier boomtowns	3.3
Blue-Chip Blues	The wealthiest blue-collar suburbs	6.2
Bohemian Mix	Inner-city bohemian enclaves a la Greenwich Village	1.0
Levittown, USA	Aging, post World War II tract subdivisions	2.9
Gray Power	Upper-middle-class retirement communities	3.1
Black Enterprise	Predominantly black, middle- and upper-middle class neighborhoods	0.7
New Beginnings	Fringe-city areas of singles complexes, garden apartments, and trim bungalows	4.1
Blue-Collar Nursery	Middle-class, child-rearing towns	2.3
New Homesteaders	Exurban boom towns of young midscale families	4.8
New Melting Pot	New immigrant neighborhoods, primarily in the nation's port cities	0.8
Towns & Gowns	America's college towns	1.6
Rank & File	Older, blue-collar, industrial suburbs	1.3
Middle America	Midscale, midsize towns	3.2
Old Yankee Rows	Working-class rowhouse districts	1.4
Coalburg & Corntown	Small towns based on light industry and farming	2.0
Shotguns & Pickups	Crossroads villages serving the nation's lumber and breadbasket needs	1.9
Golden Ponds	Rustic cottage communities located near the coasts, in the mountains, or alongside lakes	5.0
Agribusiness	Small towns surrounded by large-scale farms and ranches	2.1
Emergent Minorities	Predominantly black, working-class city neighborhoods	1.5
Single City Blues	Downscale, urban, singles districts	3.2
Mines & Mills	Struggling steeltowns and mining villages	3.0
Back-Country Folks	Remote, downscale, farm towns	3.4
Norma Rae-ville	Lower-middle-class milltowns and industrial suburbs, mainly in the South	2.3
Smalltown Downtown	Inner-city districts of small industrial cities	2.2
Grain Belt	The nation's most sparsely populated rural communities	1.2
Heavy Industry	Lower-working-class districts in the nation's oldest industrial cities	2.4

PRIZM Cluster	Thumbnail Description	% of U.S.Households
Share Croppers	Primarily southern hamlets devoted to farming and light industry	3.8
Downtown Dixie Style	Aging, predominantly black neighborhoods, typically in Southern cities	2.9
Hispanic Mix	America's Hispanic barrios	1.6
Tobacco Roads	Predominantly black farm communities throughout the South	1.2
Hard Scrabble	The nation's poorest rural settlements	1.5
Public Assistance	America's inner-city ghettos	2.5

©1992, Claritas/NPDC, Inc. PRIZM is a registered trademark of Claritas/NPDC, Inc. The 40 PRIZM cluster nicknames ("Blue Blood Estates," "Money & Brains," and so on) are trademarks of Claritas/NPDC, Inc.

EXHIBIT 6-6: A COMPARISON OF TWO PRIZM CLUSTERS

	Pools & Patios	Heavy Industry
You are	45 to 64	55 plus
You have	A college degree, grown children	Some high school education, grown children
Your home is in	Fairfield, CT, or Los Angeles, CA	Newark, NJ, or Pawtucket, RI
Your job is	White collar	Blue collar
You travel by	Cruiseship	Railroad
You like	Civic clubs, golf, mutual funds	Asthma remedies, ale, auto racing
You don't like	Roller derbies, gospel music	Compact pickup trucks, billiards
You read	The Wall St. Journal, The New Yorker	The Star, Modern Bride
You don't read	Hot Rod, Essence, Harper's	Nation's Business, Grit
You drive	Alfa Romeos, BMWs, Peugeots	Dodge Aries, Chevrolet Citations
You don't drive	Ford Fairmonts, Dodge Diplomats	Audis, Saab 9000s
You eat	Natural cereal, dry soup	Meat sticks, English muffins
You don't eat	Whole milk, meat sticks	Popcorn, frozen yogurt
You watch	60 Minutes	Donahue, Nightline
You don't watch	Another World	Today Show

©1992, Claritas/NPDC, Inc. PRIZM is a registered trademark of Claritas/NPDC, Inc. The 40 PRIZM cluster nicknames ("Pools & Patios," "Heavy Industry," and so on) are trademarks of Claritas/NPDC, Inc.

EXPANDING THE ANALYSIS
AND THE IMPORTANCE OF TRENDS

The demographic and socioeconomic groupings bring order to the basic statistical population measures by clustering factors that exhibit similarities in character. The variables discussed are not the only ones available to the marketer. The Census Bureau compiles additional breakdowns that may be useful depending on the needs of the study. A list of the population items (appears on all forms) and sample components (data collected from approximately one in six housing units) from the 1990 Census of Population and Housing is provided in Exhibit 6-7. Another excellent reference for selecting appropriate demographic variables for segmentation is the American Association of Advertising Agencies' "Recommended Audience Segments for Consumer Media Data," which is reproduced in the chapter's appendix.

Trend analysis is the projection of relevant demographic and socioeconomic variables to predict future characteristics of a market. This additional step is sometimes neglected or relegated to a minor component of the analysis. However, if prudently used, trend analysis can be a powerful marketing tool for intermediate and long-term planning. Businesses that ignore population and market trends are "flying blind." If they are not fortunate, they will likely to be out of business within two years.[12]

The trend report shown in Exhibit 6-8 reveals two important changes from 1992 to 1997: an increase in minority populations (Black, Asian, and Hispanic) and an increase in household income. As you can see from this report, trend analysis is an important part of demographic segmentation.

EXHIBIT 6-7: SUBJECT ITEMS INCLUDED IN THE 1990 CENSUS OF POPULATION AND HOUSING

100 Percent Components

Population Items

Household relationship

Sex

Race

Age

Marital status

Hispanic origin

Housing Items

Number of units in structure

Number of rooms in unit

Tenure (owned or rented)

Value of home or monthly rent

Congregate housing

Vacancy characteristics

Sample Components

Social Characteristics

Place of birth, citizenship

Education

Ancestry

Migration-1985 residence

Language spoken at home

Veteran status

Disability

Fertility

Housing Items

Year moved into residence

Number of bedrooms

Plumbing & kitchen facilities

Telephones in unit

Vehicles available

Heating fuel

Source of water and method of sewage disposal

Year structure built

Condominium status

Farm residence

Shelter costs with utilities

Economic Characteristics

Labor force

Place of work and journey to work

Year last worked

Occupation, industry, and class of worker

Work experience in 1989

Income in 1989

95

EXHIBIT 6-8: A TREND REPORT

DMIS Internal Horseshoe Bend

American Profile 10/27/92
Trend Report (1)

	1990 Census	1992 Estimate	1997 Projection
Total Population	667,490	702,820	789,443
White	63.3%	61.9%	59.4%
Black	5.0%	5.1%	5.4%
American Indian	1.1%	1.1%	1.1%
Asian	8.6%	9.4%	10.7%
Other	22.0%	22.5%	23.4%
Hispanic	35.5%	36.3%	38.1%
Total Households	220,933	231,781	258,590
Household Population	654,970	690,300	776,923
Average Household Size	2.96	2.98	3.00
Household Income			
$ 0 - $ 9,999	17.2%	16.0%	13.2%
$ 10,000 - $ 14,999	10.9%	10.4%	9.1%
$ 15,000 - $ 24,999	19.4%	18.7%	16.8%
$ 25,000 - $ 34,999	15.9%	15.9%	14.3%
$ 35,000 - $ 49,999	16.3%	16.5%	17.1%
$ 50,000 - $ 74,999	12.6%	13.2%	15.5%
$ 75,000 - $ 99,999	4.2%	4.8%	6.5%
$100,000 - $149,999	2.3%	3.0%	5.0%
$150,000 +	1.3%	1.6%	2.5%
Total	100.0%	100.0%	100.0%
Median Household Income	$ 26,377	$ 27,962	$ 32,537
Aggregate HH Inc ($000)	7,782,740	8,768,809	11,543,490
Median Family Income	$ 30,012	$ 31,815	$ 37,021
Per Capita Income	$ 11,883	$ 12,703	$ 14,858
Median Age Total Pop	29.3	29.7	30.2
Median Age Adult Pop	38.9	39.3	40.3
Median Age Female Pop	30.4	30.8	31.5
Median Age Adult Female Pop	39.9	40.3	41.4
Median Age Male Pop	28.2	28.5	29.0
Median Age Adult Male Pop	38.0	38.4	39.2

96

USING GEODEMOGRAPHICS

To maximize the value of the physical dimensions, you should use a composite geodemographic model for segmentation analysis. A synergistic premise behind geodemographics is that the sum of the whole is more powerful than the individual parts (geography, demographics, and socioeconomic factors). This technique consists of the following four steps:

1. *Define the trade or service area.* As discussed in Chapter 5, the first step is to use relevant market scope and/or geographic market measures to define the market.

2. *Specify pertinent demographic and socioeconomic bases to analyze.* Generally, one or two variables will not be sufficient for segmenting markets. An analysis of all potentially useful dimensions should be planned prior to beginning the analysis.

3. *Determine where to obtain the geodemographic data.* This information is available from a variety of sources (to be discussed in detail in the next section). These include public and academic libraries; local, county, or state planning departments or data centers; universities (business development centers and computerized information centers); other computerized services; marketing research/consulting firms; demographic research firms; and in-house primary research projects. The cost of such data can vary from free of charge (excluding the cost of time) to thousands of dollars, depending on a company's research needs and the scope of the analysis. Exhibit 6-9 illustrates the type of demographic information found in a sample report from CACI, a private-sector firm.

EXHIBIT 6-9: A DEMOGRAPHIC AND INCOME FORECAST

Anytown, U.S.A.	Site:	Circle	Radius:	3.00 miles
4TH & Elm	Latitude:	38,52,10	Degrees North:	38.87
0 - Any Size Radius	Longitude:	77,09,20	Degrees West:	77.16

	1990 Census	1993	1998	1993-1998 Change	Annual Change
Population	165187	166683	168519	1836	0.2%
Households	67207	68005	69085	1080	0.3%
Average HH Size	2.44	2.43	2.42	-0.01	-0.1%
Families	40412	40462	40476	14	0.0%
Per Capita Income	$ 23473	$ 26000	$ 26415	415	0.3%

	1990 Number	%	1993 Number	%	1998 Number	%
Households by Income						
HH Income Base	67330	100.0	68001	100.0	69081	100.0
less than $15,000	6103	9.1	5178	7.6	5175	7.5
$15,000-$24,999	7205	10.7	6227	9.2	6294	9.1
$25,000-$34,999	9181	13.6	8390	12.3	8523	12.3
$35,000-$49,999	12916	19.2	12400	18.2	12579	18.2
$50,000-$74,999	15227	22.6	15867	23.3	15902	23.0
$75,000-$94,999	8777	13.0	9612	14.1	9747	14.1
$100,000-$149,999	5756	8.5	7431	10.9	7730	11.2
$150,000 +	2165	3.2	2896	4.3	3131	4.5
Median HH Income	$ 47551		$ 52038		$ 52243	
Average HH Income	$ 57263		$ 63297		$ 64011	
Population by Age						
0-4	10774	6.5	10368	6.2	9404	5.6
5-14	16297	9.9	18335	11.0	20443	12.1
15-24	21183	12.8	17577	10.5	16319	9.7
25-44	65441	39.6	64903	38.9	59357	35.2
45-64	31268	18.9	34909	20.9	41963	24.9
65-74	11991	7.3	11467	6.9	10876	6.5
75-84	6532	4.0	7079	4.2	7664	4.5
85+	1702	1.0	2046	1.2	2492	1.5
Median Age	34.6		36.2		38.7	
Population by Race						
White	125851	76.2	123597	74.2	119791	71.1
Black	11372	6.9	12096	7.3	12876	7.6
American Indian	541	0.3	514	0.3	471	0.3
Asian/Pacific	15978	9.7	17757	10.7	20677	12.3
Other Races	11445	6.9	12719	7.6	14703	8.7
Hispanic Origin*	25367	15.4	30887	18.5	39367	23.4

Income data from the 1990 Census are sample data; all other 1990 data are complete-count. Sample data are subject to sampling variability and may differ from complete-count totals. Income amounts are expressed in current dollars for 1990 and 1993; 1998 amounts are in 1992 dollars.
*Persons of **Hispanic Origin** may be of any race.
©1993 CACI (800) 292-CACI FAX: (703) 243-6272 4/20/93

4. *Analyze and evaluate the marketing information.* This most critical stage depends to a great extent on the three previous ones. The major objective you are pursuing is obtaining practical information. Does it assist you in solving specific marketing problems? If you answer this question no, it is likely that the study was not planned as well as it could have been. Assuming the study provided the needed information, the next step is to translate the findings into segmentation strategy.

SOURCES OF DEMOGRAPHIC DATA

Low-Cost Demographics

Good demographic data does not have to be expensive. There are some excellent secondary sources of demographic information that are available at no charge through your local public or university library. Researchers should not limit themselves to libraries in the search for secondary demographic data. Other good sources for low- and no-cost demographics include government agencies (federal, state, and local branches), universities, and various other local sources. Take a look here at some places you can call on to acquire demographic data.

99

Library References. *Library demographics* are both underused and underestimated as planning tools. Library demographics represent one of the best avenues for securing market information for small companies or those with a limited research budget. There are dozens of quality demographic references readily obtainable at most public libraries. Exhibit 6-10 shows the widespread acceptance of consumer demographic sources, based on a survey conducted of 50 public and academic libraries throughout the U.S. (27 responded). Brief abstracts of the most important sources of consumer and industrial demographics can be found in Appendix A (Major Sources of Demographic/Marketing Information).

EXHIBIT 6-10: LIBRARY DEMOGRAPHICS, CONSUMER SOURCES

Reference	% of Libraries Where Available
County and City Data Book	96
U.S. Statistical Abstract	96
Sales and Marketing Management's Surveys/Special Issues	93
State and Metropolitan Area Handbook	93
Census of Population & Housing	89
Editor and Publisher Market Guide	89
Rand McNally Commercial Atlas and Marketing Guide	85
American Demographics	85
CACI's Sourcebooks	74
Statistical Reference Index	59
Statistical Handbook Series	56
State Statistical Abstracts	48
Data from Local/County/State Agencies	37
Donnelley's Market Profile Analysis	22
SRDS' Lifestyle Market Analyst*	22
REZIDE: National Encyclopedia of Residential ZIPCode Demography	15
Zip Code Sale Information Guide	11

*This source was a "write-in" (not listed on the questionnaire). It is likely that this reference is more widely available than survey figures indicate.

Ask yourself how much you really know about U.S. demographics—Segmentation Skillbuilder 6 can help you assess your knowledge. All of the answers to this quiz can be found by consulting the *U.S. Statistical Abstract*—one of the best sources for consumer demographics—at your local library.

100

Please answer the following 10 questions based on data from the *1991 U.S. Statistical Abstract*. All questions relate to 1990 statistics. The goal is to "guesstimate" within +/-20% (except question 3). Partial credit is allowed. Check your score at your local library.

1. What is the U.S. population?_____ million

2. What percentage of the population live in the:
   Northeast (New England, Mid-Atlantic) _____
   Midwest (E. North Central, W. North Central) _____
   South (S. Atlantic, E. and W. South Central) _____
   West (Mountain, Pacific) _____

3. Name the three largest and smallest states based on population.
   Largest _____ Smallest _____
   Largest _____ Smallest _____
   Largest _____ Smallest _____

4. What state has the most farms? _____ How many? _____

5. What is the average household size?_____

6. What is the median age of the population? _____

7. What percentage of the labor force is female?_____

8. What percentage of all households have incomes of more than $50,000 ?
   _____ under $20,000 ? _____

9. What is the average per household expenditure for motor fuel (gasoline) annually? $ _____

10. What is the annual per capita consumption for bananas? _____ lbs.

Rating:

9-10 Demo expert! (most impressive, you should have written this quiz)

7-9 Good demo guesstimator (nice job—all skill, no luck)

5-7 Average (not bad, a monthly dose of *American Demographics* should improve your score)

<5 Demo, don't know (you're sentenced to read the *U.S. Statistical Abstract* from cover to cover)

Federal Agencies. The Census Bureau's resources were reviewed earlier; some are summarized in Appendix A. These and a host of others are available for purchase at a reasonable cost from the Washington office or any of the regional data centers. Also, don't neglect other federal agencies. Many times demographic information may be obtained through the Department of Commerce, Small Business Administration, or other government agencies. It is interesting to note that the U.S. government is the single largest gatherer of statistical information in the world and publishes thousands of books and reports annually.

State and Local Agencies. Although the amount of state- and local-generated statistical information is considerably less than that available in federal publications, these smaller agencies still can be a good source to tap in assembling consumer demographics. A good starting point at the state level is your state data center. All 50 states have a designated data center that can assist marketers in obtaining demographic information. American Demographics' *Insider's Guide to Demographic Know-How* publishes a comprehensive directory of state and local resources (as well as federal agencies).[13]

There is also a great deal of information available locally to assist in your demographic planning needs. Many cities and counties can provide demographics that are often more pertinent to your situation, because they are localized. For example, a former client of mine, who was relocating his office supply store, went to the Dade County (Florida) Planning Department to "try" to obtain some demographic information. A couple of hours later and only $36 poorer, he left the agency with an armful of reports, maps, and statistical publications. This information was vital in making future strategic marketing decisions for his business.

Universities. Colleges and universities can also be a prime source of demographic information. At Florida International University, for example, demographics are available from no fewer than three different places: the library, the computer center (detailed census information down to the block level is available for a fee), and the Small Business Development Center. Although it is often difficult to find a demographic specialist, marketing faculty can be effective consultants in many projects. Also, students can be used to collect primary data or gather and interpret secondary research (this can be done on a fee basis or for course credit).[14]

Other Sources. Additionally, you can often check with local chambers of commerce, professional associations, shopping center developers or management, and/or the local media to obtain demographic data.

Purchased Demographics

Suppose you don't want to do it yourself. Although some technical assistance may be available from the low-cost sources, most of the data compilation and analysis is your responsibility. What are your other demographic options? You can purchase one of two types of demographic studies: canned or custom. *Canned,* or *packaged, demographics* is relatively low-cost data using predetermined census areas or other geographical classifications for virtually all of the recognized demographic variables. Typically, this information is provided by research firms specializing in demographics who have compiled extensive in-house data banks, generally derived from the census. Because these companies serve many clients, savings can be passed on by utilizing similar formats for most applications. Services offered by these demographic specialists are listed in Appendix B.

Custom demographics, the more costly alternative, is recommended when your research needs vary markedly from what is generally provided, or further analysis is called for to analyze a market situation. Demographic consultants may repackage census information, analyze it, supplement it with some primary research, and prepare a report of their findings/recommendations for management's review. You can sometimes obtain canned demographics (numbers only, no analysis) for as low as $100, but custom demographics will generally cost several thousand dollars and up, depending on the scope of the project.

KNOW YOUR TRADE-OFFS

Again, it all goes back to the central issue: your research needs. Perhaps the low-cost demographic sources meet your information needs, but you may need a project consultant to assist in research design and interpretation of the findings. When using demographic consultants, you should always work closely with them to maximize the value of the marketing information. Segmentation Action List 6 provides a list of a dozen important questions to ask your demographic specialist before you start any project.

Segmentation Action List 6: Buying Demographics

1. Where does the consultant/vendor obtain the demographic data?
2. How is the trade area defined?
3. What are the appropriate demographic variables?
4. How current is the information?
5. How accurate is the information?
6. Are forecasts included? How are they derived?
7. How will the information be presented (reports, tables, maps, graphics, or other)?
8. Is the output flexible—available in formats other than paper reports (CD-ROM, computer tapes, floppy diskettes, microfiche)?
9. Is assistance in understanding and implementing the findings available?
10. How practical is the information?
11. How much will it cost?
12. How frequently are updates needed?

Computer Demographics

If you expect to use demographic data on a regular basis, you may want to consider purchasing computerized databases. Most of the demographic research vendors now offer a wide variety of demographic software and related products (maps, reference sources, and so on) that are quite good.

Desktop demographics is a recent innovation that helps businesses integrate, manipulate, and analyze a wide variety of information via databases. CACI, Claritas/NPDC, Donnelley, and National Decision Systems sell desktop systems with entry-level prices of less than $15,000.[15] For example, Donnelley's CONQUEST is a personal computer-based geodemographic marketing information system that provides access to the company's demographic, economic, and geographic databases. Claritas' COMPASS system integrates PRIZM data with demographics and mapping, and client information files. This desktop marketing system has been used for trade area analysis and presentation by local cable companies, General Motors, and CitiCorp.[16]

SUMMARY

Once you have specified a geographic market area, you can apply demographic and socioeconomic segmentation bases and variables. A popular and effective approach for understanding descriptive characteristics in consumer markets—demographic analysis—is a major segmentation weapon used to win marketing wars. This chapter reviewed major demographic (market size factors; age and stage; men and women; and race, nationality, and religion) and socioeconomic (monetary factors, homeownership factors, and social class) segmentation bases and variables.

Geodemographic clustering systems such as the PRIZM service are gaining in popularity and importance and were examined. Insights from the 1990 census, trend analysis, and a four step-process for using geodemographics were also discussed. The chapter paid considerable attention to sources of demographic information. These included no/low-cost options (library references; federal, state, and local agencies; universities; and other sources), purchased demographics (canned vs. custom demographics), and computer demographic products.

APPENDIX: RECOMMENDED AUDIENCE SEGMENT DATA

The following guide provides standard breakdowns for demographic characteristics according to the American Association of Advertising Agencies. The purpose of this guide is to provide advertising and marketing professionals with a tool for collecting and analyzing media and marketing data with comparable reporting standards.

These breakdowns reflect recent demographic, economic, and sociological changes in the population. In addition, consideration has also been given to data refinements that enable you to further differentiate between the marketing media characteristics of population segments, such as reporting the number of children under the age of 18. This type of data will help to distinguish differences between the living patterns of families that have children and those that do not have any children.

This appendix can be used as a handy checklist to be sure that you are considering all demographic variables in your segmentation studies.[17]

AAAA's Recommended Standard Segments for Demographic Characteristics in Surveys of Consumer Media Audiences

Data to be gathered and reported (if possible, to be directly accessible)

			Data to be reported for:			
Characteristic	Minimum Basic Data to be Reported	Additional Data — Highly Valued	Persons	Homemakers	Household Head	Households
I. Persons Characteristics						
A. Household Relationship	Principle Wage Earner in HH (Defines HH Head)		X	X	X	
	Principle Shopper in HH (Defines Homemaker)			X		
	Spouse					
	Child					
	Other Relative					
	Partner/Roommate					
	Other Non-Relative					
B. Age	Under 6	2—5	X	X	X	
	6—11	6—8				
	12—15	35—49				
	16—20	25—49				
	18—20					
	16 or older					
	18 or older					
	18—24					
	25—34					
	35—44					
	45—49					
	50—54					
	55—64					
	65—74					
	75 or older					

Characteristic	Minimum Basic Data to be Reported	Additional Data — Highly Valued	Data to be reported for:			
			Persons	Homemakers	Household Head	Households
C. Sex	Male		X	X	X	
	Female					
D. Education	Last Grade Attended:					
	Grade School or Less (Grade 1—8)		X	X	X	
	Some High School					
	Graduated High School					
	Some College (At least 1 Year)					
	Graduated College	Any Post Graduate Work				
	If Currently Attending School.	—(If Pertinent to Study)—				
		Live Home				
		Live Away				
		—Live in Student Housing				
		—Live Off Campus				
	Full-Time Student					
	Part-Time Student					
E. Marital Status	Married	Spouse Present	X	X	X	
		Spouse Absent				
	Widowed					
	Divorced or Separated	Spouse Working				
	Single (Never Married)					
	Parent	Engaged				
	Pregnant					
	"Living Together"					

107

Demographic and
Socioeconomic Segmentation

Characteristic	Minimum Basic Data to be Reported	Additional Data — Highly Valued	Persons	Homemakers	Household Head	Households
					Data to be reported for:	
F. Religion—Political		Protestant ⌐ Active (Practicing) Catholic └ Inactive (Nonpracticing) Jewish Other None Political —Conservative —Liberal —Moderate	X	X	X	
G. Race	White Black Other		X	X	X	
H. Principle Language Spoken At Home	English Spanish Other		X	X	X	
H1. Other Languages Spoken At Home	English Spanish Other		X	X	X	

I. Individual Employment Income

Characteristic	Minimum Basic Data to be Reported	Additional Data — Highly Valued	Persons	Homemakers	Household Head	Households
		Data to be reported for:				
I. Individual Employment Income	Under $10,000	$75,000—99,000	X	X	X	
	$10,000—14,999	$100,000 and over				
	$15,000—19,999					
	$20,000—24,999	IEI Income by Quintile as				
	$25,000—29,999	Determined by the Survey Ziptiles				
	$30,000—39,999	Other Income				
	$40,000—49,999					
	$50,000—74,999					
	$75,000 and over					

IEI by Quintile
Income Interval

Quintile	% Adults	Low	High	Median Income
1	20	—	10,156	6,391
2	20	10,757	19,999	13,959
3	20	20,000	29,999	24,953
4	20	30,000	43,243	34,967
5	20	43,244	—	60,150

Characteristic	Minimum Basic Data to be Reported	Additional Data — Highly Valued	Persons	Homemakers	Household Head	Households
					Data to be reported for:	
J. Occupation as Defined by Bureaus of the Census	**Armed Forces**		X	X	X	
	Civilian Labor Force					
	Employed	Hold More Than One Job				
	—Part-Time (35 or More Hours Per Week)	In Home				
	—Part-Time (Less Than 35 Hours Per Week)	Out-Of-Home				
	Self-Employed	Private Company				
	Unemployed—Looking for Work	Government				
	Major Occupational Categories	Predominantly—Day Work				
	—Managerial, Professional	—Evening/Night Work				
	—Technical	Technical				
		Related Support Occupations				
	—Admin. Support (Incl. Clerical)					
	—Sales					
	—Operative, Non-Farm Laborers, Service Workers, Private Household Workers					
	—Farmers, Farm Managers, Farm Laborers					
	—Craftsmen					
	—Other					
	Industry of Employment					
	Job Title					
	Not Employed					
	Retired					
	Student (Full-Time)					
	Homemaker (Not Employed Outside Home)					
	Disabled					
	Temporarily Unemployed					
	Other					

Characteristic	Minimum Basic Data to be Reported	Additional Data — Highly Valued	Persons	Homemakers	Household Head	Households
II. Household Characteristics						
A. County Size	A County B County C County D County		X	X	X	X
B. Geographic Area as Defined by Bureau of the Census	Inside Metropolitan Statistical Area . . . —MSA Central City —MSA Suburban —MSA Other Outside Metropolitan Statistical Area	Metropolitan Statistical Area Populations 4,000,000 and over 1,000,000—3,999,999 500,000 — 999,999 250,000 — 499,999 100,000 — 249,999 50,000 — 99,999				
	Urban	Urban: Urbanized Area —Central City —Urban Fringe —Other Urban —Places of 10,000—50,000 Population —Places of 2,500—9,999 Population				
	Rural					
C. Geographic Region	As Defined by Bureau of the Census —Northeast —North Central —South —West Nielsen Geographical Areas —Northeast —East Central —West Central —South —Pacific	Census Geographic Division —New England —Mid Atlantic —East North Central —West North Central —South Atlantic —East South Central —West South Central —Mountain —Pacific Major Market Unduplicated TV Coverage Areas	X	X	X	X
D. Presence/Age of Children in Household	No Children Under 18 Youngest Child 6—17 Youngest Child Under 6	Youngest Child 12—17 Youngest Child 6—11 Youngest Child 2—5 Youngest Child Under 2	X	X	X	X
E. Household Type		Family Members Only Nonfamily Members Only Both Family and Nonfamily Members	X	X	X	X

Data to be reported for: Persons, Homemakers, Household Head, Households

Demographic and Socioeconomic Segmentation

Characteristic	Minimum Basic Data to be Reported	Additional Data — Highly Valued	Persons	Homemakers	Household Head	Households
			Data to be reported for:			
F. Household Size	1 Member 2 Members 3 Members 4 Members	Number of Adults (Persons 18 and over) Male/Female HH Female Only HH Male Only HH	X	X	X	X
G. Number of Children Under 18 In Household	None One More Than One	Number of Children 6—17 Number of Children Under 6 Number of Children by Household Size	X	X	X	X
H. Household Income	See I., Individual Employment Income	$75,000—99,999 $100,000 and over Household Income by Quintile as Determined by Survey Zipitles	X	X	X	X
I. Other Household Characteristics		Number of Adults Employed Full-Time	X	X	X	X
J. Home Ownership	Own Home —Private Ownership —Cooperative Ownership —Condominium Rent Home	Residence Five Years Prior to Survey —Lived in Same House/Home —Lived in Different House/Home —In Same County —In Different County —In Same State —In Different State	X	X	X	X
K. Type Housing Unit	Single Family Home Multiple Family Home Apartment Mobile Home or Trailer		X	X	X	X

NOTE: The recommended minimum and additional data standards apply to generalized surveys. Those surveys done to more specific purposes—e.g. particular geographic sections of the country, affluent markets, publications directed towards a specific target, etc.—may choose to collapse or expand characteristic segments as appropriate to their context.

NOTES

1. Joe Mandese, "Who Are the Targets?" *Marketing & Media Decisions,* July 1989, pp. 29-31, 34-35.

2. Jeff Ostroff, "An Aging Market," *American Demographics,* May 1989, pp. 26-28, 33, 58.

3. Bernard Gavzer, "What Is a Family?" *Parade Magazine,* November 22, 1992, p. 16.

4. Horst H. Stipp, "What Is a Working Woman?" *American Demographics,* July 1988, pp. 24-27, 59.

5. Betsy Spethmann, "Census Data Base Adds Up to Success," *Advertising Age,* April 15, 1991, p. 6.

6. Elisa Soriano and Dale Dauten, "Hispanic 'Dollar Votes' Can Impact Market Shares," *Marketing News,* September 13, 1985, p. 45.

7. "Cereal Targets Hispanics," *Marketing News,* June 7, 1993, p. 1.

8. Cyndee Miller, "Researcher Says U.S. Is More a Bowl Than a Pot," *Marketing News,* May 10, 1993, p. 6.

9. Peter Kerr, "Shift for Marketers: Yup to Grump," *New York Times,* August 27, 1991, p. D1, D6.

10. Neil Howe, "As Boomers Get Power, USA Should Worry," *USA Today/International Edition,* August 8, 1992, p. 10A.

11. Michael J. Weiss, *The Clustering of America* (New York: Harper and Row, Publishers, 1989), pp. xii, 2.

12. William Dunn, "Survival By Numbers: Small Business Marketing for Changing Demographics, *Nation's Business,* August 1991, pp. 14-21.

13. *Insider's Guide to Demographic Know-How: Everything Marketers Need to Know About How to Find, Analyze, and Use Information About their Customers,* Penelope Wickham (ed.) (Ithica, N.Y.: American Demographics Press, 1988), pp. 113-150. See third edition for further updates.

14. Art Weinstein, Bruce Seaton, and J. A. F. Nicholls, "Students as Marketing Consultants," *Journal of Marketing Education,* Summer 1991, pp. 36-44.

15. Russell J. Kirchner and Richard K. Thomas, "Desktop Decisions," American Demographics, August 1989, pp. 34-37.

16. "Customization with Compass," GDT News (Lyme, N.H.: Geographic Data Technology, Inc., Summer/Fall 1989), p. 1.

17. Reprinted with permission of the American Association of Advertising Agencies, New York.

114

PSYCHOGRAPHICS

There are times when I look over the various parts of my character with perplexity. I recognize that I am made up of several persons and that the person that at that moment has the upper hand will inevitably give place to another. But which is the real one? All of them or none.

—*W. Somerset Maugham, 1874*

Previous chapters explained that what people are (their age, family structure, income, occupation, and so on) and where they live provide useful information for segmenting markets. This chapter will explore behavioral approaches to segmentation. These bases recognize that what people do (their activities, buying behaviors, interests, and media exposure) and how they feel about life (their attitudes, opinions, and values) are often strong determinants of their use of goods/services. Unlike physical dimensions, the behavioral bases— psychographics, benefits, product usage, and others—assist the marketer by probing into specific product category and brand decisions by consumers.

Segmentation dimension decisions are not an either/or proposition. Both physical and behavioral bases can be used to find and capitalize on market niches. Psychographics is explored in this chapter. Psychographics can explain why Anheuser-Busch's Natural Light bombed while Bud Light was a huge hit.[1] When you travel, are you a happy camper, worry wart, or grumpy guest? An exploratory, national study found that 41% of businesspersons enjoyed traveling, an equal percentage worried about airline and hotel safety, and 18% had little good to say about business trips.[2] Product usage, benefits, and other behavioral bases (perceptions/preferences, media exposure, image-concept, and marketing mix factors) are examined in Chapter 8.

PSYCHOGRAPHICS: AN OVERVIEW

One of the more powerful segmentation approaches—psychographics—has come a long way since the term was coined by Emanuel Demby, a marketing researcher, nearly 30 years ago. Demby's definition (edited) of *psychographics* is:

> The use of psychological, sociological, and anthropological factors, self-concept, and lifestyle to determine how the market is segmented by the propensity of groups within the market—and their reasons—to make a particular decision about a product, person, or ideology. . . .[3]

Yes, But What Is Psychographics?

Also called *lifestyle or activity and attitude research*, psychographics combines the objectivity of the personality inventory with the rich, consumer-oriented descriptive detail of the qualitative motivation research investigation.[4] Even today, there is a great controversy among marketing practitioners and academics about what constitutes psychographics.

Many researchers in psychographics limit themselves to lifestyles or AIOs (activities, interests, and opinions),[5] whereas others endorse personality,[6] values,[7] and trends.[8] Although there are differences among these concepts, they should be considered collectively to provide meaningful marketing information. Although personality can be used to segment markets, it is difficult to reach targets found by such traits as sociability, self-reliance, or assertiveness. Recently, consumer personalities were classified by five geometric shapes:

- *Boxes* are neat, organized, and highly structured (accountants, computer programmers)

- *Triangles* are self-assured, respected, and leaders (executives, entrepreneurs, politicians)

- *Rectangles* are going through life changes and are unpredictable (college graduates, new employees)

- *Circles* are concerned about good interpersonal relations and peace (nurses, secretaries)

- *Squiggles* are creative idea-people who are not detail-oriented (artists, scientists)[9]

Despite the progress made in personality-based segmentation, lifestyle factors are considerably more important to marketers; therefore, they are the focus for most of this chapter.

PROS AND CONS OF PSYCHOGRAPHIC SEGMENTATION

Advantages of Psychographics

Psychographic research is being used more frequently in market segmentation studies for four reasons, which are explored here.

Target Market Identification. Although used more in advanced analyses than initial segmentation studies, psychographics can prove valuable for finding and explaining markets. Consumer differences extend beyond demographics; researchers must understand individuals' state-of-minds (their AIOs) to piece together the total "market puzzle." Furthermore, a more complete profile of your target market is possible. Lifestyle characteristics and quantitative factors, such as size and scope of the market, can be assessed in a new way.

Take a look at the bicycle market from a psychographic standpoint. Consumers buy bikes for a variety of nondemographic reasons. The adult exercise segment of the market is a case in point. There are fitness buffs, joggers and cyclists, antijoggers, recreational riders, and nature lovers.

Understanding Consumer Behavior. Markets are people. By analyzing purchase motives, marketers can better understand why buyers act the way they do in the marketplace. Psychographic research assists in this objective. Brand choice, company loyalty, motivations and needs, attitudes, and perceptions/preferences can be explored via this segmentation approach. The value of such information is readily apparent.

A firm may know who the heavy users of its product are, but not why they buy. Through psychographic research, the firm can study this small core of loyal customers. Such information can be used in designing future promotional appeals, as well as offering similar benefits to potential new users. Is the shopper who regularly patronizes a particular retailer going there because of convenience or friendly sales help? One psychographic study found that there are seven types of shoppers consistently found across geographic markets: inactive, active, service, traditional, dedicated fringe, price, and transitional shoppers.[10]

Strategic Marketing. The additional marketing information available through psychographic analysis can be employed in planning successful marketing strategies for the firm. Psychographics is most useful for companies that sell products that are expensive (such as automobiles or boats), discretionary (such as camcorders or health club memberships), or somewhat indistinguishable (soft drinks or beer). Strategic information gathered through a psychographic analysis can permeate all marketing areas of the company. Some examples include:

- Positioning new products/repositioning existing products

- Improving products or services to better meet segment needs

- Recognizing the importance of price factors in a given market

- Promotional strategies, in particular selecting appropriate media vehicles, advertising messages, and sales appeals

- Exploring new distribution methods or improving existing channels of distribution

Minimizing Risk. The cost of a new product introduction, brand line extension, or proposed venture can be substantial. Furthermore, the vast majority of such projects fail; recently, the new product failure rate has been estimated at 90%![11] By incorporating psychographics into your firm's product testing and R & D program, project successes are more likely. Often the key ingredient is locating the subtle product or concept variations that customers desire.

Limitations of Psychographics

Although using psychographic research in segmentation studies can be very beneficial, there are also two key shortcomings the marketer must be aware of.

Data Collection and Analysis. Unlike demographics, psychographics is primary research and is a more complex approach to obtaining the marketing information sought by management. Data collection can be problematic because of the large number of questions asked via the survey instrument.

Compounding this is the analysis of a voluminous amount of data, requiring the use of multivariate statistical techniques in seeking key marketing relationships.

Cost Factors. A well-designed psychographic study is on the upper rung of the pricing ladder compared to other types of segmentation research. Expect to invest $50,000 and up for a complete research package. If cost is a major consideration for your company, this type of analysis is not an appropriate use of marketing funds.

CONDUCTING A PSYCHOGRAPHIC STUDY: NINE GUIDELINES

There is no single preferable approach for conducting the psychographic study. However, here are nine guidelines that you will find helpful in planning the research project.

1. *Seek detail.* Lifestyles are a complex area. Focus groups can be an effective means for identifying relevant issues for the psychographic survey instrument. The more test data collected (determining what is pertinent is a judgment call), the better the expected value of the subsequent marketing information.

2. *Personal interviews work best.* Because of the wealth of data that needs to be collected, telephone surveys are often inappropriate. Similarly, direct mail often cannot be used. It suffers from a low return rate, with many unusable or incomplete questionnaires. Therefore, personal interviews are usually the best choice. Through this approach, the necessary data can be collected, alternative concepts can be tested, and even visuals can be used as needed.

3. *AIO statements are the heart of the survey.* To develop viable lifestyle segment profiles, a large number (anywhere from several dozen to several hundred) of activity, interest, and opinion (AIO) statements are the primary means of gathering information. These issues should relate to the purchase decision. Some typical AIO statements from an automobile study can be seen in Exhibit 7-1.

EXHIBIT 7-1: SAMPLE AIO STATEMENTS

My family knows I love them by how well I take care of them.

My choice of a car affects how I feel about myself.

I take a look at many of the new cars that are introduced.

I'm willing to pay a higher price for a car that I'm satisfied with.

Advertisements for automobiles are an insult to my intelligence.

I take pride in doing my own car maintenance and repair whenever I can.

Reprinted with permission of Applied Research Techniques, Inc., Parsippany, NJ.

4. *Measure AIO statements on a scale basis.* In many psychographic studies, Likert multipoint scales (or similar scales) are constructed to determine the degree of agreement/disagreement for each statement (see Exhibit 7-2). The magnitude of the response is the critical measure of personality traits and lifestyles.

Although 5- or 7-point scales are common, Art Boudin of Applied Research Techniques, Inc., frequently uses 11-point scales in segmentation studies. Because measuring dispersion (deviations from the mean) is a method for determining segment formation, a good case for the more detailed scale can be made.

EXHIBIT 7-2: AN AIO SCALE

	Very Important	Important	Average Importance	Somewhat Important	Not Important
	5	4	3	2	1
How important to you is the availability of While-You-Wait-Service?		X			

5. *Use multivariate analysis.* Given the large number of statements queried, factor and cluster analyses are suitable for reducing the personality and lifestyle issues to a more manageable number of factors or groups. The resultant marketing information defines and describes segments. See Exhibit 4-5 (Multivariate Statistical Techniques) for further comments on R- and Q-factor analysis and cluster analysis.

6. *Incorporate secondary data into the study.* A good psychographic analysis is built on well-executed primary research. This does not mean that secondary data should be ignored in the process. Secondary information from past studies, as well as published or syndicated sources, is a welcome accompaniment to the project and can contribute immensely to the explanation of the research findings.

7. *Add in other physical and behavioral dimensions.* You have already seen the value of psychographics in market segmentation analysis. However, this technique should not be used in isolation. To maximize the validity of segment profiles, you should use additional bases. Demographics and product usage are two of the more frequently used dimensions. Other bases might be indicated, depending on the particular type of analysis conducted. Exhibit 7-3 describes a market segment for banking services from a psychographic perspective. Note how demographic, media preference, and usage dimensions are incorporated into the profile. This target market summary provides a starting point for strategy development.

EXHIBIT 7-3: SEGMENT PROFILE FOR "GROUP A" FOR BANKING SERVICES

These are lower-middle to middle-income people with great concerns about money. Their financial objectives center around having sufficient assets to "live comfortably," which they describe in very modest terms. They feel the pace of social change has been too fast over the past several years. And they are either unable or unwilling to keep up with it. Although they must be very careful about their money, they don't really know how to manage it or spend it properly. They seek advice from many sources before committing themselves to any financial course of action. But this reasoned approach often produces conflicting or confusing information for them. So most of their financial decisions end up being made at irrational or emotional levels.

Their parents, who were born outside of the United States, never had checking accounts, bank loans, or bank credit cards. Similarly, Group A uses only the bank's savings services, preferring to pay cash for all purchases. They enjoy coming to the bank and very likely have a favorite teller whom they try to see. In fact, a trip to the bank is something of a special occasion for them.

They pay close attention to advertising. But because they do not trust it much, they rarely act upon it. They do seem more responsive to image-oriented, rather than product-oriented, messages. Their media preferences include a great deal of indiscriminate television watching and some family magazines.

This group composes 15% of the total market.

Psychographics

8. *Avoid preconceived notions.* In addition to setting research objectives, it is also helpful to develop some hypotheses prior to conducting the study. This forces you to consider the consequences and potential implications of the findings. Be open-minded about the outcome of a study. Although in most cases the results are informative and add a new perspective to present marketing planning initiatives, sometimes you find unexpected or unusual insights. Preconceived bias must be overcome to maximize the value of the information.

9. *Name the segments.* Once a reasonably accurate segment portrait has been established, it is advisable to tag a descriptor to the designated segment. For a running/exercise shoe manufacturer, a name like "Weekend Athletes" clearly represents a particular segment of the market that the firm might actively pursue. Given segment names, you can readily identify some key lifestyle and usage characteristics of the videocassette recorder buyer groups listed in Exhibit 7-4.

EXHIBIT 7-4: PSYCHOGRAPHIC PROFILE OF THE "BRAND X" VCR PURCHASER

Segment # and Name	% U.S. Male Household Head	% "Brand X"	Index
1. The Inconspicuous Social Isolate	8.1	31.3	386
2. The Silent Conservative	16.5	2.0	12
3. The Embittered Resigned Worker	12.8	0.7	5
4. The High-Brow Puritan	13.5	0	0
5. The Rebellious Pleasure Seeker	9.3	7.3	78
6. The Workhard-Playhard Executive	10.7	4.0	37
7. The Masculine Hero Emulator	18.8	43.7	229
8. The Sophisticated Cosmopolitan	10.4	12.0	115
TOTALS	**100.0**	**100.0**	**100***

Reprinted with permission of Applied Research Techniques, Inc., Parsippany, NJ.
*Average index.

SYNDICATED LIFESTYLE RESEARCH

The marketer in need of psychographic data doesn't have to opt for a custom segmentation study. Many companies are now using syndicated research services as a complement to other segmentation findings. The best known lifestyle services are SRI International's VALS (Values and Lifestyles) and Yankelovich's Monitor.

VALS 2

SRI's VALS 2 program is a revised lifestyle segmentation system that categorizes consumers based on self-orientation and resources.[12] Three powerful self-orientations are principle, status, or action. Principle-oriented consumers are driven by their beliefs (principles) rather than feelings, events, or desire for approval. Status-oriented individuals are heavily influenced by others—their actions, opinions, and approval. Action-oriented people seek social or physical activity, desire variety, and are risk-takers. Consumer resources are based on factors such as education and intelligence, income, health, self-confidence, eagerness to buy, and energy level. Expressed as a continuum from minimal to abundant, consumer resources increase through middle-age and decrease with old age, depression, major financial setbacks, and physical or psychological impairment.

The VALS 2 typology consists of eight consumer segments that differ in attitudes, behavior, and decision-making (Exhibit 7-5). A summary of some key descriptors for these groups follows:

Actualizers (Act)—independent, leaders, risk-takers

Fulfilleds (Ful)—organized, self-assured, intellectual

Believers (Bel)—literal, respectful, loyal

Achievers (Ach)—conventional, brand conscious, pragmatic

Strivers (Stv)—eager, social, trendy

Experiencers (Exp)—impatient, impulsive, spontaneous

Makers (Mak)—self-sufficient, practical, family oriented

Strugglers (Str)—cautious, conservative, conformist

EXHIBIT 7-5: THE VALS 2 SEGMENTATION SYSTEM

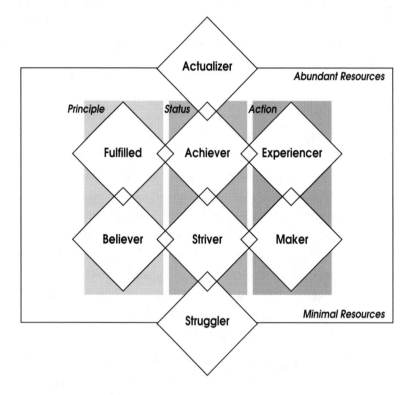

Source: SRI International.

A demographic profile of the VALS 2 segments is detailed in Exhibit 7-6.

Exhibit 7-6: Demographics of the VALS 2 Segments

(Percent, Except as Noted)	Act	Ful	Bel	Ach	Stv	Exp	Mak	Str	Av
Age									
18-24	7	1	3	14	24	61	25	7	18
25-29	5	4	3	17	15	16	17	6	10
30-34	13	15	10	20	16	11	16	7	13
35-44	27	32	16	29	22	8	17	13	20
45-54	22	17	15	13	11	2	11	13	13
55-64	14	15	21	6	7	2	8	18	12
65+	12	17	32	2	5	<1	6	34	14
Median Age (years)	45	49	60	37	33	26	33	61	41
Sex									
Female	43	54	43	63	57	37	39	68	51
Marital Status									
Married	68	69	63	81	59	31	61	49	60
Single	16	9	8	13	20	50	21	13	18
Separated/divorced	9	11	11	3	13	7	9	15	10
Widowed	2	9	13	1	5	1	2	21	7
Education									
Did not graduate from high school	<1	<1	24	1	1	8	11	27	10
Graduated from high school	7	12	50	36	55	32	53	37	37
Attended college	24	25	9	26	30	41	26	3	22
Graduated from college	27	32	0	31	10	14	4	0	13
Graduate school	42	31	0	5	2	3	2	0	8
Household Size									
One	12	17	19	3	16	12	9	28	15
Two	38	40	41	26	24	29	30	34	33
Three	16	16	12	25	24	24	26	18	20
Four or more	34	28	28	46	36	35	35	20	33
Have Dependent Children									
Under 6	15	15	9	35	26	19	26	14	20
6-11	17	20	12	28	21	11	20	15	18
12-17	19	20	19	19	23	17	16	9	18
Own Home	78	85	73	82	59	34	66	62	67
Household Income									
Less than $10,000	0	5	15	0	13	20	14	54	16
$10,000-$19,999	2	11	29	0	51	25	27	31	19
$20,000-$29,999	6	16	20	<1	27	21	28	12	16
$30,000-$49,999	27	39	25	35	33	22	27	3	26
$50,000-$99,999	47	24	11	56	6	12	3	0	19
$100,000 or more	19	5	0	8	0	1	0	0	3
Median Income ($000)	58	42	24	54	28	31	27	11	32
Occupation									
Professional/technical	44	36	3	25	15	15	7	5	17
Managerial	13	10	4	10	6	4	3	2	6
Clerical/sales	9	10	10	26	18	19	10	7	14
Crafts/trades	4	3	5	6	8	13	14	3	7
Laborers/operators	3	3	18	5	12	13	27	18	13
Other employed	3	3	7	8	8	11	9	8	7
Homemaker/student/retired	23	35	53	19	34	25	30	57	36

Source: VALS 1989 Leading Edge Survey.

125

Fueled by a reported $1.5 million investment and two years in retooling, VALS 2 is a significant improvement over the original typology. Key advantages are that new groups are more balanced in size and better discriminate brand usage by consumers, and that VALS 2 has advanced from a priori lifestyle segmentation (groups are specified before the research is conducted) to a post hoc (after the fact) system.[13] Unlike the original VALS program launched in 1978, the new system places less emphasis on values and more emphasis on psychological, economic, and educational resources.[14]

VALS information has been used successfully to develop new products, create product positioning strategies, target new markets, design ad campaigns, measure media audiences, and predict consumer and business trends. Additionally, SRI has joint venture agreements with the leading geodemographic clustering firms—CACI, Claritas, Donnelley, and National Decision Systems— and product usage/media information providers such as Simmons and Mediamark. Hence, a powerful PRIZM/VALS linked analysis is possible.[15]

Other Syndicated Lifestyle Services

The *Yankelovich Monitor* is an annual survey of more than 50 social trends relevant to consumer marketing. The recognition of the impact of key trends in a given market can prove to be valuable for a company's strategic marketing planning. Examples of some recent Monitor trends include personalization, physical self-enhancement, health orientation, meaningful work, new romanticism, return to nature, antibigness, concern about environment, responsiveness to fantasy, and emphasis on winning.[16] Yankelovich's generalized typology is more useful in understanding value systems operating today in the U.S. rather than specific product markets.

The *List of Values (LOV)* developed at the University of Michigan is an alternative to VALS that is gaining favor in academic marketing circles. Advantages of LOV are that it is in the public domain and was shown to relate closely to consumer behavior and predict trends.[17] Values such as self-respect, security, warm relationships, sense of accomplishment, self-fulfillment, being well-respected, sense of belonging, and fun/enjoyment/excitement have been tracked via LOV.[18] Other syndicated lifestyle services include DYG's Environmental Scanning Program and leading advertising agency services such as DDB Needham's Life Style Study, Ogilvy and Mather's New Wave, and Backer Spielvogel Bates Worldwide's Global Scan.[19]

SYNDICATED LIFESTYLE RESEARCH: AN ASSESSMENT

Syndicated services are gaining in popularity. Yet, marketing practitioners sometimes question their effectiveness. This form of generalized lifestyle research is market- or consumer-driven, as opposed to product-driven. Individuals are analyzed as to their overall attitudes, values, and desires. Product-specific data, the more important information from a market segmentation perspective, is not obtained. Marketers can only infer how consumer segments will respond to their product offerings. Ideally, you want to know this information. Because consumers react differently when exposed to alternative product stimuli, the need for situation-specific data focusing on unique markets, product classes, and product items is paramount.

Despite this shortcoming, syndicated lifestyle research is beneficial to a company as a supplemental means of customer analysis. It is an economical (but by no means inexpensive) alternative to designing a customized psychographic study. Lifestyle services are useful for selecting advertising media and designing creative strategies. Furthermore, they can be quite helpful to foreign-based companies seeking to quickly understand the American consumer market.

LIFESTYLE ANALYSIS: OTHER CONSIDERATIONS

Consumer lifestyles are dynamic, evolving, and culture-specific. Marketers must not only observe and anticipate changes in lifestyle but also react quickly with product introductions and on-target promotional campaigns. Segmentation Skillbuilder 7 puts you in the marketer's hot seat; how would you cope with changing American lifestyles?

Lifestyles relate to how people live and allocate their resources (time and money). Simply stated, lifestyles are consumers' activities, interests, and opinions (AIOs). Unlike values that endure, lifestyles change rapidly as societies change. During the past decade, Americans have witnessed dramatic changes. Astute marketers can find new business opportunities from market shifts. It is a three-step process: identify trends, recognize the marketing implications, and create goods/services to respond to the new needs. A list of some changing U.S. lifestyles is shown here. Your challenge is to determine marketing implications and propose responsive new product offerings (number one was started for you).

Lifestyle Trend	Marketing Implications	Product
Convenience-seeking	Not willing to wait	ATMs, 24-hr. supermarkets
	Want quick service	One-hour photos, airport
Enhancement of physical self		curbside check-in
Enhancement of psychological self		
Environmentalism and interest in societal causes		
Cocooning		
Pleasure-seeking		
Variety-seeking		
Having fewer children		
Blurred sex roles		
Alternative types of households		
Working women		

Suggested Reading: Popcorn, Faith. *The Popcorn Report.* (New York: Doubleday, 1991).

An extension to lifestyle analysis is *lifestyle change marketing* or *synchrographics*. According to Robert Perlstein, timing (when people buy) is an innovative and profitable way to segment markets in the 1990s. He states that consumers spend the most when faced with a major lifestyle change. Examples of relevant lifestyle changes include going to college, starting a new job, getting married, having a baby, getting divorced, moving, and losing a loved one.[20]

Now that you are well informed about psychographics and lifestyle research, you may be ready to initiate a project in your company. Sixteen points to consider prior to negotiating for this type of behavioral research are listed in Segmentation Action List 7.

Segmentation Action List 7: Contracting for Psychographic Research

1. Is custom or syndicated lifestyle research required?

2. Is there in-house capacity to assist in the project?

3. Specifically, what are your research objectives (see Chapter 3)?

4. Have you spoken with at least two research firms or consultants with expertise in psychographics?

5. Do they have experience in your market or a closely related market?

6. What are the professional and academic qualifications of the researcher(s)?

7. Did you review detailed proposals from these research providers?

8. From a methodological perspective, exactly what is entailed in the study?

9. Will the psychographic research be used to identify new market segments, describe existing segments, or predict differences in customer behavior?

10. Can the psychographic research be validated against other syndicated services or your own primary research?

11. What supporting dimensions (in addition to the psychographics) will be used in the study?

12. Will this psychographic segmentation approach respond to changes in the marketplace?

13. How closely will the researcher work with your company in project design, implementation, and strategy development?

14. Is this a one-shot effort, or do you seek an ongoing relationship with the research firm?

15. What value do you expect from this study?

16. How much is this answer worth to you?

SUMMARY

As marketers have realized that demographics are seldom adequate to understand today's complex markets, psychographic research has moved to the forefront in recent years. This powerful lifestyle-based technique can be very useful for identifying markets, explaining consumer behavior, devising strategic marketing, and minimizing risk. Recognize however, that this technique is complex and costly. Nine practical guidelines to conducting psychographic studies were offered in this chapter.

You might want to consider syndicated lifestyle services such as VALS 2 or The Monitor to get a better understanding of your customers. Synchrographics (lifestyle change marketing) offers a new way to reach prime prospects. The next chapter looks at some additional approaches to behaviorally segment markets (usage, benefits, and so forth).

130

NOTES

When Natural Light failed where Bud Light succeeded

- 1. Bickley Townsend, "Psychographic Glitter and Gold," *American Demographics*, November 1985, pp. 23-29.

2. Dan Wascoe Jr., "Firm Recommends Catering to Travelers' Different Needs," *Minneapolis Star Tribune*, July 21, 1989, p. 1D.

3. Emanuel H. Demby, "Psychographics Revisited: The Birth of A Technique," *Marketing News*, January 2, 1989, p. 21.

4. William D. Wells, "Psychographics: A Critical Review," *Journal of Marketing Research,* May 1975, pp. 196-213.

5. William D. Wells and Douglas J. Tigert, "Activities, Interests, and Opinions, *Journal of Advertising Research,* Number 11, 1971, pp. 27-35.

6. Joseph T. Plummer, "How Personality Makes a Difference," *Journal of Advertising Research*, December/January 1984/1985, pp. 27-31.

7. Wagner A. Kamakura and Thomas P. Novak, "Value-System Segmentation: Exploring the Meaning of LOV," *Journal of Consumer Research*, June 1992, 119-132.

8. Faith Popcorn, "Fresh Popcorn," *Express Magazine,* Winter 1992, p. 32.

- 9. Susan Dellinger, *Psycho-Geometrics* (Englewood Cliffs, N.J.: Prentice-Hall, 1989).

10. Jack A. Lesser and Marie A. Hughes, "The Generalizability of Psychographic Market Segments Across Geographic Locations," *Journal of Marketing*, January 1986, pp. 18-27.

11. Cyndee Miller, "Little Relief Seen for New Product Failure Rate," *Marketing News*, June 21, 1993, pp. 1, 10-11.

12. Values and Lifestyle Program. Descriptive materials for the VALS 2 Segmentation System (Menlo Park, Calif.: SRI International, 1989).

13. Lewis C. Winters, "SRI Announces VALS 2," *Marketing Research*, June 1989, pp. 67-69.

14. Judith Graham, "New VALS 2 Takes Psychological Route," *Advertising Age*, February 13, 1989, p. 24.

15. Martha Farnsworth Riche, "Psychographics for the 1990s," *American Demographics*, July 1989, pp. 25-26, 30-31, 53-54.

16. *Yankelovich Monitor: Technical Description Reference Book*, (Westport, Conn.: Yankelovich Clancy Shulman, 1985).

17. Lynn R. Kahle, Sharon E. Beatty, and Pamela M. Homer, "Alternative Measures of Values: List of Values (LOV) and Values and Lifestyle Segmentation (VALS)," *Journal of Consumer Research*, Vol. 3, 1986, pp. 405-409.

18. Lynn R. Kahle, Basil Poulas, and Ajay Sukhdial, "Changes in Social Values in the United States During the Past Decade," *Journal of Advertising Research*, February/March 1988, pp. 35-41.

19. Rebecca Piirto, "Measuring Minds in the 1990s," *American Demographics*, December 1990, pp. 30-35.

20. Robert Perlstein, "Synchrographic Marketing—Market Identification Based on Time: When Consumers Become 'Must Buy' Markets," *First Annual Conference on Database Marketing Proceedings*, Miami, June 4-6, 1989, pp. 463-490.

8

Usage, Benefits, and Behavioral Segmentation

Twenty percent of the customers account for 80% of the turnover.

—*Vilfredo Pareto, 1911*

Why does one consumer drink Coke, another Pepsi, and a third prefer iced tea? Demographics and psychographics can provide many clues, but it is often helpful to consider additional segmentation bases. We will examine how usage, benefits, perceptions/preferences, image-concept, media exposure, and marketing mix factors can be used to segment markets.

PRODUCT USAGE SEGMENTATION: AN OVERVIEW

If you analyze your individual purchase behavior—thinking, say, about groceries—you will notice that there are many products that you buy on a regular basis or in large quantities. Many other items you purchase less frequently, with a vast majority (tens of thousands) of goods seldom if ever bought. This scenario is the basis for product usage segmentation—segments are identified and targeted based on a compilation of product consumption levels within a given market.

Usage dimensions also recognize that individuals act differently depending on their situation or use occasion. For example, a purchasing agent may be a conservative, fact-seeking buyer at the office and at home be an impulsive free-spender. Similarly, a woman who shops for her wardrobe at a discount clothing store may not think twice about spending $80 for a bathing suit at a specialty shop, if she is planning a Caribbean vacation. These segmentation bases acknowledge the complexities, and at times contradictions, evidenced by all people to varying degrees.

Florists and card shops are businesses built around occasions. Holidays (Valentine's Day, Easter, Mother's Day, and Christmas), memorable days (birthdays, anniversaries, and weddings) and illness or funerals account for the vast majority of florists' sales. To smooth seasonal demand, greeting card manufacturers have turned their energies toward nonoccasion cards—whose message is friendship or humor.[1]

Conceptualizing Product Usage

Product usage analysis consists of two components: usage frequency (how often the product is used) and usage variety (the different applications for which a product is used).[2] Two consumers may both play their stereo systems two hours daily (same usage frequency). One person may listen only to the radio; the other enjoys the radio, plays compact disks, and records cassettes (greater usage variety).

To analyze markets based on usage patterns, it is first necessary to classify users into specific consumption categories. An often-used method is heavy users versus medium users versus light users versus nonusers for a particular good or service. For example, in the nonfrozen yogurt market, heavy users were defined as those purchasing six or more cups per month, medium users two to five, and light users one or less. A yogurt consumption profile indicates that users are almost twice as likely to be women than men; users are generally young, college educated, and have above average incomes (many professionals/managers). Regionally, consumption levels in the West and Northeast are significantly higher than in the north-central and southern areas of the United States (see Exhibit 8-1).

Exhibit 8-1: Yogurt Consumption

Yogurt Consumption Charts

WHO EATS YOGURT?

YOGURT CONSUMPTION
(STANDARD CROSS TABULATION)

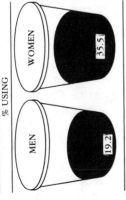

% USING

MEN 19.2 WOMEN 35.5

% VOLUME

MEN 35.6 WOMEN 64.4

INSIGHT: Women are the primary users. But which women? Who are they?

WHAT ARE THEIR GENERAL DEMOGRAPHIC CHARACTERISTICS?

YOGURT CONSUMPTION -
DEMO GROUP
(FEMALES)

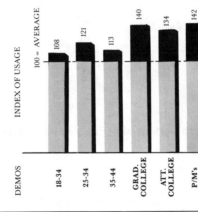

INDEX OF USAGE

100 = AVERAGE

DEMOS

18-34	108
25-34	121
35-44	113
GRAD. COLLEGE	140
ATT. COLLEGE	134
P/M's	142
CLERICAL SALES	115

INSIGHT: College educated and professional/managerials are heavy yogurt consumers, 34% to 42% above average. (That's a good clue for the advertising copy and the media you'd use to reach them.)

WHERE DO THEY LIVE?

YOGURT CONSUMPTION - BY REGION
(FEMALES)

% USING

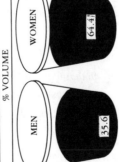

NORTH-EAST	40.2
NORTH CENTRAL	31.1
SOUTH	28.1
WEST	49.6

INSIGHT: Market potential levels vary markedly by region.

Reprinted with permission of Simmons Market Research Bureau

Do you recall the 80/20 rule? This states that approximately 80% of your sales come from only 20% of your customers or products. Hence, knowing who your best customers are and which products are your fast sellers offers you a major marketing edge. A corollary to this is the 80/50 rule. This means that approximately 80% of a firm's sales are likely to come from the 50% of the users that compose the heavy half.[3] If 40% of the potential consumers for a product were nonusers, you would analyze the other 60% of the market. The light half (30% of the market) might purchase 20% of the product, whereas the heavy half (also 30% of the market) would account for the lion's share, or 80%, of the sales. See Exhibit 8-2. Recognize that these theorems are guideposts and are not appropriate in every marketing situation.

EXHIBIT 8-2: LIGHT VERSUS HEAVY HALF SEGMENTATION

Segment	% of Population	% of Product Consumption
Nonusers	40	0
Light users (1/2)	30	20
Heavy users (1/2)	30	80
TOTAL USERS	60	100

Product Usage Analysis: Pros and Cons

Pros. Segmenting markets based on usage categories provides four major benefits:

1. *Studying usage categories is a useful dimension for understanding consumer or industrial markets.* For example, golfers buy golf clubs, balls, tees, golf gloves, and (fashionable?) pants. Computer users purchase diskettes, laser paper, printer ribbons, service contracts, and so on.

2. *Targeting by usage category can increase consumption among heavy users in moderately competitive markets.* One study identified five different approaches by which heavy user indexes could be calculated.[4] These solutions impact the allocation of marketing resources and efforts.

3. *Targeting by usage category can increase consumption among light and medium users in highly competitive markets.* Whereas heavy viewers are clearly the primary target for early evening television news

programs, research found that the late evening news was dominated by light and moderate viewers.[5] Hence, the programming and advertising aimed to the 10:00 p.m. audience should differ from that of the 5:30 p.m. broadcast.

4. *By providing new benefits, it is possible to attract nonusers or neglected segments.* One leading hotel chain identified 12 market segments based on differing group and individual visitation motives. Systematic segment tracking and evaluation provides direction for reaching overlooked market opportunities.

Cons. The marketer needs to be cognizant of three shortcomings associated with the product usage dimension:

1. *Product usage segments are often difficult to explain through traditional demographics only.* In many markets, additional segmentation bases should be employed (psychographics, benefits, and/or media exposure). If you analyzed the piano market on a demographic basis, you would notice that income is the key variable affecting purchase behavior. However, there are many affluent households that do not own or want a piano. Obviously there are nondemographic variables that greatly affect consumers' purchase decisions. These factors include such issues as:

  a. Does anyone in the household currently play piano?

  b. Are there any children in the family that might take piano lessons?

  c. What is the potential customer's music appreciation level?

  d. Did the customer own a piano when he or she was growing up?

  e. How does the customer feel about a piano as a piece of decorative furniture?

2. *There are several inherent problems associated with targeting the heavy user segment:*

  a. Other companies may also recognize the value of the heavy user. Therefore, competition for customers in this segment can be great.

b. All heavy users are not purchasers for the same reasons. Customers may want price, performance, service, or quality. Because customers have different needs, further subsegmentation within the heavy user category is usually advisable.

c. Heavy users are not product-loyal. They tend to buy heavily within a product class but often have little allegiance to individual products, services, or companies. There is more loyalty in industrial markets, however.

3. *There are some definitional problems in product usage analysis.* For instance, how do you distinguish between a heavy, medium, and light user? Also, what criteria should be used in specifying consumption segments? These and other questions must be answered by the marketing analyst.

Applications and Implications of Usage Segmentation

Exhibit 8-3 illustrates how the eight VALS 2 segments differ in product consumption for 18 popular consumer products. An index of 100 is the national average for a particular product category. Therefore, an index of 200 is twice the norm, 50 is half of what would be expected, and so on. For example, Actualizers are nearly four times (usage index = 363) as likely to own a foreign luxury car as the overall population. In contrast, virtually no Strugglers (index = 3) would own a Lexus or similar vehicle. Simmons and MRI (Mediamark Research Inc.) are good sources of syndicated usage data for marketers.

EXHIBIT 8-3: REPRESENTATIVE CONSUMER INDICATORS

Item	Base Rate	Segment							
		Actualizer	Fulfilled	Believer	Achiever	Striver	Experiencer	Maker	Struggler
Own SLR camera	0.34	163	124	80	138	83	88	115	29
Own bicycle >$150	0.25	154	116	90	33	83	120	88	43
Own binoculars >$100	0.15	173	139	110	134	65	73	69	63
Own compact disc player	0.14	133	108	119	97	96	94	94	69
Own dishwasher	0.38	157	142	118	138	89	51	78	42
Own fishing equipment	0.46	87	91	114	87	84	113	142	67
Own backpacking equip	0.19	196	112	64	100	56	129	148	29
Own food processor	0.36	148	138	111	121	72	71	89	63
Own home computer	0.19	229	150	59	136	63	82	109	20
Own home security	0.08	196	136	119	146	74	29	74	51
Own <$13K import car	0.24	172	128	80	143	68	109	89	44
Own >$13K import car	0.11	268	105	70	164	79	119	43	32
Own med./small car	0.35	133	117	89	101	112	92	112	54
Own living room furn.	0.56	120	107	110	112	97	68	102	84
Own foreign luxury car	0.04	363	154	39	141	57	136	22	3
Own new car >$20,000	0.08	196	141	87	211	58	84	39	33
Own pick-up truck	0.33	72	96	115	104	103	91	147	52
Own sports car	0.05	330	116	43	88	102	112	90	5

Note: Figures in the base rate column are the proportion of the population in Survey 2 using the product or service. Figures under each segment are the index for each segment (100 = base rate usage).

Source: SRI International.

139

Assessment of the Usage Dimension. Although product usage segmentation has at times been treated as a step-child as a segmentation base, this "sleeper" is still a viable technique that can provide you with great insight in many markets. Its use does not have the widespread acceptance of demographics, nor the explanatory value of psychographics or benefit segmentation. Additional research is needed to maximize the value of product usage analysis in the marketplace. This can be accomplished by treating product usage measures as both a primary segmentation base and as a complementary tool that can extend other segmentation findings. Product usage analysis is also a flexible, low cost, and easy to use marketing research technique. Goods and services can be analyzed for consumption levels on both a unit or dollar volume basis.

BUILDING LOYALTY

Marketing implications regarding usage segmentation relate to brand/company loyalty, promotion, and marketing information. Loyalty can be built through ongoing customer programs (frequent fliers) and offering long-term services (cable TV subscriptions, book-of-the month clubs, and so on). Advertising and selling efforts can be customized to meet the needs of various customer groups. Many firms have a small core of key accounts (perhaps 10 or 20) that account for a substantial proportion of their sales. In industrial markets, heavy users require regular sales calls and perhaps a dose of LGD (lunch, golf, and dinner) marketing. Infrequent customers can be informed of your company's activities and new products through quarterly newsletters or occasional telephone calls. And former users are easier to win back than creating new customers.

A *marketing information system (MKIS)* captures the vital information needed for analyzing product usage groups. In addition to recording key demographic and psychological characteristics, one business consultant tracks clients' key advisers (attorneys, bankers, and CPAs), publications they read, organizational affiliations, and the trade shows and seminars they attend.[6] This information separates prospects from suspects. A strong MKIS must be able to produce segmentation data at various levels of aggregation—a requirement that is easily met with today's technologies.[7] A complete MKIS consists of the following four subsystems:

1. A marketing records system tracks recurring sales and customer data (remember, your customer is your most important marketing asset!).

2. A marketing intelligence system monitors market conditions (competition, syndicated data, sales rep input, and so on).

3. A marketing research system obtains and inputs primary data about your customers (review Chapter 4).

4. A marketing tools support system consists of databases, graphics programs, statistical packages, and other computer software. This enables you to access and analyze customer data from subsystems 1-3. You can find segments of greatest marketing opportunity; is it heavy, medium, light, or nonusers?

BENEFIT SEGMENTATION

Robert J. Ringer offered a formula on how people can make their lives more pleasurable by focusing on individual happiness and personal needs.[8] In a sense, benefit segmentation is similar to this philosophy by asking a related question, "What is this product going to do for me?" Benefits are the sum of product advantages or satisfactions that meet a customer's needs or wants. They extend beyond product features and serve to satisfy physical, emotional, or psychological needs. Two clear examples of what a benefit is are often cited in personal sales training:

"Sell the sizzle, not the steak."

"People don't buy drill bits, they buy round holes."

Benefit segmentation probes users' buying motives and is linked directly to the marketing discipline of consumer behavior. A compilation of key benefits is analyzed in determining pertinent market segments. A primary benefit or a summation of benefits is often featured and used for segment identification purposes—for example, the Value Seekers. Ten benefit segments for categorizing prospective MBA students based on their educational motives/preferences are listed in Exhibit 8-4.

Exhibit 8-4: 10 MBA Benefit Segments*

1. **Quality Seekers.** Typically part-time students pursuing their MBA several years after earning their undergraduate degree. They want a first-rate education at an AACSB-accredited program.

2. **Specialty Seekers.** Desire a specialized education to become experts in their fields (insurance, health care, and so on).

3. **Career Changers.** Believe that the MBA will give them opportunities for career advancement and mobility. The benefit they seek is career flexibility.

4. **Knowledge Seekers.** Want to learn and feel that knowledge is power. They feel that the MBA will be an asset in their social, corporate, or political lives.

5. **Status Seekers.** Feel that the MBA means more income and prestige.

6. **Degree Seekers.** Believe that the bachelor's degree is insufficient and the MBA is essential to being "job-competitive" in today's business world. This segment has the highest proportion of full-time students.

7. **Professional Advancers.** Strive to climb the corporate ladder. They want careers with their current employer and seek higher income and upward mobility.

8. **Avoiders.** Seek the MBA program that requires them to do the least work. They seek low-cost, low-quality programs.

9. **Convenience Seekers.** Enroll in MBA programs that are close to their homes or jobs and have simple registration procedures.

10. **Nonmatriculators.** Want to evaluate whether they should participate in an MBA program. Seek schools that allow them to take courses without completing formal applications or GMAT exams.

*George Miaoulis and Michael D. Kalfus, "10 MBA Benefit Segments," *Marketing News,* August 5, 1983, Section 1, p. 14. Reprinted with permission of the American Marketing Association.

Arm and Hammer Baking Soda, a product that was in the decline stage of its product life cycle as a baking aid, was successfully repositioned by appealing to a variety of new benefit segments. These include its uses as a refrigerator deodorizer, plaque remover, and bleach booster (for sweeter smelling clothes), to name a few additional applications. More typically, a product will have one primary usage. However, through effective research, more than one potentially profitable benefit segment can often be identified. In many cases, the composition of benefit segments may differ markedly from demographic classifications alone.

A study of nonintelligent data terminals indicated that traditional business segmentation bases such as company size and standard industrial classification codes do not act as surrogate measures for benefits sought.[9] See Chapter 9 for further discussion on industrial benefit segmentation.

It is only appropriate that we have previously explored psychographic and product usage bases, because benefits are closely allied to these dimensions. An individual's lifestyle, values, and habits (past purchase behavior) generally have a great impact on subsequent benefits sought by that person. According to the confirmation-disconfirmation paradigm, a positive experience means that the customer will seek repeat satisfaction; a negative experience leads to avoidance.

Recognizing the renaissance of the marketing concept (placing customer satisfaction first, while generating a profit), more and more companies are now cultivating the long-term, benefit-seeking customer. The marketing concept should be more than a slogan such as "USAir Begins with You." It must be a management commitment to customer service—starting at the top, from the CEO to the janitor.

Advantages of Benefit Segmentation

The prudent use of benefit analysis provides marketers with a new perspective and added insight into market situations. When properly executed, this approach is one of the most powerful means to identify and exploit markets. For example, research conducted in collaboration with American Express found that demographic variables (with the exception of household income) were not effective for describing tourism markets. In contrast, however, 11 benefit variables—scenic beauty, shopping, rest and relaxation, cuisine, history/culture, accommodations, sports facilities, water sports facilities, attitudes of the people, entertainment/nightlife, and airfare cost—were useful for profiling three benefit segments: "passive-entertainment," "sports-types," and "outdoor-types."[10]

Some of the benefits of benefit segmentation are the following:

1. *Widespread application.* Benefit segmentation is an appropriate segmentation base for consumer, industrial, and international markets. It can be effective for assessing markets for goods, services, and ideas (such as nonprofit organization marketing).

2. *Causal basis.* Unlike most other segmentation bases, benefit segments are based on cause-and-effect factors rather than descriptive factors. Because benefits recognize why customers buy—their purposes and product desires—a direct relationship exists between motivations and purchasing patterns. Russell Haley, the father of benefit segmentation, advocates a three-step approach consisting of exploratory research, scale development work, and quantitative measurement.[11]

3. *Flexibility.* Benefit segmentation is a method with great adaptability. Here are three examples:

   a. Benefit segments can be derived through a variety of approaches—including but not limited to focus groups— the Delphi technique (a group of expert opinions), in-depth interviewing, and quantitative research (mail surveys, telephone, and personal interviews). Analytical methods for forming benefit segments can span the gamut from tabulation of opinion to multivariate analysis.

   b. Common or custom segment classifications can be used in the study. In past segmentation studies, some generic benefit segment groups have been called the Rational Man, Swingers, Hedonists, Conservatives, Sociables, Worriers, and a host of other explanatory segment names.[12] A customized typology builds on the results of past research projects and maximizes the value of the segmentation findings.

   c. Benefit segmentation can be used in collaboration with several other closely related segmentation bases. These include demographics, psychographics, usage, perceptions/preferences, and so on. Segmentation Skillbuilder 8 gives you the tools you will need to apply benefit analysis to your market situation.

Limitations of Benefit Segmentation

In many respects, the shortcomings of benefit segmentation resemble those of psychographic research—namely, problems in data collection and analysis, and cost factors. An additional limitation of concern to marketers is human behavior. Although individuals may want specific rational benefits from products, they sometimes do not act as they indicate, and deviate from their stated purchasing behavior.

This exercise (adapted from Russell Haley's work) presents a six-step process to identify customer market segments for your firm. Although the focus of this approach centers on benefit segmentation, other physical and behavioral dimensions are incorporated into the planning and research framework to provide a detailed segment profile.

Methodology

1. List several major benefits that customers are likely to seek in choosing your firm's goods or services (record these benefits in Table A).

2. Show this list to a prospective customer and ask the respondent if there are any additional benefits important to him or her in selecting your firm's products. Add these new benefits to Table A and record all of them in Table B.

3. Ask this respondent to rate the benefits numerically in Table B using the following importance scale:

   Most important benefit = 4

   Second most important benefit = 3

   Third most important benefit = 2

   Fourth most important benefit = 1

   All other benefits = 0

4. Collect similar marketing data from a sample of other respondents using steps 1 through 3. Add in new benefits and continue recording this data in Table B.

5. After all data has been collected, note respondents with similar response patterns (numerical highs and lows). These respondents are members of specific market segments.

6. List key benefits by segment on the segmentation grid (Table C). Using your keen judgment, complete the segment description given the attributes provided (note: typically, marketing research findings assist you in this process). When the segment column is completed, provide a name representative of the overall market characteristics for the segment. Continue with this approach for the other market segments.

Table A: Major Benefits

1.
2.
3.
4.
5. (or more?)

Usage, Benefits, and Behavioral Segmentation

Table B: Respondent Benefit Grid

Customer:	1	2	3	4	5	6	7	8	9	10 & more
Benefit_____:										
1.										
2.										
3.										
4.										
5.										
6.										
7.										
8.										
more ?										

Table C: Segmentation Grid for Your Company

Segment:	1	2	3	4	5
Attribute _____:					
Motivations/benefits					
Usage situations					
Usage by product type					
Frequency of usage					
Degree of loyalty					
Image of your firm					
Media preferences					
Adopter categories					
Key demographics					
Geographics					
Other descriptors					
SEGMENT NAME					
SEGMENT SIZE					
STRATEGIC IMPLICATIONS					

Suggested Reading: Haley, Russell I. *Developing Effective Communications Strategy: A Benefit Segmentation Approach*. (New York: John Wiley and Sons, 1985).

OTHER BEHAVIORAL BASES

So far, the discussion has explored in detail three of the major behavioral segmentation bases for segmenting markets: psychographics, product usage, and benefits. Although these dimensions are some of those more commonly employed in segmentation analysis, by no means are these the only options. The marketer has literally dozens of alternatives to choose from in addition to the aforementioned bases. In most segmentation studies, the use of several segmenting bases (both physical and behavioral) is recommended. A brief overview of some other worthwhile behavioral dimensions follows.

Perceptions and Preferences

A cross between psychographics and benefit segmentation, *perceptions* are concerned with how individuals mentally observe and comprehend brands, product categories, companies, competitors, or other marketing issues. In many cases, these perceptions can differ significantly from expectations. An evaluation of marketing research interviews from respondent and practitioner perspectives revealed that the public rated the experience more positive than did the researchers. Specifically, the respondents found that questions were easy to understand, interviewers were skilled, subject matter was interesting, and the time was convenient. However, unlike the researchers, the public thought interviews were too long and too personal.[13]

Perceptions are important, but customer *preferences* are even more valuable to marketers. This knowledge can greatly assist you in tailoring products to specific segment needs and wants. For example, in a study of nine product attributes, color, firmness, crispness, and garlic flavor were found to be key discriminators in determining the ideal frankfurter.[14] A major advantage of perceptual and preference research is that they are extremely useful for developing positioning strategies. Often, multidimensional perceptual mapping techniques are used to understand and graphically depict potential market segments.

Image-Concept

Consumers are often driven by emotion or nonrational influences rather than rational ones. Examples of emotional needs and (related product satisfactions) include: happiness (beer), success *(The Wall Street Journal)*, beauty (cosmetics), love (flowers), belonging (fashion), and fantasy (travel). Marketers can research these emotional needs and form unique image-oriented market segments through clustering techniques.

A manufacturer of special-effect clothing for the entertainment industry crossed over into the volatile consumer market with the introduction of its satin, embroidered "Miami Vice" jacket. Despite expectations that the majority of customers would be teenagers, most buyers were older than 25. About 10% were "Miami Vice Fanatics," and the remaining 90% were "Miami Vice Watchers." The former segment cared little about the product; they would purchase anything related to the television show. The latter group liked the show but were more interested in making a fashion statement.[15]

A five-step process for conducting, executing, and controlling an image-concept study follows:

1. Qualitative research—Conduct focus groups or in-depth interviews.

2. Quantitative research—Devise primarily an attitude research project.

3. Develop an image-concept premise (ICP) through data analysis/reduction.

4. Pretest the ICP. Develop promotional campaigns, refine the distribution mix, and review pricing strategy (holding focal product constant).

5. Implement, monitor, and revise ICP-based program.

Media Exposure

Broadcast, print, and other media provide one of the strongest influences on modern society. Consumers are exposed to hundreds of advertising messages daily through television, radio, newspapers, magazines, and periodicals, billboards and signage, direct mail, and other media classes. Armed with the knowledge of which media vehicles (the specific radio station listened to or trade journal read) people respond to, it is then relatively easy to reach prospective market segments.

Here are some examples of highly targeted radio/broadcast audiences. In New York City, sports addicts can listen to the FAN and debate the merits (or lack thereof) of the local teams with talk show hosts at any hour of the day or night. In Fort Lauderdale, the Winners News Network (WNN) is all motivation; instead of three-minute songs, the station features short self-help tips, business and sales strategies, health and lifestyle guidelines, and related achievement-oriented vignettes. Lifetime Cable Television bills itself as the women's network. The anticipated expansion of cable TV to 500 stations in the not-too-distant future means that media preferences will increase in importance as a segmentation base.

Even so-called mass media such as newspapers are turning to target marketing. The Palm Beach Post compiles and conducts research on virtually all aspects of its market (retail sales, demographics, leisure activities, and so on) to meet the information needs of area businesses.[16]

Marketing Mix Factors

Markets can be segmented based on the marketing controllables: product, promotion, price, and distribution. Some possible approaches emerging from the marketing mix include ones described here.

Product. Product segmentation focuses on product attributes, perceived quality, brand loyalty, innovativeness of new product acceptance, and/or purchase intentions. Recall the earlier discussion of product usage and perceptions and preferences, which could also be considered in this context. Additionally, product segmentation can occur through analyzing the five senses (sight, sound, smell, taste, and touch). Consider the impact the senses can have on food products and related purchasing behavior. Is the packaging attractive? Does it have snap, crackle, and pop? Is the aroma pleasing? Do you like the taste? Do the melons feel ripe? Prior to the emergence of market segmentation as an important marketing discipline, product differentiation (still a viable strategy in many markets) was the primary means of concentrated marketing.

Promotion. Media exposure, the flagship promotional segmentation base, was previously described. Other segmentable promotional avenues include sales territories (usually analyzed as a geographic base), copy platforms and sales appeals, and promotion acceptance/response rates (premiums, coupons, special offers, and so on).

Price. Markets can be segmented by price sensitivity/elasticity, price/quality relationships, and the importance of various price incentives on the purchase decision.

Distribution. Channels of distribution alternatives can serve to segment markets. Some examples of marketing channel options illustrate this approach:

- Selling direct to consumers (bypassing traditional channel members)
- Wholesaling and retailing (taking on another channel member's function, forward or backward integration)
- Selling via mail order, catalog, online computer services, cable television, and so on (adding new distribution methods)

- Selling to vertical niche markets or the government (penetrating new markets)

- Global expansion (international segmentation)

MANAGING THE BEHAVIORAL SEGMENTATION STUDY

At this point, segmentation decisions should be made in two areas: selecting appropriate behavioral bases and the need for outside assistance.

Selecting Bases

As you can clearly see, there are many alternatives to consider as behavioral segmentation dimensions. No one choice is necessarily better than the next until it is carefully evaluated in a specific market setting. The Behavioral Segmentation Matrix helps you to assess and evaluate all eight major behavioral segmentation bases (see Exhibit 8-5). In most projects, multiple dimensions (physical and behavioral) should be used. Some recommended behavioral segmentation bases for a dental practice are shown in Exhibit 8-6.

EXHIBIT 8-5: A BEHAVIORAL SEGMENTATION MATRIX (PROS AND CONS OF THE ALTERNATIVE BASES)

Base	Primary or Secondary*	Importance as a Base	Research Complexity	Cost
Psychographics, Custom	P	4	5	5
Psychographics, Syndicated	S	4	2	3
Product Usage	P, S	5	2	3
Benefits	P	4	4	5
Perceptions/Preferences	S	3	4	4
Image-Concept	S	2	4	4
Media Exposure	S	3	2	3
Marketing Mix Factors	S	2	3	3

*P = primary segmentation base. S = secondary base. P,S = base commonly used in both applications.

The 1 to 5 scale: 5 = the most important, complex, or costly; 1 = the least important, difficult, or costly base relative to the other behavioral options (3 = average). A low score should not necessarily be disregarded nor a high score embraced. These are general guidelines only, and subject to further review given your market situation.

EXHIBIT 8-6: TYPICAL BEHAVIORAL VARIABLES FOR A DENTAL PRACTICE

Variables	Categories
Lifestyle	Traditional family, single parent family, single/married professional, upwardly mobile, status seeker.
Benefits Sought	Economy, convenience, prestige, dependability, enhanced appearance.
Patient Status	Nonpatient, potential patient, new patient, regular patient, occasional patient, former patient.
Frequency of Dental Visits	Three or more times a year, twice a year, once a year, once every 18 months, once every 2 years, less than once every 2 years.
Loyalty to Practice	None, medium, strong, absolute.
Dental Health I.Q.	Low, medium, high.
Motivation to Seek Regular Care	Low, medium, high.
Fear of Dental Treatment	No fear, mildly fearful, very fearful but manageable, dental phobic.

Reprinted from the *Dental Marketing Planner*, 1983, pp. 69-70, with permission of the American Dental Association, Chicago.

Outside Assistance

Who should design and implement the behavioral segmentation study? Recognize that this type of research is more complex than physical attribute segmentation (geographics or demographics). In most cases—unless of course, you have in-house talent to handle all or part of the project—it is advisable to use a competent marketing research firm or marketing consultant. Segmentation Action List 8 lists 20 key questions to ask your prospective research supplier prior to contracting for a behavioral study.

Segmentation Action List 8: Contracting for Behavioral Research

1. Does the research firm have experience in this market or a related one?

2. How does that firm view the purpose of the project?

3. From a methodological perspective, what is involved in this segmentation study?

4. Will the research company work closely with you in the project?

5. What types of primary and secondary segmentation bases are advised?

6. Have all appropriate bases and variables been considered?

7. Will secondary or syndicated data and/or physical attribute dimensions be used?

8. Are national databases required?

9. What data collection methods will be employed?

10. How will the survey instrument be pretested?

11. What size sample will be used?

12. Is the research product-driven?

13. Is the research design based on causal, descriptive, or exploratory factors?

14. What analytical methods will be employed?

15. How reliable will the findings be?

16. How practical will the information be?

17. Is assistance available in understanding and implementing the findings?

18. What information will be provided, analysis only or analysis plus recommendations?

19. Will there be an oral and written report of the findings?

20. How much will it cost?

SUMMARY

If you are thinking about conducting behavioral research, there are three major segmentation bases to consider: psychographics (discussed in the previous chapter), product usage, and benefits. Product usage segmentation classifies users into specific consumption categories (for example, heavy, medium, light, or nonusers). Usage analysis also assesses frequency, variety, and usage situations. It is a flexible, low cost, and easy to use approach to understanding and evaluating markets.

Benefit segmentation groups customers by similarities in buying motives. It has widespread application, a causal basis, and is highly flexible. Other options that are used less often in segmentation analysis include perceptions and preferences, image-concept, media exposure, and marketing mix factors. These approaches were briefly reviewed.

There is no single best behavioral dimension. Marketing analysts and information users should be familiar with the various bases (know their advantages, limitations, and applications) and select those that are most appropriate for given market situations.

NOTES

1. Judith Waldrop, "Funny Valentines," *American Demographics,* February 1989, p. 7.

2. S. Ram and Hyung-Shik Jung, "The Conceptualization and Measurement of Product Usage," *Journal of the Academy of Marketing Science,* Winter 1990, pp. 67-75.

3. Dik Warren Twedt, "Some Practical Applications of Heavy-Half Theory," in James F. Engel, Henry F. Fiorillo, and Murray A. Cayley (eds.), *Market Segmentation: Concepts and Applications,* (New York: Holt, Rinehart, and Winston, 1972), pp. 265-271.

4. Steven J. Anderson and David W. Glascoff, "Index Number Calculation Procedures Involving Product Usage and Volume Segmentation Approaches to Market Segmentation," in L. M. Capella, et al. (eds.), *Progress in Marketing Thought,* (Mississippi State, Miss.: Southern Marketing Association, 1990), pp. 5-10.

5. Michael A. Jones, Jerry J. Ingram, and Donald R. Self, "Use Segmentation of the Local TV News Audience," in Jon M. Hawes and John Thanopoulos (eds.), *Academy of Marketing Science Conference Proceedings*, Orlando, May 17-20, 1989, pp. 556-559.

6. Gerry Foster, "Bulls-Eye Marketing—The Key to Profitability," *Home Office Computing*, April 1991, pp. 24-25.

7. Charles W. Stryker, "The Sales Information System: Putting the System to Work," *Business Marketing*, July 1985, pp. 80, 82, 84.

8. Robert J. Ringer, *Looking Out for Number One* (New York: Fawcett Crest Books, 1977).

9. Rowland T. Moriarty and David J. Reibstein, "Benefit Segmentation in Industrial Markets," *Journal of Business Research*, December 1986, pp. 463-486.

10. Jonathan N. Goodrich, "Benefit Segmentation of U.S. International Travelers: An Empirical Study with American Express," in D. E. Hawkins, et al. (eds.), *Tourism Marketing and Management Issues* (Washington, D.C.: George Washington University, 1980), pp. 133-147.

11. Russell I. Haley, "Benefit Segments: Backwards and Forwards," *Journal of Advertising Research*, February/March 1984, pp. 19-25.

12. Russell I. Haley, "Benefit Segmentation: A Decision-Oriented Research Tool," *Journal of Marketing*, July 1968, pp. 30-35.

13. "About the Interview Experience," *Walker Industry Image Study*, Ninth Edition (Indianapolis: Walker Research, Inc., 1990), p. 4.

14. Based on a research study of packaged frankfurter users conducted by Applied Research Techniques, Inc., Parsippany, N.J..

15. Marvin Nesbit and Art Weinstein, "Image-Concept Segmentation Targets Nonrational Needs," *Marketing News*, July 31, 1987, pp. 4, 30.

16. "The Marketing Campaign," *Marketing Palm Beach County and the Treasure Coast* (West Palm Beach: The Palm Beach Post, March 1988), p. 6.

9

SEGMENTING BUSINESS MARKETS

In developing our industrial strategy for the period ahead, we have had the benefit of much experience. Almost everything has been tried at least once.

—Tony Benn, 1974

Should a computer chip manufacturer such as Intel use the same methods that a potato chip company such as Frito-Lay uses to analyze markets? This brings to mind two related questions. How similar or different are business markets compared to consumer markets? What segmentation bases should be used in industrial market situations? These dual, important issues are the focus of this chapter.

Previous chapters reviewed physical and behavioral segmentation dimensions from a consumer marketer's perspective. This approach is valuable for retailers, personal service firms (banks or hair salons), and some professional services (doctors or dentists) whose goal is to sell their goods or services to the final consumer. But what about the manufacturer, wholesaler, or business service firm (printer or marketing research company) whose goods or services will be used by another company? In several respects this is a different marketing problem and, as such, requires a different planning and strategic marketing approach. Exhibit 9-1 identifies the customer focus for the segmentation analysis in consumer and industrial markets. As this diagram illustrates, all channel members focus on the final user in consumer markets. In contrast, there are many targets for intermediate marketing activity in business markets.

WHY BUSINESS MARKETS ARE DIFFERENT

Before you design the industrial segmentation research plan, it is important to recognize the four major differences between consumer and business-to-business markets: the scope of the geographic trade area, product/market factors, the nature of the purchase decision, and closeness of the customer.

Scope of the Geographic Trade Area

The area an industrial marketer serves is typically larger than the one served by neighborhood retailers or personal/professional service firms. Megaretailers such as Kmart and McDonald's and service organizations such as Merrill Lynch and H & R Block are found nationally but appeal to localized customer groups. It is not uncommon for an industrial firm to conduct business in several states, regions, or countries. Despite this larger trade area focus, the customer base for an industrial firm is generally highly concentrated. For example, a supplier and distributor of industrial pumps and motors serviced accounts throughout the southeastern United States, but the majority of its sales came from its own backyard (South Florida). As another example, Silicon Valley (California), Route 128 (Boston), and the Research Triangle (North Carolina) are all areas of intensive high-tech activity.

It should also be recognized that industrial market areas are often easier to quantify and target than consumer markets. A distributor of graphic supplies can identify a target market (such as advertising agencies) through readily obtainable trade directories. In addition to providing sales leads by name and location, these sources often list other vital marketing data such as the size of the company, media specialization, key management personnel, and services offered.

Exhibit 9-1: Who Is Your Customer*?

A. Consumer Markets

Manufacturer Wholesaler Retailer/Service Provider

Consumer*

B. Business Markets

Manufacturer -> Manufacturer*

Manufacturer -> Wholesaler*

Manufacturer -> Retailer*

Manufacturer -> Service Firm*

Wholesaler -> Wholesaler*

Wholesaler -> Retailer*

Wholesaler -> Service Firm*

Retailer -> Retailer*

Service Firm -> Service Firm*

Note: Although there is occasional upward channel movement in business markets (for example, a large retailer selling to a small wholesaler), virtually all marketing efforts are directed horizontally (such as manufacturer to manufacturer) or downward (such as manufacturer to wholesaler)

* denotes a customer.

Product/Market Factors

Most industrial sales are larger than those in consumer markets. Of course, there are consumer purchases of automobiles, boats, or houses. But for individuals, these are rare purchases. Most consumer sales are relatively small compared to industrial sales of equipment, materials, components, products, or services (periodic reorders of industrial parts and supplies may be small orders, however).

As a corollary to this point, there are generally fewer potential customers for the company to target in industrial markets. For example, Boeing's customer base consists of only a limited number of prospective aircraft buyers. At times, this smaller customer pool can wreak havoc with the best laid marketing plans. Dependency on a small core of customers often leads to large variations in revenues and profits (greater peaks and valleys), as the firm acquires or loses a major account. Industrial sales come from derived, not final, demand, which makes the firm more susceptible to cyclical market pressures. Steel producers, for example, are greatly dependent on automobile sales.

Nature of the Purchase Decision

A complex consumer decision may be a joint one between a husband and wife to buy new bedroom furniture. In industrial markets, complex decision making occurs on a regular basis. Often, many people will be involved in purchase decisions. Special justifications, authorizations, and approvals will be needed, and months can pass before a sale is transacted. The industrial salesperson is confronted with more intelligent, calculating, and rational buyers than are typically found in the consumer sector. On the positive side, once a customer has been "sold," loyal, lasting customers are often the result.

Closeness of the Customer

In their highly acclaimed book, *In Search of Excellence,* Peters and Waterman stressed the importance of getting close to customers and listening to their needs and wants.[1] Industrial companies are naturally closer to their customers, although their satisfaction levels vary from poor to excellent depending on how well the companies implement the marketing concept (an organization-wide effort to satisfy customers at a profit). Closeness in industrial markets is nurtured because: personal selling is the most effective promotional strategy, the sales force typically goes on-site to the buyers' premises, and long-term customer relationships often develop. In addition, it is easier to stay in touch with your market through trade journals that comprehensively cover industry news and views, trade directories that provide detailed marketing information about firms, and trade associations that share knowledge about markets. But, action—a responsive, customer-centered marketing program—is needed to truly meet the needs of the customer.

BASES FOR SEGMENTING INDUSTRIAL MARKETS

For the most part, the segmentation options for the business marketer are similar to those of the consumer marketer. There are three major differences, however. First, although most of the bases are generally the same, the value of their application varies by market situation. For example, psychographics are very important in consumer research, yet relatively unimportant in most industrial analyses (in contrast, benefits are generally more important in segmenting business markets). Second, the specific variables used within particular segmentation dimensions differs in industrial segmentation analysis. Demographics provide a good example of this point. Let's assume the variable in question is income. In consumer markets, your concerns may be household, family, or per capita income. In industrial markets, your interest would turn to basic financial statistics about the organization (total revenues, sales by division or product line, and so on). Third, there are some additional segmenting bases particularly suited for industrial markets: Standard Industrial Classification (SIC) codes, end-use analysis, and adopter categories. Major business segmentation bases are discussed next.

Physical Dimensions

Geographics. Geography, the starting point in an industrial segmentation study, is used to divide markets by market scope factors (local/regional, national, or international) and geographic market measures. Potential customer density, standardized market areas, and census classifications are of primary importance to the business-to-business marketer. Also, such sources as *Sales and Marketing Management* magazine and the business census reports help firms target specific industries and states or counties. Through these resources, industrial marketers can better identify market areas, define and measure sales area potential, direct promotional activities, and evaluate the success of strategic marketing initiatives.

Demographics. The next step, after geographic bases have been specified and determined, is to analyze a battery of relevant demographic variables. These "business demographics" are similar in concept and purpose to consumer demographics but vary in their application. You can compare business demographic bases and variables to the applicable, traditional consumer demographics and socioeconomics. Exhibit 9-2 shows the relationship between these two groupings using the basic framework developed in Chapter 6.

EXHIBIT 9-2: BUSINESS VERSUS CONSUMER DEMOGRAPHICS

Category	Business Demographics	Consumer Demographics
Market Size	Number of potential customers; number of stores, locations, plants; the number of employees	Population, number of households/ families, household/family size
Age and Stage	Number of years firm has been in business, stage of product/industry life cycle	Age distribution, stage of family life cycle
Monetary Factors	Financial factors (sales, profits), type of business/SIC, management style	Income, occupation, education
Ownership Factors	Own building/property versus lease establishment type (store, office, plant, warehouse), length of time at facility	Homeowner versus renter, type of dwelling, household mobility/stability
Social Class (Industry Stature)	Market or industry position, high-tech versus low-tech	Lower-lower to upper-upper, cluster approach

It should be mentioned that consumer demographics still plays a role in industrial market segmentation. Once all relevant data has been collected (business demographics plus product usage, benefits, and other information), you should seek personal information about the decision-maker for a higher-level, more complete analysis. However, at this time the issue at hand is business demographics. Where can you obtain this information? Exhibit 9-3 shows the availability of key business demographic sources, based on a survey of libraries throughout the United States. You are also advised to refer to Appendix A, "Major Sources of Demographic/Marketing Information," Part V, for brief summaries of some of the best business demographic references.

EXHIBIT 9-3: LIBRARY DEMOGRAPHICS, BUSINESS SOURCES

Reference	% Libraries Where Available
County Business Patterns	93%
U.S. Business Census Reports (such as Wholesale Trade)	78%
Dun's Census of American Business	44%
State Business Censuses	37%
Business Demographics from State Agencies	26%
Business Demographics from Local/County Agencies	19%
Markets of the U.S. for Business Planners	7%

Behavioral Dimensions

Product Usage. Analyzing consumptive patterns of existing and potential customers can be an important segmenting dimension in industrial markets. The first step is to divide the market into two groups: users and nonusers. Next, workable classifications and definitions of users must be determined. Some possibilities include the following:

- Heavy versus medium versus light users (based on unit or dollar sales, or number of orders)

- Users of your product or service versus users of competitors'

- Loyal versus nonloyal customers (the degree of loyalty shown)

- The applications of product usage by user group

- Geographic differences by market (comparing customer penetration and growth patterns of two or more market areas)

As these categories indicate, the product usage dimension is by no means limited to a buy or no-buy decision. Through careful research, a wealth of valuable data can be gathered about past purchase behavior. Often, this information is close at hand—customer invoices and credit records can be checked, industry directories and trade papers studied, and primary or secondary data collected where needed. Equipped with this knowledge, you are in a much better position to develop strategies to target various user segments of the industrial market.

Here's a small business example. Medic-Aid is a healthcare forms processor specializing in Medicaid and Medicare reimbursements. Pharmacies, hospitals, physicians, nursing homes, and other healthcare-related providers can benefit from their computerized billing service. After further analysis, the company defined its primary target market as independent drug stores in areas with a large concentration of poor and/or elderly consumers.

Benefit Segmentation (Common Buying Factors). What is a business looking for when it considers buying a facsimile machine? There are many factors that may enter into this purchasing decision. Examples include: transmission/print capabilities, particular features (such as size or weight of the unit, size of the automatic document feeder, automatic paper cutter, anticurl system, and fax/phone changeover), price, manufacturer's quality (is it a brand name or a no-name?), and service and support. Hence, different customer segments are attracted to various models based on the package of benefits offered to them. Benefit segment analysis can assist management in identifying technology gaps in the current product offering and can provide guidelines for product development.[2]

CompuRent leases computer equipment to banks, hospitals, schools, nonprofit organizations, and industry. Advantages of renting/leasing versus purchasing include these: customers can try before they buy; customers may have a short-term need for the equipment; cash flow is controlled; and expenditures can be applied toward purchase.

Recognizing the proliferation of computer retailers and the subsequent market shakeout, CompuRent was able to carve a niche in its market by providing an alternative approach to computerization. Entrepreneurs are also appealing to other benefit segments such as those seeking used computer equipment.

By segmenting an industrial market through analyzing common buying factors (benefits sought), marketing strategies can be tailored to the needs of specific customer sectors. Hence, customer action (interest, inquiries, and sales) and post-sale satisfaction are more likely to result through this approach than through unfocused marketing initiatives. An electrical components producer segmented its market based on common buying characteristics. One segment consisted of high-volume buyers that were extremely price sensitive.

162

Another segment of small-lot buyers insisted on high quality and special features, but were not noticeably price-conscious. The manufacturer was able to meet the low price requirements of the former segment by raising prices in the latter 25%, with no appreciable loss of business.[3]

Other Behavioral Bases. Generally, lifestyle and personality factors are not that critical in an initial segmentation study for an industrial market. However, since individuals ultimately make all purchase decisions, psychographics can be an important dimension in understanding purchase behavior and influences. This higher level analysis assumes that the industrial marketer already has a good perspective on the market situation, and wants to expand the analysis to include characteristics of the target firm's decision-maker(s). A recent industrial psychographics study was useful for matching salespeople with clients based on personality traits and business-related factors.[4]

Other behavioral dimensions may prove insightful in business markets. Perceptions is a base requiring an understanding of individuals' awareness and attitude levels for a particular product, service, or company. In industrial markets, the key people to analyze for perceptions and preferences include purchasing agents, users, influencers, and decision-makers. Similar in some respects to psychographics, these dimensions are typically not used in basic segmentation studies, but they can be incorporated into advanced analyses, where personal characteristics are of prime concern.

As in consumer markets, media exposure can be an important secondary segmenting dimension. In industrial markets, however, personal selling is a more important promotional strategy than advertising. Industrial advertising is generally used to build a company's image, to remind customers and potential customers about the firm's goods and services, and to generate leads for the sales force. A paramount industrial media/promotion mix might include direct mail, trade journals, and trade shows. Given the smaller market base and the relative ease with which potential customers can be reached, media preference can be very effective in supplementing other segmentation findings.

The marketing mix factors described in the previous chapter—product, promotion, price, and distribution—can also be quite useful in industrial applications. Research on the industrial transmissions market found that

163

including marketing controllables (strategic responses) in the study improved the usability and implementation of the segmentation findings.[5] In business markets, customized products for specific applications are frequently needed. Precise product requirements must be met, negotiation of price is a factor, face-to-face communication is critical, and distribution changes from a product movement function to one of service delivery.

Special Industrial Dimensions

Standard Industrial Classification (SIC) Codes. One of the simplest and potentially most valuable industrial segmenting bases, SIC codes have evolved from a statistical government data collection facilitator to a customer/supplier classification tool for industrial marketers. *The Standard Industrial Classification Manual,* a publication of the U.S. Government Office of Management and Budget, is the master reference for defining American industries.[6] This publication is periodically updated (generally every 10 years, although the 1972 version was not revised until 1987). The SIC system spans the gamut of U.S. economic activities including, but not limited to, the divisions of agriculture, mining, construction, manufacturing, transportation, wholesale trade, retail trade, finance, services, and public administration.

Major two-digit groups (for example, wholesale trade are categories 50 and 51, durables and nondurables, respectively) are the first industry level breakdown. Exhibit 9-4 provides a list of all of the two-digit SIC codes. Next, a three-digit industry group code is assigned (501 represents the wholesaling of motor vehicles and automotive parts and supplies). Finally, a four-digit industry-specific number indicates an even finer distinction (5012 is the appropriate category for the wholesale distribution of automobiles and other motor vehicles).

Exhibit 9-4: The Two-Digit SIC Codes

SIC Code #	Industry Description
01	Agricultural production—crops
02	Agricultural production—livestock
07	Agricultural services
08	Forestry
09	Fishing, hunting, and trapping
10	Metal mining
12	Coal mining
13	Oil and gas extraction
14	Mining and quarrying of minerals
15	Building—general contractors
16	Heavy construction
17	Special trade contractors
20	Manufacturing—food and kindred products
21	Manufacturing—tobacco products
22	Manufacturing—textile mill products
23	Manufacturing—apparel and fabric products
24	Manufacturing—lumber and wood products
25	Manufacturing—furniture and fixtures
26	Manufacturing—paper and allied products
27	Manufacturing—printing and publishing
28	Manufacturing—chemicals
29	Manufacturing—petroleum refining
30	Manufacturing—rubber and plastics
31	Manufacturing—leather and leather products
32	Manufacturing—stone, glass, clay, and concrete
33	Manufacturing—primary metal industries
34	Manufacturing—fabricated metal products
35	Manufacturing—machinery and computer equipment
36	Manufacturing—electronic/electrical equipment and components
37	Manufacturing—transportation equipment
38	Manufacturing—measuring/controlling instruments
39	Miscellaneous manufacturing industries

SIC Code #	Industry Description
40	Railroad transportation
41	Highway passenger transportation
42	Motor freight transportation
43	U.S. Postal Service
44	Water transportation
45	Air transportation
46	Pipelines, except natural gas
47	Transportation services
48	Communications
49	Electric, gas, and sanitary services
50	Wholesale trade—durable goods
51	Wholesale trade—nondurable goods
52	Retail building materials, hardware, garden supply
53	Retail general merchandise stores
54	Retail—food stores
55	Retail—automotive dealers and gas stations
56	Retail—apparel and accessory stores
57	Retail—furniture/home furnishings
58	Retail—eating and drinking places
59	Miscellaneous retail
60	Banking institutions
61	Credit institutions
62	Security and commodity brokers
63	Insurance carriers
64	Insurance agents, brokers, and service
65	Real estate
67	Holding and other investment offices
70	Hotels and lodging places
72	Personal services
73	Business services
75	Automotive services
76	Miscellaneous repair services
78	Motion pictures
79	Amusement and recreation services

SIC Code #	Industry Description
80	Health services
81	Legal services
82	Educational services
83	Social services
84	Museums, art galleries, botanical, and zoological
86	Membership organizations
87	Engineering, accounting, research, and management
88	Private households
89	Miscellaneous services
91	Government
92	Justice, public order, and safety
93	Public finance, taxation, and monetary policy
94	Human resources programs
95	Environmental quality and housing programs
96	Administration of economic programs
97	National security and international affairs
99	Nonclassifiable establishments

Source: Standard Industrial Classification Manual 1987, U.S. Office of Management and Budget.

The beauty of the SIC system is its widespread acceptance. A number of marketing references, both public and private, use the SIC code as a basic data-gathering unit. Therefore, market analysis through multiple sources is possible. Anecdotal evidence recommends the use of SIC codes as tools for segmenting and targeting business markets. Because product complementarity and technological association are clearly significant in many SIC categories, such codes offer a useful starting point for defining markets.[7] This approach may be especially valuable when there are no strong demand-side factors delineating market boundaries. Furthermore, SIC analysis helps industrial managers avoid the error of drawing market boundaries too narrowly.

The SIC system does have some key limitations, however. First, the basic manual is updated infrequently—the 1987 manual was the latest one available at the time of this publication. Many marketing professionals feel that the SIC system is not responsive to today's service-based, high-tech, and global economy. Second, product classes don't always correspond with marketer's needs (often too broad or narrow). Some four-digit codes have 20 or more subcategories. For example, examine SIC 5012 again. In addition to automobiles, other vehicles are included such as buses, campers, mopeds, motorcycles, motor homes, snowmobiles, taxicabs, trucks, and vans. With the SIC system, you are forced to "buy" the whole code—you cannot select specific segments of a predefined industry. Third, SIC data does not necessarily correspond to actual geographic market boundaries. It assumes all markets are domestic and neglects import competition. A final limitation is the nondisclosure rule imposed by government publications. This means that information for a sole establishment in a geographic area cannot be released. If that firm was a potential customer of yours, you would not have access to data from public sources about that company.

Although the SIC approach is a convenient tool for analyzing markets, more detailed general and proprietary coding systems are needed for business markets. In its current form, SIC analysis is probably best used as a secondary industrial segmentation variable.

End Use. With this approach, the final application of the product is the segmenting base. Industrial products can take many forms, including raw materials, work-in-process, and finished goods. The end use of the product has a definite impact on the purchase decision (is it a relatively insignificant, perhaps replaceable part or is it a critical component of a machine?).

A five-step segmentation process can be useful for industrial and high-tech markets.[8] Product type (systems/equipment, components, or materials) is the first consideration. Original equipment manufacturers (OEMs) or aftermarkets (maintenance, repair, and overhaul market or MRO) provide the second segmentation cut. Steps three and four are SIC level and customer applications. Finally, geography, common buying factors, and buyer size complete the segmentation analysis in business markets.

Input-output analysis is closely related to product end use. This technique recognizes that most industrial transactions pass through a channel of users. By analyzing a series of intermediary sales, a company can more accurately focus in on actual target markets. You now know how much of your product is being used, and by whom. This production/consumption data is available from such sources as the *U.S. Industrial Outlook, County Business Patterns, Survey of Current Business, Sales and Marketing Management,* Department of Commerce publications, trade associations, and private research firms.

The *Thomas Register of American Manufacturers* is a multivolume directory useful for targeting industrial markets. Although most businesspeople use it as a supply source, you can find new customers through the register, too. Assume that you developed an industrial component that was of interest to aircraft or automotive jack producers. The directory identifies about five dozen prospects for your product. Customer searches can also be narrowed down by state, area code, or specific words mentioned in company descriptions. The *Thomas Register* is now available on CD-ROM, which enables you to receive ads by fax, view textual information, print labels, and telephone prospects—all from the convenience of your friendly PC.[9]

Adopter Categories. Markets can be segmented based on the rate of customer acceptance for new product concepts. Adopter category segmentation is based on two key ideas: the diffusion of innovations and the identification of lead users. According to the diffusion literature, there are five categories of new product acceptance—innovators, early adopters, early majority, late majority, and laggards.[10] Lead users face strong market needs months or years before the bulk of the marketplace and expect to benefit significantly by finding a solution to those needs.[11] Although adopter category segmentation is useful in many industrial market situations, it is particularly insightful in high-tech markets. The following example illustrates this process based on a segmentation research project conducted by this author (and a colleague) in the cardiac pacemaker market.

The market for cardiac pacemakers has stabilized in the last decade due to pricing pressures caused by diagnostic-related groupings (DRGs) and institutional buyers, intense competition, investigations into the need for the products, and regulatory problems. In the short-term, manufacturers can improve their market position at the expense of competitors. New product development is a major priority. An automatic pacemaker (pacer) is an implantable device that does not require preprogramming and has sensor inputs that maintain the safest level of patient care.

Semistructured depth interviews with physicians provided adequate data for an exploratory segmentation analysis of the automatic pacing submarket (segment identification was the research objective). Based on the qualitative research, six potential market segments for automatic pacing emerged. Three of these customer segments—the progressives, black box-devotees, and show-mes—were likely adopters (worth targeting for future marketing activity). Two segments—the nonbelievers and ones with no perceived need—may eventually adopt the product, although they were not good choices to target for short to intermediate term marketing activity; and one segment—the techies—were likely to never adopt the automatic pacer. Although a battery of factors were considered in segment formation, one major attitudinal variable (user orientation) was most useful in understanding the automatic pacing market. A brief description of the characteristics of the physician-customer segments is shown in Exhibit 9-5.

EXHIBIT 9-5: ADOPTER CATEGORIES FOR AUTOMATIC PACING

Variables	Progressives	Black-box Devotees	Show-mes
Segment Profile	View pacer as technological advancement, will try unproven products, innovators	"Nontinkerers," want simple and reliable product, early adopters	Like concept, need support/case studies, followers, a large segment
User Orientation	Technology	Simplicity	Conservative
Type of Physician	Implanting cardiologists	Implanting cardiologists	Surgeons, referring cardiologists, electrophysiologists
Hospital Type	Teaching	Nonteaching	Nonteaching
Usage Rate	High	Average-high	Average
Sources of Information	Professional journals sales reps/materials, colleagues	Sales reps, colleagues	Primarily colleagues
Need for Manual Overrides	Yes	Uncertain—further research required	Yes

SEGMENTING BUSINESS MARKETS: SOME CONSIDERATIONS

Traditionally, industrial marketers have been more product-oriented than have consumer marketers. An emphasis on segmentation is needed to become truly customer-focused. Market identification and selection is the primary strategic decision area for the business firm.

How do industrial segmentation research designs compare to consumer ones? There are some differences, but essentially they are similar in concept and in practice (see the 10 planning and research guidelines in Chapters 3 and 4).

The major difference between industrial and consumer segmentation analysis is the segmentation bases (the heart of this chapter). Many options are available. Generally speaking, you should use several layers of segmentation dimensions to best find and describe your target markets. You have now been exposed to these tools and should be able to choose several appropriate dimensions for your market situation. Segmentation Action List 9 gives you an opportunity to put this knowledge into practice. In addition, Segmentation Skillbuilder 9 provides financial guidelines and a worksheet for choosing industrial market segments.

Segmentation Action List 9: Business Segmentation Dimensions

1. How do you define your market geographically? How could you define your market geographically?

2. Describe your target market(s) by the following business demographic variables:

   a. type of business
   b. sales volume
   c. number of employees
   d. number of locations
   e. number of years in business
   f. market position

3. Can you identify key user categories (heavy versus light users, loyal versus nonloyal customers, user group needs, geographic discrepancies)?

4. Have you assessed key benefit segments? What are the common buying factors present in the market?

5. Are other behavioral segmentation dimensions (that is, industrial psychographics, perceptions, media exposure, marketing mix factors) relevant and used in your analysis?

6. Have you identified and researched your target markets by SIC code?

7. Have you conducted a product end-use analysis?

8. How can you apply adopter category segmentation to your market situation?

9. Are your target markets based on segmentation research?

10. Are multiple business segmentation bases used?

SEGMENTATION SKILLBUILDER 9: EVALUATING INDUSTRIAL MARKET SEGMENTS*

Prior to selecting target markets, you should consider the short-term and long-run profit potential of the various segments. In markets where your company does not have a presence, profit estimates can usually be developed through published financial data, interviews with investment analysts, and competitive monitoring.

The accompanying table shows how market size, profit margins, and growth rate can be combined to determine the relative value of industrial market segments. The profit value of a share point is determined by multiplying 1/100th of the market by the current profit percentage (such as Segment A—Medical Instrumentation is $1 million x 12% = $120,000). The projected market size is determined by multiplying the size of the current market by the estimated growth rate over that given period. Segment A, currently worth $100 million, is expected to grow 15% annually. Therefore, its projected market size in 5 years is about $200 million. Note, you must also account for estimated changes in profit percentages, where applicable.

This basic worksheet indicates that several key variables must be considered in evaluating market segment opportunities. In addition to the data provided here, other useful types of information are desirable. Historical size and growth patterns (during the past five years), lists of major competitors and their market shares, and major customers and their annual purchases—for key industry segments—also provide insight into business markets. Obviously, simply completing this form is not an end unto itself. The form is designed to help marketers evaluate and cross-check the various market segment trade-offs (in particular, the impact of profit in the decision) and choose segments that are presently most attractive, as well as future business opportunities.

1. Based on the attached worksheet, compute the profit value per share point and projected segment size (lines 3 and 5) for market segments B through E—segment A was done to get you off to a fast start.

2. Which of the five market segments would you target now? In five years?

CURRENT AND 5-YEAR MARKET SEGMENT FORECASTS

Market Segments	(A) Medical Instruments	(B) Process Controls	(C) Test Equipment	(D) Mainframe Computers	(E) Microprocessors
1. Segment Size (millions)	100	350	200	400	60
2. Current Profit (%)	12	9	14	15	20
3. Profit Value per Share Point (thousands)	120	—	—	—	—
4. Estimated Growth Rate (%)	15	7	8	5	20
5. Projected Segment Size (millions)	201	—	—	—	—

*This exercise was adapted from Ames, B. Charles and Hlavacek, James D. *Managerial Marketing for Industrial Firms*, (New York: Random House, Inc., 1984), pp. 134-136.

Segmenting Business Markets

SUMMARY

Industrial markets differ from consumer markets in four respects: (1) the scope of the geographic trade areas (larger, but more concentrated), (2) product/market factors (larger sales, fewer customers), (3) the nature of the purchase decision (more complex), and (4) the closeness of the customer (more personal contact). You must carefully consider these differences when you are segmenting business markets.

You can use an arsenal of segmentation dimensions in these markets. The primary options include geography, business demographics, product usage, benefits (common buying factors), SIC codes, end-use factors, and adopter categories. In some market situations, other, secondary behavioral bases may be useful (such as industrial psychographics, perceptions, media exposure, or marketing mix factors). Consider using multiple business segmentation bases to provide the richest view of potential market segments and target markets.

NOTES

1. Thomas J. Peters and Robert H. Waterman, Jr., *In Search of Excellence:Lessons from America's Best-Run Companies* (New York: Warner Books, 1982), pp. 156-199.

2. Cornelis A. de Kluyver and David B. Whitlark, "Benefit Segmentation for Industrial Products," *Industrial Marketing Management,* November 1986, pp. 273-286.

3. Robert A. Garda, "How to Carve Niches for Growth in Industrial Markets," *Management Review,* August 1981, p. 19.

4. Seymour H. Fine, "Buyer and Seller Psychographics in Industrial Purchase Decisions," *Journal of Business and Industrial Marketing,* Winter-Spring 1991, pp. 49-58.

5. Jay L. Laughlin and Charles R. Taylor, "An Approach to Industrial Market Segmentation," *Industrial Marketing Management,* May 1991, pp. 127-136.

6. *Standard Industrial Classification Manual* (Washington, D.C.: U.S. Office of Management and Budget, 1987).

7. James W. McKie, "Market Definition and the SIC Approach," in Franklin M. Fisher (ed.), *Antitrust and Regulation: Essays in Memory of John J. McGowan* (Cambridge, Mass.: MIT Press, 1985), pp. 85-100.

8. James D. Hlavacek and B. C. Ames, "Segmenting Industrial and High-Tech Markets," *Journal of Business Strategy*, Fall 1986, pp. 39-50.

9. For further information about the *Thomas Register* on CD-ROM, contact the Thomas Publishing Company, New York, at (212) 695-0500.

10. Everett M. Rogers, *Diffusion of Innovations*, Third Edition (New York: The Free Press, 1983).

11. Eric von Hippel, *The Sources of Innovation* (New York: Oxford University Press, 1988).

175

10

SEGMENTING INTERNATIONAL MARKETS

**If you ever want to get anything done in a foreign country,
you'd better understand their culture.**

—Ross Perot, 1987

Marketing has evolved from being a highly localized activity to one global in scope. In the 1990s, marketing's expanded range means that successful small and large companies will often seek profitable business opportunities in distant lands. Heineken, which bills itself as the world's most international brewery, uses a global positioning strategy of premium pricing and high quality. Although favorably perceived as a fine export worldwide, Heineken is viewed similar to Miller (an average quality brew) in its homeland. In Holland, the beer is positioned as a popularly priced product, typically costing no more than mineral water or a Coke in most bars and restaurants. Speaking of Coca-Cola, Diet Coke is known as Coca-Light throughout the European Community (EC).

WHY GO INTERNATIONAL?

The primary reason multinational companies (MNCs) and exporters seek to enter new markets is to increase sales and profits. Other firms avoid potentially lucrative international opportunities because of a lack of customer knowledge, limited information on foreign business practices and uncontrollables (political, economic, technological, and competitive environments), unwilling or untrained international executives, and considerable start-up expense.

Can companies afford to focus their efforts on only domestic markets? Generally speaking, an ethnocentric business orientation does not make sense. In increasingly competitive markets, an international or global emphasis is highly desirable. Consider these examples:

- Apple Computer is committed to being a leading distributor in the EC. European sales account for 60% of its international turnover and about 20% of its worldwide sales.[1]

- Harris Corporation, a global leader in electronic systems, semiconductors, communications, and office equipment, increased its sales from outside of the United States from 20% in fiscal 1989 to 28% in 1990.[2]

- Pier 1 Imports Inc., a retailer of products from Indonesia, Italy, Thailand, and more than 40 other countries, recently entered the international arena via a joint venture with a British company. By the year 2000, Pier 1 hopes to have about 250 stores outside of the U.S. and Canada.[3]

There are three key reasons why firms should pursue global markets:

1. *To develop a competitive advantage.* World markets have become highly competitive. Marketers face strong challenges from global competitors in their domestic markets. As David Horowitz and Charles Kuralt might say, we can "fight back" by taking our business "on the road." This means selling the Japanese cars, the Swiss chocolate, the English tea, and so on. Recognize that markets are people and purchasing power, as well as products. Given that the United States accounts for less than 5% of the world's population and less than 25% of its purchasing power, American firms cannot afford to miss 75% to 95% of the market. Whereas huge countries such as China (with more than a billion people) and India (nearly a billion more) appear attractive superficially, per capita income is relatively low. For example, it is estimated that less than 20% of China's population (primarily the urban sector) represents a viable market for consumer export products.

2. *New markets have new product/technological life cycles.* Although there are similar market needs for many products throughout the world (such as automotive air filters, bleach, and credit cards), a globalization or straight extension strategy doesn't always work. Companies in the United States and other industrialized nations can take mature products such as computers and introduce them to less-developed countries (LDCs) where there is a vast, untapped market potential. Although 386- and 486-based computers are the industry standard in advanced nations, LDCs may still benefit from early generation 8086 and 8088

chip products. New markets also present new needs. Cognizant of language differences, IBM markets more than 20 variations of PC keyboards in Europe (product adaptation is a frequent outcome of international segmentation).

3. *Technology has made the world smaller.* Improvements in telecommunications, transportation, computerization, information services, and media options have made it almost as easy to do business from Tokyo to Toronto as it is from New York to New Jersey. American marketers' newfound technological sophistication allows companies to quickly find and respond to global market trends. International markets are no longer divided solely by political, cultural, or language barriers but often along lifestyle or usage dimensions. As an example, marketers can target the EC youth market and reach them via multicountry advertisements on European MTV to sell compact disks (CDs) and related products by such global recording stars as Phil Collins/Genesis, U2, Michael Jackson, and Madonna.

INTERNATIONAL SEGMENTATION ISSUES AND DECISIONS

The benefits of consumer and industrial segmentation in domestic markets have been established. Market segmentation and targeting decisions are equally vital in foreign markets, because customer needs and characteristics frequently vary. Here are two examples:

- When they say things go better with Coke in Lapland (near the arctic circle), it's likely they mean reindeer rather than hot dogs or hamburgers. Also given the inclement climate, this soft drink is often served in warmers rather than coolers.

- The French are strong believers in properly documenting business and personal records. Photocopy (reproduction) services are popular in Paris—they seem to be located on almost every street. In addition, writing paper is frequently sold with duplicates enclosed!

Geodemographics and Macrosegmentation

There are many ways to segment international markets. One of the best methods is the two-step approach. *Macrosegmentation,* the first step, divides the world into country segments. The second step, *microsegmentation,* integrates product-market factors into the analysis. Now look closer at the idea of macrosegmentation. Using a diverse set of 18 economic indicators (energy usage, education, motor vehicle ownership, the number of televisions and radios in a household, import/export trade, GNP, government spending, the number of hospital beds, and so forth), a recent study found six clusters of macro/nation segments.[4] These clusters could be further reduced to generate three broad groups based on stage of economic development: highly developed (United States, Japan, EC), developing (trade-dependent nations in the Pacific Rim), and LDCs (many countries in Africa, Asia, Latin America, and the Caribbean).

Levels of economic development are not the only way to form macrosegments. International marketers can also use physical attribute segmentation dimensions such as geography, demographics, and socioeconomics (is a nation's per capita income $2,500 or $25,000 annually?). Recognize, however, that foreign censuses differ significantly from the U.S. reports. Here are some major differences:[5]

- Many nations offer bilingual reports (some are in English). Most provide only their native language.

- Germany prints a good deal of information on noncitizens, and Canada collects data on religion (topics ignored in U.S. censuses).

- Income data is often the key segmentation variable in U.S. consumer studies. Unfortunately, this topic is generally taboo in most national censuses (Japan, UK, France, Spain, and others).

- Although the 10-year period between reports in the United States is fairly typical, Japan and Canada conduct their censuses at 5-year intervals. Other countries, such as France and Germany, are unpredictable and gather demographic data irregularly.

Behavioral Dimensions and Microsegmentation

The value of product-specific microsegmentation is evident based on a product usage study prepared for Budget Rent-a-Car on the short-term car hire market in Europe (Exhibit 10-1).[6] Although the primary purpose of behavioral attributes is to form product-specific microsegments, several ad agencies and marketing research firms have developed syndicated psychographic services to better understand foreign markets. Backer,

Spielvogel & Bates Worldwide's Global Scan identifies five value-based segments—strivers, achievers, pressured, adapters, and traditionals—in 18 countries. Young & Rubicam's Cross Cultural Consumer Characterization (4Cs) offers seven needs-based segments in 12 nations.[7]

EXHIBIT 10-1: BUDGET'S PROFILE OF THE EUROPEAN CAR HIRE BUYER

- 24% of respondents rented for business purposes.

- The typical business renter in the UK is male, under 35, social grade AB or C1, and lives in the South-East. Women account for 13% of British business rentals.

- The average distance covered was 150 km, except in Italy, where it was 450 km.

- Demand for one-way rental varied from just 3% in Italy to 33% in France.

- Market penetration varies from only 12 rentals per 1,000 people in Italy to 81 per 1,000 in Sweden.

- Customer usage varies from 2 to 3 days in France, Germany, Sweden, and the UK to 5 to 7 days in the Netherlands.

- France, Germany, Italy, the Netherlands, Sweden, and the UK account for 79% of the West European car hire market.

SRI's VALS service is also applicable to international markets. Japan VALS (a customized project) is a variation that reflects changing values and social behavior in Japan. The 10 Japan VALS segments and accompanying demographic profiles are shown in Exhibits 10-2 and 10-3, respectively. Other country-specific VALS research efforts are in the works.

EXHIBIT 10-2: THE JAPAN VALS SEGMENTS

Segment Name/Symbol	Count (000s)	% of Population
Integrator/Int	3,441	4.0
Tradition Innovator/TrI	4,813	5.6
Tradition Adapter/TrA	8,585	10.1
Ryoshiki Innovator/Ryl	5,051	5.9
Ryoshiki Adapter/RyA	8,555	10.0
Self Innovator/Sel	5,589	6.6
Self Adapter/SeA	9,744	11.4
High Pragmatic/HPr	12,126	14.2
Low Pragmatic/LPr	14,638	17.2
Sustainer/Sus	12,803	15.0
Totals	85,345	100.0

Source: 1991 Japan VALS Survey.

Exhibit 10-3: Demographics of the Japan VALS Standard Segments

Variable	Sus	LPr	HPr	SeA	Sel	RyA	Ryl	TrA	Trl	Int
Sex (male)	41	51	57	51	47	45	43	62	60	58
Age (years)	56	43	35	29	29	44	47	45	47	40
Education										
Less than high school	48	26	5	8	6	4	7	13	16	3
High school	47	58	45	53	55	41	33	60	55	30
Technical school	3	7	10	11	14	7	7	4	10	7
College or postgraduate	3	8	41	28	26	48	53	22	19	60
Income										
Annual income (YM)	3.42	4.43	6.95	4.74	4.84	7.39	7.59	6.75	7.62	13.89
Annual budget (YK)	288	348	539	544	588	522	620	485	641	1162
Marital Status										
Never married	4	16	31	51	54	11	9	7	9	25
Married	88	79	68	47	43	87	90	90	90	75
Housing										
Live with spouse	84	76	66	46	38	83	86	86	87	72
Live with own children	58	68	60	37	35	73	66	81	71	66
Live with parents	17	30	43	54	66	32	28	31	27	46
Own home	76	63	63	55	67	67	74	69	74	76
Own condo	3	4	5	5	3	9	7	3	3	5
Rent home	6	7	6	8	10	4	4	7	5	4
Rent condo, apt/room	10	17	16	25	17	9	8	11	8	8
Own other real estate	16	15	20	15	21	27	32	27	35	37
Occupation										
Primary industries	10	3	2	1	0	1	2	3	3	3
Retail/manufacturing	11	10	10	5	12	8	13	10	12	10
Manage own business	1	2	2	1	2	3	5	4	5	11
Senior management	1	1	3	1	3	3	2	3	4	12
Middle management	2	3	6	3	2	9	12	10	11	11
Professional	1	5	9	8	8	12	14	6	8	8
Sales/Clerical	5	11	22	28	25	14	10	16	10	14
Laborer	14	20	9	11	10	6	5	14	12	1
Services	3	5	6	10	11	5	2	4	5	5
Freelance	0	1	1	3	1	1	1	0	0	1
Part-time	10	8	6	6	5	10	5	6	4	3
Housewife	28	22	17	11	9	23	26	17	19	10
Student	1	2	7	10	11	3	1	3	3	10
Unemployed/Retired	13	5	1	2	1	2	1	4	5	2

NOTE: Column percent is shown unless figures are in italics. Source: 1991 Japan VALS Survey.

Other International Segmentation Dimensions

Language, culture, and political risk should also be considered as potential international segmentation variables. Recognizing the multilingual orientation of Belgium, Uncle Ben's rice mixes can be found with usage directions in three languages in Brussels—English, French, and Dutch (German is also an official language but not one found on the box). In the Netherlands in the early 1990s, Americana culture is alive and well; fashion is 1960s vintage (remember bell bottoms and tie-dyed t-shirts?), Holland has the world's largest non-U.S. Elvis Presley fan club, and Michael Jordan/Chicago Bulls memorabilia are quite popular. Ranking countries on the basis of political risk prior to new market entry facilitates global market expansion. Political risk segmentation can be a starting point and key factor in site selection decisions when you evaluate two or more countries.[8]

INTERNATIONAL SEGMENTATION STRATEGIES

Multinational firms can use segmentation strategies as a basis for formulating overall international marketing mixes. Companies can pursue a concentrated or diversified country strategy and a concentrated or diversified business strategy.

The global banking industry provides an interesting study in contrasting business styles. Two of the top 20 banks (in assets) are the Dutch-based ABN-AMRO Holding N.V. and the New York-based Citicorp. Although each is successful in its own right, the former concentrates on its core business in limited countries. ABN-AMRO views Europe as its domestic market and competes to a lesser extent in North America by using different names for its banks (such as European American Bank and LaSalle National Bank). In contrast, Citibank also sticks to a primary business but is more global in scope, competing in 92 countries. The company appeals to customers with its standardized brand name, Citibank, and core product mix consisting of Citicard Banking Centers, Citibank ATM network, and Citiphone Banking.[9]

Companies can also enter new businesses in limited markets or employ the ambitious strategy of both country and business expansion. Circuit City, an expanding electronics chain, is toying with the idea of using its proven selling and distribution expertise to market used cars in the United States. Companies like General Electric, Matsushita, and Sony are global giants, seeking profitable opportunities in dozens of businesses (strategic business units) throughout the world.

SEGMENTING INTERNATIONAL MARKETS: STRATEGIC CONSIDERATIONS AND GUIDELINES

A strong international marketing program is built on a foundation of effective target marketing. Recognize that costs and complexity increase significantly as new markets are researched, evaluated, and attacked. To succeed overseas, marketing investment must be controlled, product quality needs to be appropriate for customer needs, strategic alliances should be actively sought, and a mega-approach to marketing employed (this extends beyond basic strategy components and considers such issues as cultural sensitivity, political systems, infrastructures, technical standards, and media availability). A summary of key issues to evaluate when you are thinking of international expansion is presented in Segmentation Action List 10.

Segmentation Action List 10: International Segmentation Issues

1. Which international markets are you considering? Why?

2. What is your firm's international degree of involvement (infrequent, selected markets, regional, global)?

3. What is your best market entry strategy (exporting, joint venture, licensing/franchising, wholly owned subsidiary/manufacturing)?

4. Is your firm's international marketing orientation ethnocentric (adhering to the home strategy), polycentric (strategy tailored to each market), or geocentric (a global strategy)?

5. Does your company stress standardization or specialization with regard to foreign markets?

6. How committed is your firm to international markets? This is evidenced by the allocation of corporate resources—human, financial, and technological.

7. From an organizational, planning, managerial, and control perspective how prepared is your firm to enter new markets?

8. Have you studied key market dimensions such as market size, demographic distribution, growth rates, product market potential, business customers, and economic climate?

9. Do you understand key environmental factors— political, economic, competitive, social/cultural, and infrastructure?

10. How will you research new markets? What type of research will you use? What sources of data? What research difficulties do you expect to encounter?

11. What dimensions will you use to segment international markets?

12. Will you use a concentration or differentiation strategy?

13. What are the likely strategic changes needed for your target markets with respect to product offerings, pricing, promotional mix, and distribution?

14. How will you measure the effectiveness of your international marketing program?

Leading global companies such as Coca-Cola, Hewlett-Packard, Intel, Merck, Philips, Sony, and Toyota (and tens of thousands of other small and large companies) earn substantial portions of their revenues and profits from nondomestic markets. Although North America, the EC, and Japan/Asia are generally favorite marketing targets, many companies find great success in less competitive markets such as Latin America, Eastern Europe, Oceania (Australia and New Zealand), Africa, or the Middle East. Given your business situation, how do you view opportunities for international market expansion? Segmentation Skillbuilder 10 should help you make this assessment.

SEGMENTATION SKILLBUILDER 10: SELECTING INTERNATIONAL MARKETS

You just received the following fax from the Vice President of International Markets for your company.

"Due to continued economic pressures and increased competition domestically, sales are flat again this year. We need to explore and exploit new market opportunities. I want to hear your thoughts ASAP."

1. Identify one country/region that merits attention and a second geographic area that can be eliminated from consideration. Discuss the rationale for your choices.

2. Note important international marketing considerations when a firm does business in the selected nation/region.

3. Describe how your product-market should be segmented (appropriate international segmentation dimensions) in the selected nation/region.

Suggested Reading: Cateora, Philip. *International Marketing*, Eighth Edition, (Homewood, Ill.: Irwin, 1993).

An International Segmentation Primer

The major difference between domestic and international segmentation is the increased scope of the market. Hence, defining the geographic market is the first step in an international segmentation analysis. Is your company competing in selected nations (like many exporters), international regional areas (such as Latin America or Asia), or worldwide?

Preliminary country screening on the viability of doing business in foreign markets is the first step. Informal market analysis can help your company make a "go" or "no-go" decision at this stage. This broad-based evaluation assesses country characteristics—political climate, stage of economic development, and so on—rather than specific consumer or product-related factors. This *macro filter* rejects those countries with undesirable political and economic environments.

An investigation of market characteristics and size, growth trends, and culture is accomplished through the *mini filter*. Here, your concern is how well the market will relate to your products. The *micro filter* features an analysis of competition, distribution channels, and product acceptance. Unlike the other two screens, which are based on secondary data, the micro filter relies on first-hand experience and an on-site evaluation of a country's potential. The *fine-tune filter* completes the initial international research needed for market selection. By examining all data and impressions gained through research and travel, returns on investment can be calculated. This leads to further decisions regarding foreign market priorities and corporate resource allocation.[10]

The next step is applying the usual (consumer or business) segmentation dimensions to prospective markets. Consumer marketers will use the typical geodemographic variables and appropriate behavioral dimensions. Industrial marketers will typically use business demographics, product usage, and benefit segmentation. According to Marvin Nesbit, a business consultant who specializes in Latin America, "the lack of available data in third world countries means that marketers need to be creative in their international market analyses." In many cases, he recommends the use of general economic and social statistics (such as UN reports) rather than traditional market-driven demographics.

Finally, add the international segmentation dimensions to the analysis, including language and culture-related factors. Culture is a complex aggregate that includes art, beliefs, customs, knowledge, ideas, laws, morals, music, religion, social institutions, technology, values, and other facets of a society's personality. Understanding both *etics* or *culture-general concepts* (opportunities for product extension) and *emics* or *culture-specific concepts* (opportunities for product adaptation) are important areas to research.[11]

The aforementioned three-step process is adequate for a basic within-market segmentation study (such as analyzing the feasibility of introducing a breakfast cereal in France or opening a marketing research firm in Ecuador). In the global marketplace of the 1990s, however, many segmentation decisions are not limited to single country markets. Political boundaries have declined somewhat in importance; regional or global market segments are often formed based on similar lifestyles or needs. This suggests a clustered approach to international segmentation. Once discriminating variables have been determined, the company then markets to selected segments, irrespective of national borders. Microsoft Corporation used global segmentation (user experience, usage situation, benefits sought, and language) to successfully introduce the Microsoft Works integrated software package into the EC in the late 1980s.[12]

SUMMARY

In today's changing and competitive marketplace, companies realize that business success often hinges on the strength of their international presence. International segmentation is not just for global giants; small and medium-sized firms can reap significant profits in overseas ventures. This chapter first reviewed the benefits of international expansion: competitive advantage, new product life cycles/needs, and improved technological access to world markets. International segmentation bases and syndicated services were next discussed. Finally, strategic considerations for starting or improving your international segmentation program were offered.

NOTES

1. Sean Milmo, "Are You Ready for 1992?" *Business Marketing,* September 1988, pp. 66, 70, 72, 74.

2. *Harris Corporation Annual Report* (Melbourne, Fla.: Harris Corporation, 1990), pp. 2.

3. Stephanie Anderson Forest and Ruth Golby, "A Pier 1 in Every Port?" *Business Week,* May 31, 1993, p. 88.

4. Ellen Day, Richard J. Fox, and Sandra M. Huszagh, "Segmenting the Global Market for Industrial Goods: Issues and Implications," *International Marketing Review 5,* Autumn 1988, pp. 14-27.

5. Donald B. Pittenger, "Gathering Foreign Demographics is No Easy Task," *Marketing News,* January 8, 1990, pp. 23, 25.

6. John Law, "Hire Expectations," *Executive Travel,* July 1992, pp. 21-24.

7. Lewis C. Winters, "International Psychographics," *Marketing Research,* September 1992, pp. 48-49.

8. Roberto Friedmann and Jonghoon Kim, "Political Risk and International Marketing," *Columbia Journal of World Business,* Winter 1988, pp. 63-74.

9. *Citicorp Annual Report* (New York: Citicorp, 1991).

10. Richard L. Leya, Export Now: *A Guide for Small Business* (Grants Pass, Ore.: Oasis Press, 1990), pp. 3-6-3-12.

11. Richard Brislin, *Understanding Culture's Influence on Behavior* (Fort Worth, Tex.: Harcourt Brace Jovanovich College Publishers, 1993), pp. 71-76.

12. Thomas J. Kosnik, "Microsoft Corporation: The Introduction of Microsoft Works," *Harvard Business School Case 9-588-028* (Boston: Publishing Division, Harvard Business School, March 7, 1991).

11

SEGMENTATION MODELS
AND PROCEDURAL GUIDELINES

Small opportunities are often the beginning of great enterprises.

—Demosthenes, 343 B.C.

As this book has stated throughout, there is no singular approach to conducting a segmentation study. If you look at other disciplines, it is often possible to clearly identify procedures for accomplishing given tasks. Consider photography, for example. The basic steps invariably are these: (1) load the camera (insert film, flash, and batteries), (2) focus on the subject, (3) shoot the picture, and (4) develop the photographs. Segmentation is more difficult, because every business situation is unique, requiring specific manipulation of corporate resources and research methods. This chapter discusses two important models you can use to facilitate segmentation analysis—the 8-S Formula and the nested approach, an industrial segmentation model. The chapter also offers five guidelines to assist you in executing the segmentation process.

THE 8-S FORMULA

A practical approach to segmenting markets consists of eight steps, called the 8-S Formula. This flexible framework is useful in consumer or business markets and is relevant for physical attribute and behavioral segmentation. The eight Ss include

- **S**elect the market to evaluate
- **S**egmentation planning
- **S**ecure information

- **S**egment formation I
- **S**ituational segmentation
- **S**egment formation II
- **S**elect target markets
- **S**trategy formulation

This section discusses how to implement the eight Ss in a step-by-step manner.

Step 1. Selecting the Market: Defining Your Presegmented Market

Geography provides the starting point for physical attribute segmentation. In behavioral analyses, the markets to be examined are generally not geographically based. These studies often use "state-of-mind" (such as the fashion-conscious woman) or "state-of-action" (for example, the frequent flyer) indicators to define markets. The challenge at this initial juncture is to adequately define your "presegmented" market. Markets consist of customer groups, customer needs/functions, and technologies.[1]

As Exhibit 11-1 shows, market definition is a three-step process. Assume a manufacturer of computer boards, microprocessors, and microcontrollers (product market) is offering its products to computer and related industries (generic market) in North America and Europe (geographic market). The relevant market is the market appropriate for a firm, given its resources and objectives. In this case, the computer components company might define its relevant market—level I—as leading-edge original equipment manufacturers (OEMs).

EXHIBIT 11-1: MARKET DEFINITION MODEL

Level I: The Relevant Market

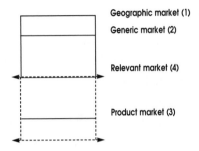

Geographic market (1)

Generic market (2)

Relevant market (4)

Product market (3)

Level II: The "Defined" or Presegmented Market

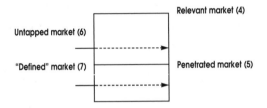

Relevant market (4)

Untapped market (6)

"Defined" market (7)

Penetrated market (5)

Level III: The Target Market(s)

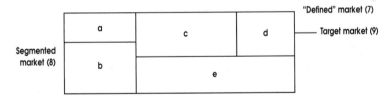

"Defined" market (7)

Target market (9)

Segmented market (8)

The firm then assesses its current customer base (penetrated market) and noncustomers (untapped market). Often the defined market—level II—will include most of your current customers (although there are some customers it is not profitable to serve) and many new prospects. For example, the revised market definition may be leading-edge OEMs that are growing 5% or more annually. Level III takes this presegmented market definition and applies the principles discussed in this book to segment and target specific market segments.

Step 2. Segmentation Planning

The 10 planning and research guidelines developed in Chapters 3 and 4 provide a sound foundation for planning a segmentation study. Although this step has been detailed earlier, a few additional comments regarding behavioral segmentation are offered.

There is little difference between research objectives and target population measurement units for physical and behavioral attribute segmentation analyses. You need to specify both of these planning elements in a successful study. Relevant definitions, however, are more problematic in a behavioral project. These might include trade area definitions (physical and nonphysical); measures for evaluating lifestyles, benefits, or perceptions; consumptive classifications; defining marketing mix elements in terms of segmentation variables; and so forth. Segmentation viability and formation criteria can be more difficult or easy to assess and construct, depending on the segmentation base(s) employed. For example, psychographics is generally more complex, whereas a product usage analysis may only require basic tabulation by consumption into user groups. As far as actual dimensions are concerned, there are many more options available to the marketing analyst, with creative approaches to "old" problems often possible.

The research process itself is usually more complex, because most of the information is primary in nature. This may require designing survey instruments, developing field procedures to collect data, using sampling methods to provide representative findings, and employing computer-based analytical methods. Also, behavioral projects (depending on the scope of the research) often are many times more costly than demographic studies. Because the research results may differ markedly from what is expected, marketing managers should be flexible and open-minded.

Step 3. Secure Information

When confronted with a marketing problem, too often the natural tendency of managers is to call for a study. In this sense, secondary data lives up to its nomenclature, because it is frequently relegated to a supporting or nonexistent role. The temptation to jump right into primary research should be avoided when secondary data can provide the information desired. For example, secondary research might tell you that the automobile market can be subdivided into five segments: the status/luxury, performance, utility, economy, and used car markets. Nissan looked at demographic factors such as income and age in 108 U.S. markets prior to launching its upscale Infiniti in Boston, New York, Philadelphia, and Washington, D.C.[2] The incorporation of syndicated data, particularly in the lifestyle area, is also gaining in popularity.

Step 4. Segment Formation I

In many projects, there may be some historical precedent for segment formation. A past study may have been conducted by your company, aspects of a competitor's planning strategy could have been featured in a trade journal article, or information might have been obtained through a trade association presentation. Sometimes valuable lessons can be learned from other companies operating in similar, but distinct, industries. A good example is the marketing strategies that hospitals have adapted from the hotel industry: Both industries are dependent on room occupancy, work closely with intermediaries (doctors or travel agents), are highly labor-intensive, and are in extremely competitive markets.[3]

A prior knowledge base can be used as a foundation for building a new segmentation model; seek information building blocks. Rather than trying to reinvent the wheel, use other valuable findings, expand on them, and adapt the research to your current situation. These findings can provide a basic understanding of a market, its driving forces, and input on customer needs. Also, explore your own hypotheses and hunches. A priori determinations for testing can be useful in providing the segmentation model direction. "Gut feel" is often sound business judgment based on years of experience.

Step 5. Situational Segmentation

A major difference between physical and behavioral segmentation is that in the latter case, explanatory links to purchase behavior (dependent variables) are obtainable through analyzing key segmentation factors (independent variables). Independent variables can include all demographic characteristics, and behavioral variables such as lifestyle data, benefits, perceptions/preferences, media exposure, and marketing mix factors. Dependent variables are generally usage measures (such as sales by units, customer category, and product/brand). This causal relationship can be expressed mathematically as

$$aX1 + bX2 + cX3 + dX4 + \ldots nXn = Y$$

where X1 is the first independent variable, X2 the second, and Xn the nth; a, b, c, or n is the degree of impact of that variable; and Y is the dependent variable.

Demographic analysis falls short, because only general characteristics of a population are surveyed. It is also important to gauge product-driven and situation-specific factors to complete an overall market picture.

Step 6. Segment Formation II

Whereas you develop an initial or rough cut segmentation scheme in Steps 4 and 5, additional analysis leads to improved categorization. Here are two key points to remember. First, analyze segments by chosen segmenting dimensions. If these factors are consistently evidenced in all (or most) segments, they are not good segmenting dimensions—they are market descriptors. Second, seek unique segmenting dimensions to find your competitive edge. Exhibit 11-2 (which rates 10 product characteristics desired by potential buyers of a desk lamp) and the accompanying discussion clarifies this issue.

Exhibit 11-2: Purchasing a Desk Lamp

Benefits Sought	Segment 1	Segment 2	Segment 3	Segment 4
Adjustability			X	X
Brand Name		X	X	
Color		X		
Fluorescent Lighting		X	X	X
Functional	X	X	X	X
High Intensity		X	X	X
Hi/lo Switch		X	X	
Low Cost	X			
Minimal Space Requirements			X	X
Style		X	X	

Four consumer markets can be identified. Segment 1, The Price Shoppers, want an acceptable desk lamp at the lowest cost. Segment 2, The Quality Shoppers, are most concerned about the brand name or manufacturer, the type of lighting provided, and the style of the lamp. Segment 3, The Special Features Seekers, view desk lamps as a commodity. Their purchase choice depends primarily on what unique advantages one lamp provides over another as it relates to their needs (features such as adjustability, space needed, and special high-intensity lighting or a hi/lo switch). Finally, Segment 4 comprises The Light Conscious. These consumers are most interested in a product that offers them the best possible lighting. Segment 4 people spend a lot of time at their desks and will carefully shop for a desk lamp that meets their rigorous standards.

As you can note from Exhibit 11-2, the desired product characteristics of fluorescent lighting, functional, and high-intensity would not be good segmenting dimensions, because these benefits are sought by most or all of the segments. Also, if most of the desk lamp manufacturers and distributors were targeting the Price and Quality Shoppers segments, potential might exist in pursuing the Special Features or Light Conscious segments. (Of course, further research into the size and accessibility of these segments is necessary.)

Step 7. Select Target Markets

Based on the market segmentation analysis and available resources, one or more market segments will be chosen as targets for market activity (see Exhibit 11-1, level III). Segmentation analysis requires strategic choices. The objective is to pursue the most attractive target market opportunities (using differentiated marketing strategies and tactics) at the possible expense of less desirable segments. A segment profile derived from a demographic study conducted for a South Florida dentist is shown in Exhibit 11-3.

EXHIBIT 11-3: SEGMENT PROFILE OF UP-AND-COMERS

→ This segment is characterized by professionals, managers, and administrators who are heading toward or at their earnings peak.

→ This segment comprises census tracts 11.04, 12.02, and 97.01.

→ The geographic location of this segment is in Miami Shores (11.04 and 12.02) and the Ojus area (97.01).

→ The total population in this segment is 21,873.

→ The total number of households in this segment is 8,397.

→ The average household size of this segment is 2.6 persons, which is above the market area average of 2.3.

→ The distribution by age for this segment is

<18	18-24	25-34
5,290/24.2%	1,663/7.6%	2,775/12.7%
35-44	45-54	55 and over
2,982/13.6%	2,976/13.6%	6,187/28.3%

→ The household income distribution for this segment is

<$25,000	$25,000-$49,999	>$50,000
3,658/44.7%	2,816 / 33.6%	1,823 / 21.7%

→ 70% of the residences are single family units, and 82% of all residences are owner occupied.

→ This segment has an average mobility turnover ratio of 0.22 which is well below the county average of 0.32.

→ 28.4% of this segment are college graduates, which indicates an education level significantly above the market area, with 14.6%.

However, segments not targeted for marketing activity might, at times, respond to marketing initiatives. The segmentation spillover effect means that consumers in nontargeted segments may relate to the promotional message, for example, and wish to take advantage of the good or service offered.[4]

Step 8. Strategy Formulation

The final step in the 8-S Formula is to develop short- and long-term strategies based on the segmentation findings. Given the target market profile in the dental study (Exhibit 11-3), examples of marketing strategies designed for the Up-and-Comers segment are provided in Exhibit 11-4. Target market strategy development is stressed in the next chapter and the Segmentation Strategy Cases (Part 4).

EXHIBIT 11-4: MARKETING STRATEGIES
FOR THE UP-AND-COMERS SEGMENT

Overall Strategy. Promote high-quality preventive dentistry and the benefits of cosmetic procedures.

Marketing Rationale. Patients in this segment are likely to have at least two needs for dental services. First, they are seeking the "best" available care for their family. A secondary need for these young professionals is to improve their appearance, often to enhance their careers.

Promotional Appeals. Aesthetics, vanity, attention, and humor.

Promotional Tactics

(a) **Advertising**—Highly targeted advertising to this upscale market is required. Appropriate media vehicles include a community magazine with reader demographics geared to the cosmetic thrust (upper income, expensive homes, substantial net worth, mostly managers or professionals, and primarily college graduates aged 25-54) and an affluent homeowners mailing list.

(b) **Promotions**—New promotional incentives should be considered for this segment. Possibilities include gold-plated toothbrushes, dental travel kits (containing toothbrush, toothpaste, and floss), pens, calculators, and restaurant or club passes.

(c) **Patient relations**—The dentists should treat these patients as peers. The dental staff and office should reinforce an image of high-quality professionalism.

THE NESTED APPROACH

A practical and comprehensive approach to segmenting business markets is Bonoma and Shapiro's nested approach. It consists of the following five nests (bases) and related segmentation variables:

1. Demographics—industry, company size, and customer location

2. Operating variables—technology, user status, and customer capabilities

3. Purchasing approaches—purchasing function organization, power structures, buyer-seller relationships, and purchase policies and criteria

4. Situational factors—urgency of order fulfillment, product application, and size of order

5. Buyers' personal characteristics—buyer-seller similarity, attitudes toward risk, and buyer motivation/perceptions[5]

Generally, marketers should work systematically from the outer nests (numbers 1-3) to the inner ones (numbers 4 and 5) because data are more available and definitions clearer. However, the inner nests (situational and personal variables) are often more useful. In situations where knowledge and analysis exists, marketers may begin at a middle nest and work inward (occasionally outward). A balance between the simplicity and low cost of the outer nests and the richness and expense of the inner ones is desirable to maximize the value of the segmentation analysis.[6]

An overview of the nested approach is depicted in Exhibit 11-5. In addition to the visual presentation of the model, questions relevant to the industrial segmentation variables are presented in Segmentation Action List 11. Segmentation Skillbuilder 11 helps you to apply this simple, yet valuable approach to your market situation.

EXHIBIT 11-5: INDUSTRIAL MARKET SEGMENTATION— A NESTED APPROACH

Industrial Market Segmentation Nested Approach

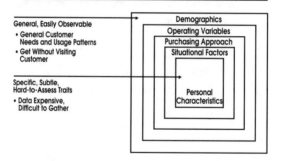

Industrial Market Segmentation Classification of Nests

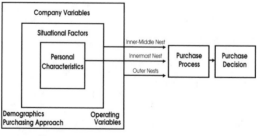

Reprinted with permission from Thomas V. Bonoma and Benson P. Shapiro.

Segmentation Action List 11: The Nested Approach

Industrial Market Segmentation

Characteristic	Segment by	Question
Demographic	Industry	Which industry to focus on?
	Company Size	Can you produce enough for large needs?
	Location	What geographical areas?
Operating Variables	Technology	What customer technologies?
	User/Nonuser Status	Heavy, medium, light, nonusers?
	Customer Capabilities	Needing many services, few?
Purchasing Approaches	Purchasing Function	Centralized or decentralized?
		national account vs field oriented
often neglected	Power Structure	Engineer dominated, finance, etc.?
	Nature of Existing Relationships	Strong relationships or most desirable companies?
	Purchasing Policies	Leasing, service, price, bid?
	Purchasing Criteria	Quality, service, price?
Situational Factors	Urgency	Quick delivery?
	Specific Application	Certain or all applications?
	Size of Order	Large or small orders?
Personal	Buyer-Seller Similarity	Values similar to ours?
people make	Attitudes Toward Risk	Risk-taking, risk-avoiding?
purchases	Loyalty	High loyalty to suppliers?

Reprinted with permission from Thomas V. Bonoma and Benson P. Shapiro.

SEGMENTATION SKILLBUILDER 11: USING THE NESTED APPROACH TO SEGMENT YOUR MARKET

Your boss, the Director of Marketing, has just returned your marketing plan draft for 199X with this comment in large red ink: "Let's look for a new approach to segmenting our market!" Recently, one of your product managers suggested that you consider using the nested approach to segment your market. The two of you meet, review notes on how this segmentation process works, and contemplate how you can adapt this approach to your industry.

Use the nested approach to identify appropriate segmentation bases and variables to segment your market. A refresher is listed here.

- Demographics—industry, company size, and customer location

- Operating variables—technology, user status, and customer capabilities

- Purchasing approaches—purchasing function organization, power structures, buyer-seller relationships, and purchase policies and criteria

- Situational factors—urgency of order fulfillment, product application, and size of order

- Buyers' personal characteristics—buyer-seller similarity, attitudes toward risk, and buyer motivation/perceptions

Suggested Reading: Bonoma, Thomas V., and Shapiro, Benson P. *Segmenting the Industrial Market.* (Lexington, Mass.: Lexington Books, 1983).

PROCEDURAL GUIDELINES FOR SEGMENTATION STUDIES

Here are five tips to assist you in conducting segmentation analyses.

- *Plan, plan, plan.* Successful segmentation projects are built on well-designed plans. The objective is to obtain usable customer-based information. Will it assist management in solving today's (and tomorrow's) marketing problems? Determine what is currently known about your market and what you need to know. The difference is the focus of your research. The planning guidelines presented throughout this book (the 4 Rs, the 10-point program for segmentation analysis, the 8-S Formula, and various segmentation action lists and exhibits) are such aids that you can use to supplement company, industry, and general planning guidelines.

- *Consult key references on a regular basis.* Thorough research is the backbone of the segmentation project. There is wealth of free and low-cost secondary sources you can use. Tapping these references can often answer many of your initial market information questions at a fraction of the cost of primary information (see Appendix A, "Sources of Demographic/Marketing Information"). Past industry and company research can also prove instrumental in the new project. The segmentation researcher must be a "student of the market." You should regularly follow movements and market trends, the industry structure, overall market performance, the competitive environment, and related factors. The quest for market insight should go on continuously—not just when the need for specific information arises.

■ *Recognize the dynamics of the market.* Just as no two people are identical, neither are two markets or companies. It is critical to acknowledge the uniqueness of business entities and situations, and act accordingly. Consumer markets differ markedly from industrial ones; personal services are not the same as professional or business services. International markets present added complexities. Within industries, individual firms must target and pursue their own niches in the marketplace. A multitude of forces are simultaneously interreacting and must be understood in order for you to fully exploit market opportunities.

SEGMENTATION AND STRATEGIC PLANNING

Integrate segmentation analysis with other marketing studies, where feasible. Additionally, you can address noncustomer marketing issues in segmentation projects. The cyclical treatment of market segmentation and marketing planning can help you recognize and respond to changing market conditions.

■ *Use a cluster of segmentation bases and variables.* To provide the most realistic profile of a market, you should use several physical and/or behavioral dimensions for defining markets. Also, one or two variables within these bases are generally insufficient for segmenting markets. An analysis of all potentially useful variables should be planned before you begin the analysis. Syndicated services analyze a battery of key factors to better understand markets. Your company should also recognize the benefits of the cluster approach.

- *Get down to basics.* The segmentation study should be designed to provide information needed for marketing decisions. Traditional approaches to segmentation, at times, emphasize rigor (methodology) over relevance. The result of such a study is a segmentation model understood only by the researcher—and not used by management. Stress practical segmentation (review Chapter 3).

SUMMARY

The 8-S Formula is a general flexible model to facilitate the market segmentation process. It is useful for both physical and behavioral attribute segmentation. The eight Ss include selecting the market, segmentation planning, securing information, segment formation I, situational segmentation, segment formation II, selecting target markets, and strategy formulation.

The nested approach is a comprehensive segmentation model designed for industrial markets. The five key segmentation bases for analysis are demographic, operating variables, purchasing approaches, situational factors, and buyers' personal characteristics. The chapter closed with procedural guidelines for conducting segmentation studies. The next chapter discusses how to turn segmentation research results into successful customer-driven marketing strategies.

NOTES

1. Derek F. Abell, *Defining the Business: The Starting Point of Strategic Planning* (Englewood Cliffs, N.J.: Prentice-Hall, 1980).

2. Joan Mooney, "Which Niche: Fitting the Car to the Customer," *Automotive Executive*, February 1988, pp. 66-67, 71-72, 75.

3. James A. Rice, Richard S. Slack, and Pamela A. Garside, "Hospitals Can Learn Valuable Marketing Strategies from Hotels," *Hospitals*, November 16, 1981, pp. 95-99.

4. Steven H. Star, "Marketing and Its Discontents," *Harvard Business Review*, November-December 1989, pp. 148-154.

5. Thomas V. Bonoma and Benson P. Shapiro, *Segmenting the Industrial Market* (Lexington, Mass.: Lexington Books, 1983).

6. Benson P. Shapiro and Thomas V. Bonoma, "How to Segment Industrial Markets," *Harvard Business Review*, May-June 1984, pp. 104-110.

PART THREE

STRATEGY & CON-
TROL

12

TRANSLATING SEGMENTATION FINDINGS INTO TARGET MARKET STRATEGY

**Take time to deliberate, but when the time
for action has arrived, stop thinking and go in.**

—*Napoleon Bonaparte, 1815*

Market segmentation can be informative, insightful, innovative, and even interesting. But its real value lies in its ability to be implications-oriented—to create profitable business opportunities from similar market situations.

Segmentation analysis and strategy planning can be likened to playing cards in several respects. All players (companies competing in a given market) must abide by the same rules (industry regulation) and are dealt cards from the same deck (overall market conditions). Each player must decide how to play the hand (strategy) given his or her resources (financial, technical skills, strengths, and weaknesses, and so on). Some players have "deep pockets" and can outspend their competitors; others are aggressive and win by using their business savvy (that is, knowing when to hold 'em and when to fold 'em). Market segmentation recognizes that all hands (marketing opportunities) should not be played equally. Rather, the players/companies should concentrate on those efforts that provide them the best chance for success. Success results from the best prospects for your goods or services—your target markets.

Building on Darwinian theory, parallels between biological competition and business competition have been drawn. Just as no two species can coexist if they make their living in the identical way, firms that offer the same products, in the same territory, under the same conditions, with the same clientele cannot coexist equally. Eventually, one will dominate.[1] While Sears and J.C. Penney struggled in head-to-head confrontations, Wal-Mart's low-cost approach to mass merchandising led to prosperity during the past decade.

Strategic marketing, the subject of this chapter, is difficult to address, because many interrelated factors (marketing, managerial, and financial) impact it. The chapter examines strategy from the segmentation perspective—that is, translating research findings into an actionable plan and tailoring the marketing mix to segment needs/desires.

TARGET MARKET STRATEGY FORMULATION: WORKING THE PLAN

Ideally, segmentation findings can be readily turned into action-oriented, strategic programs. But this is not always the case; strategy formation is not an immediate process. Although many segmentation analyses are data-based, strategy development almost requires a sixth sense. Intangible factors such as experience and creative insight play a role in strategic design. Given the limitations of one chapter of coverage, this book presents only a general framework for strategy formulation (specific strategies and tactics must be adapted to your market situation and chosen segments).

Recognize that marketing elements differ in importance in various segmentation studies. For one firm, product factors may be the primary consideration; in another, promotion or distribution can be the central controllable. Secondary issues should not be neglected either, because their impact may also be crucial to developing new marketing programs.

The Three Basic Steps to Strategy Formulation

A three-step process can be used to develop your target market strategy. This process consists of the following components: segment identification, market selection, and positioning.

Segment Identification. The first 11 chapters of the book developed a framework for planning and conducting a market segmentation analysis. The product of such a study is the determination of a given number of homogeneous market segments based on selected segmentation variables and criteria. Now the market has structure, and marketing decisions change from analytical to strategic in nature.

Although many companies (including Du Pont, Eastman Kodak, and Xerox) are spinning off strategic business units (SBUs) not related to their core businesses, Kmart's strategy for the 1990s is based on specialty store acquisition to offset flat sales in its mature discount operation (specialty chains accounted for 31% of the company's revenue in 1992 versus just 7% in 1987). Kmart has identified high-growth retail opportunities in warehouse clubs (Pace), home improvement (Builders Square), drugstores (Pay Less and Pay and Save), books (Waldenbooks and Borders), office supplies (Office Max and Bizmart), and sporting goods (Sports Authority).[2]

Market Selection. Your first major strategic decision is to select from the alternative market segments one or more groups to target for marketing activity. Each of the individual segments must be evaluated on its own merits and in conjunction with the capabilities and environmental situation surrounding the firm. This evaluation recognizes that the options are unique and have varying degrees of attractiveness to your firm. Although several submarkets may be worth pursuing, companies must balance a multiplicity of tangible and intangible factors. This includes customer needs, the internal environment (in particular, financial and other resources), the external environment, an assessment of opportunities versus problems, and corporate objectives. A measure of segment potential can then be determined. At this point, the company has decided what sectors of the market to go after.

Examine the airline industry as a case in point. Customers fly different airlines for a variety of reasons. These include economy, service and amenities, flying to the "right" destination, the airline's reputation, and catering to the business traveler. Which benefit segments should management pursue?

Positioning. It is next important to formulate a unique marketing strategy to appeal to the customers you are trying to reach. Although a "me-too" or copycat strategy sometimes works, in the majority of cases a fresh approach to marketing is required to stand out from the crowd and be successful.

Assume that research findings from a segmentation study for an automobile dealer suggest that an advertising campaign can target either young professionals or middle-aged consumers for a new sports car. If competitors are pursuing baby boomers, the firm should strongly consider the alternative submarket. The "fountain of youth" strategy, allowing mature adults to combat a midlife crisis or restore their younger days, might provide a strong competitive edge.

The overall marketing strategy employed, which includes the manipulation of the marketing mix (the 4 Ps), is the positioning aspect of strategic implementation. According to noted advertising consultants, Ries and Trout, "Positioning is not what you do to a product; positioning is what you do to the mind of the prospect."[3] The basic premise behind positioning is that the firm must have a competitive advantage to survive or thrive in the marketplace. These advantages can be real (such as a better product or lower price) or intangible (such as a product that is built to last or backed by a company's reputation).

Positioning is sound marketing decision making based on the facts—the segmentation study findings—plus business creativity. This creative process might call for searching out unique marketing advantages, seeking new market segments that competitors are not cultivating, or developing new approaches to "old" problems. The goal of the positioning strategy is to carve out a market niche for the firm. Perceptual mapping, which has long been used as a modeling technique in consumer markets, is gaining favor as a diagnostic tool in industrial settings.[4]

Positioning is increasingly critical to high-technology marketers. A three-level positioning model is shown in Exhibit 12-1. The core product (Level I) is the device that the company produces. At this short-term positioning stage, differentiating features such as quality, specifications, and price are at the forefront. These variables can be quickly emulated by competitors; hence, there is a need for intermediate positioning. The extended product (Level II) develops the marketing infrastructure and strategic relationships. The total product (Level III) is a long-term positioning strategy. It sells who the company is and what it stands for. Merck's leadership position in pharmaceuticals, Hewlett-Packard's reputation for quality, and the Xerox commitment to customer service have been built over many years and overshadow individual product successes (and occasional failures).[5]

EXHIBIT 12-1: THE HIGH-TECH PRODUCT POSITIONING MODEL

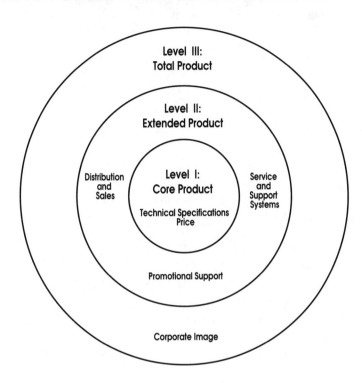

Segmentation Skillbuilder 12 provides a framework for incorporating the three-step strategy formulation process into your company's marketing plan for selected target markets.

Step 1: Identify Market Segments
(list the submarkets from the segmentation study)

Market Segment A   _____
                                     segment name

Market Segment B   _____
                                     segment name

Market Segment C   _____
                                     segment name

Market Segment D   _____
                                     segment name

Market Segment X   _____
                                     segment name

Step 2: Target Market Segments
(select key segment or segments for marketing activity)

Primary market   _____
                                segment name

Target market profile and needs:

Secondary market   _____
                                   segment name

Target market profile and needs:

Step 3: Position the Segments
(formulate a unique marketing strategy)

Primary market   _____
                                segment name

Competitive advantages:

Positioning strategy:

Secondary market   _____
                                   segment name

Competitive advantages:

Positioning strategy:

NICHEMANSHIP: SEGMENTED MARKETING AT ITS BEST

Niche marketing is a form of concentrated target marketing. Segmentation, on the other hand, discerns and responds to customer needs through concentration or differentiation (review Chapter 1). Five strategies that companies use to find their niche are product/service modification, customer service variations, different distribution channels, targeted communications, and variable pricing.[6]

Market niches are small segments that offer incremental business opportunities; they allow specialized marketers to be big fish in small ponds. According to Mediamark Research, some less obvious niche markets include shampoo for gray hair, low-alcohol beer, the under $10,000 car, and products for male homemakers.[7]

Nichemanship is the process whereby a company integrates marketing and management activities to optimize its competitive market position. A segmentation-derived positioning strategy for a focal customer target is a major part of nichemanship. Here are other characteristics of a market nicher:

- The company determines those products that it can best offer given its distinct competencies, competition, and customer needs/wants. (It is truly market-oriented.)

- The company designs specialized goods and services to meet identified market demands.

- By only focusing its energies on specific target markets, the company is more efficient than its larger counterparts in satisfying its customer base.

- Change is sought. Market niche companies are not looking to be like everyone else but to seek a new and better way to conduct business.

- A management commitment to excellence in all endeavors is the market niche company's underlying operating philosophy. An environment for growth is fostered.

- These firms are trend setters/trend spotters, market innovators, and creative marketing strategists.

True niche-based firms also recognize the value of sound research and stand the test of time. Apple Computer and McDonald's are two such firms. Although Apple might be a more obvious choice to many, McDonald's also fits this bill. In 1955, McDonald's had only one hamburger restaurant. In the four decades since, "The Golden Arches" have served billions of hamburgers, revolutionized the fast-food industry, and created a worldwide empire. Segmentation Action List 12 provides 10 questions to assess how well your firm practices niche marketing.

Segmentation Action List 12: Are You a Good Niche Marketer?*

1. Do you know your firm's strengths, weaknesses, and competitive advantage?

2. Do you understand your customer, inside and out?

3. Is your company dependent on one or a limited number of customers? Do most of your sales come from a single product?

4. Have you developed an ongoing customer information system? Does it measure sales, profits, and market response links?

5. How well do you know your competition (for example, why customers use competitive products and how you can get them to switch)?

6. What is your positioning strategy? Have you developed and communicated a clear image for your product/product line? How is your product differentiated from that of your rivals?

7. Have you created your own safe haven in the market? (Try not to compete with yourself, but create high entry barriers for others.)

8. Are your resources spread too thin? (Watch for overexpansion, attacking too many niches.)

9. Is your marketing program synergistic? Is it consistent with your financial, management, operations, and R&D strategies?

10. Are you monitoring shifts in the marketplace and responding quickly to them?

— **Adapted from Tevfik Dalgic and Maartin Leeuw, "Niche Marketing Revisited: Theoretical and Practical Issues," in Michael Levy and Dhruv Grewal (eds.), Academy of Marketing Science Proceedings, Miami Beach, May 26-29, 1993, pp. 137-145.*

STRATEGY DEVELOPMENT

Marketing strategy was described in Chapter 2 (the marketing planning section). Segmentation strategy is the process whereby a firm maximizes the marketing controllables (the 4 Ps) toward satisfying a target market's needs. Marketing strategy recognizes the dynamics of markets and the objectives, resources, and "personality" of a company. Personality means the company's business character/culture (its organizational philosophy and management style) and the importance of people functions in the marketing plan.

Hence, a master marketing program must mesh with your company's business style and be appropriate for the firm given its present situation. Marketing is not a business function to be undertaken by only the marketing researchers, advertising department, or sales force. It is an ongoing series of activities that permeates all levels of the company, from president to part-time help. Similarly, all levels of the company must be apprised of appropriate strategies or tactics relevant to their areas of responsibility.

Successful segmentation strategy consists of two phases. First, you find and pursue market niches/segments (this three-step process was just described). This strategic position activates the overall direction the company will follow. Next, you review, formulate, or revise primary and secondary marketing mix elements. These are the weapons used to win the "marketing war."

As you specify marketing strategies for a target group, three broad business areas must be carefully analyzed: customer needs, and internal and external marketing factors. Customer needs must consider how segments are defined based on the typical physical and behavioral segmentation dimensions and variables; product uses and usage patterns (note: because consumptive measures frequently are dependent variables, it is advisable to separate this into its own base); present levels of product satisfaction; and so forth. The Environmental Scorecard (in Chapter 2) is a useful worksheet for comparing the strengths or weaknesses of many corporate and industry-related issues.

Product Strategy

In segmentation studies, the customers' views toward the product or service are the driving force in shaping appropriate product decisions. In developing these strategies, a firm must analyze all of the goods or services it offers. This includes individual product items/brands, product lines, and the product mix the business handles. Segmentation strategy planning is more concerned with specific product units or families of products than entire product classes, markets, or industry sales volume. Factors that impact product strategy decisions include the nature of the product, the product life cycle, the classification of goods, product policies, and the role of product differentiation.

Nature of the Product. The nature of the product or service refers to the basic characteristics of the good or service. Some important questions to ask about this are listed in Exhibit 12-2. Once these issues are resolved, the firm has a good understanding of the intricacies of the product, its applications, and the market it is competing in—a key toward strategy formulation. Recent winners—*Time* magazine's best products of 1992—included Motorola's pocket cellular phone, Apple's PowerBook Duo Dock, Chrysler's LH series (Concorde, Eagle Vision, and Intrepid), cosmetics aimed at women of color, clear products (soaps, sodas, and so much more), the nicotine patch, the Juiceman II, Step Aerobics, and Malcolm X-related merchandise.[8]

EXHIBIT 12-2: THE NATURE OF THE PRODUCT

What type of product is it?

What is it primarily used for?

Are there any other applications for the product?

Who uses the product?

Why do customers use it?

What benefits are customers seeking?

Is there anything customers or potential customers do not like about the product? Why?

Is the product branded?

Does the product have any other favorable proprietary positions (patents, copyrights, and/or trademarks)?

How is the product manufactured?

How is the product distributed?

How is it promoted?

How is it priced?

What is the product's past performance (sales figures, strengths and weaknesses)?

Does the company produce any related products?

What is the competitive environment?

Product Life Cycle. Life cycles provide another useful tool for analyzing products or services prior to strategy development. Like people, industries and products have an aging process. This five-phase life cycle consists of birth, growth, maturity, decline, and death. It is important to assess where your industry is and where it is headed. Also, determine where your product or service is in its life cycle.

At the introductory and early growth stages of a market, products or services appeal to innovators and the early adopters. As the industry develops and matures, competition will intensify and new segmentation strategies will be needed to find a niche in the marketplace. Finally, at the decline stage, the customer pool has been severely depleted, and the remaining market segments must be nurtured and cultivated for efforts to remain profitable.

Classification of Goods. The classification of goods framework divides consumer and industrial products into groupings of similar products based on their inherent qualities or characteristics. For consumer goods, segmentation is most important for specialty goods (exotic perfumes), very important for shopping goods (VCRs), of average importance for convenience goods (frozen pizzas), and of low importance for unsought products (cemetery plots). Industrial goods can be classified into capital purchases (such as buildings or heavy equipment), tools and other equipment, raw materials, parts and materials, supplies, and industrial services. Industrial market segmentation was examined in Chapters 9 and 11 (the nested approach).

Product Policies. Product policies relate to the firm's business mission and operating philosophy. These are constraints or guideposts that govern product decisions. Product policies serve to limit product choices in a number of strategic areas. The first consideration is the markets to compete in and the broad product offerings to compete with. Other product policies can relate to the company's product testing program (planning efforts, research and development, and test marketing), new product policies (a product innovator or imitator), product mix decisions (including branding and product line extensions or deletions), packaging, warranties, and service.

Product Differentiation. The four product and service factors explored so far have provided some direction for a market segmentation program—adapting the product or service to meet the unique needs of selected target markets. But in some cases, product or service differentiation—emphasizing the products' or services' differences rather than the customer needs (if the needs for a product or service are basically the same)—is the more important marketing strategy. The Strategy Selector, given in Exhibit 12-3, can be used to assist you in this decision process.

EXHIBIT 12-3: THE STRATEGY SELECTOR

Marketing Variable	Segmentation More Important	Product Differentiation More Important
Market Size	Large	Small
	1 2 3 4 5	
User sensitivity to product differences	Low	High
	1 2 3 4 5	
Product life cycle stage	Saturation	Introduction
	1 2 3 4 5	
Type of product	Distinct	Commodity
	1 2 3 4 5	
Number of competitors	Many	Few
	1 2 3 4 5	

Adapted with permission of the American Marketing Association. R. William Kotrba, "The Strategy Selection Chart," *Journal of Marketing*, July 1966, pp. 22-25.

The soft drink industry is a clear example of a market in which segmentation is the preferable strategy. According to the criteria in the Strategy Selector, it scores a 1, 2, 2, 3, and 1, respectively. On the other hand, hearing aids is a product-market where product differentiation is the advisable strategy. Because the market is relatively small and the product is always used for the same purpose (to amplify sound), product superiority is more important than market segmentation. Hearing aid scores using this model are 5, 4, 3, 4, and 3 respectively. These results do not mean that either strategy should be used in isolation. Product differentiation is still important in the soft drink industry—there are regular versus diet products; colas versus noncolas; caffeine-free, clear, and natural products; and a variety of package sizes, to name a few distinctions. Also, segmentation is needed to reach audiologists (a prime decision-maker for selecting hearing aids).

217

Promotional Strategy

A company can reach and persuade its target markets by using a mix of four promotional elements—personal selling, advertising, publicity, and sales promotion. They are defined as follows:

Personal Selling—An individual promotional means characterized by face-to-face, two-way communication about a good or service.

Advertising—Any paid form of nonpersonal presentation of ideas, goods, or services by an identified sponsor.

Publicity—News about a product, service, institution, or person not paid for by the sponsor.

Sales Promotion—All activities that supplement advertising and personal selling efforts, such as exhibitions, displays, demonstrations, and other nonrecurrent selling activities.[9]

Personal Selling. Personal selling is a deceptively important promotional strategy. In the United States, more money is spent in this area than for advertising. Selling is where the actual dollars (or yen, Deutsche marks, pounds, francs, and so on) change hands in consumer, industrial, and government markets. Good selling is matching customer needs to a firm's goods or services. If this is accomplished, a sale is made, a satisfied customer established, and potential long-term relationships begin.

The beauty of personal selling is that its objective parallels that of market segmentation—tailoring products to meet customers' desires. The one major weakness plaguing this promotional approach is its high costs (a single industrial sales call was recently estimated at over $250).[10] Given this limitation, the other mass promotional techniques can be employed to generate highly qualified inquiries/leads to make personal selling more efficient (hence, improve the closing ratio).

Advertising. Advertising is a dynamic, interesting, and at times glamorous field that is often misunderstood by the public. It is also a complex area, with many interrelated components affecting its overall business impact (including media options, budgets, media selection and scheduling, message preparation, the role of the advertising agency, and measurement techniques). Depending on a company's promotional focus, advertising can run the gamut from being virtually nonexistent to being a major factor in determining a firm's success. From a segmentation perspective, advertising is an excellent, but not inexpensive, means of reaching out to the firm's most likely prospects, its target markets.

Successful advertising calls for investing your dollars wisely. Advertising expenditures should be allocated to media vehicles that can best deliver target markets. There are dozens of different media that can be used (one advertising professional claims that more than 14,000 choices exist!). Obviously, most of these media are obscure, impractical, or unimportant. For simplicity, media can be divided into three major classes: *broadcast* (radio, television, film, and other electronic media), *print* (newspapers and many types of periodicals), and *other media* (direct, directory, outdoor, transit, specialty, and so on). The "and so on" pertains to those remaining 14,000 options. In addition to the media classifications, there is an abundance of *media vehicles* to choose from. Some are highly selective and well suited to reaching designated market segments. Consider these examples:

- *Cable TV:* The Entertainment and Sports Programming Network (ESPN) delivers upscale men.

- *Catalogs:* L. L. Bean, The Sharper Image, and Williams-Sonoma are typical examples of some of the estimated 78 catalogs each consumer receives annually.[11]

- *Direct Mail:* How about a list of Apple computer owners (800,000), bird lovers (1.2 million), or cycling enthusiasts (2.2 million)?[12] This is not a problem. These lists and tens of thousands more are readily available for purchase from leading mailing list houses.

General media vehicles such as daily newspapers or national TV broadcasts may reach large numbers of people but are poor at delivering the desired user profile. Targeted advertising minimizes audience waste (nonprospects). In addition to media considerations, creative and copy platforms must be developed to meet segment needs.

219

Publicity. Public relations (PR) or publicity is somewhat related to advertising but is a different promotional strategy. Unlike advertising, which is company sponsored, publicity is placed by an outside organization and is perceived as being more objective. Excluding PR initiation costs, publicity is free promotion, and its exposure can provide a most favorable response to the firm. In addition to targeted media vehicles used in a well-executed publicity campaign, speaking engagements, written materials, and special events are typically featured. Accountants, attorneys, doctors, and financial planners are examples of professionals that have recognized the value of publicity as a new business generator.

Sales Promotion. Finally, sales promotion activities such as samples, price incentives, premiums, contests/sweepstakes, point-of-purchase displays, and trade shows/exhibits can be used to supplement other promotional efforts. The underlying question to answer before you use any and all promotional strategies and tactics is, "Is it right for the market segment I am trying to attract?"

Pricing Strategy

How much should you charge your customers for your product? This question is one of pricing strategy. Setting prices for your goods or services is not a simple issue. There are many marketing and financial factors affecting this decision. Price also can be viewed from several perspectives, in addition to the marketer's concept of price. Exhibit 12-4 shows how other business professionals view price.

EXHIBIT 12-4: THE MANY FACES OF PRICING DECISIONS

Business Professional	Techniques Used To Determine Price	How Price Is Set
Accountant	Analyze fixed and variable costs, perform breakeven analysis	Cost plus markup
Financial Analyst	Analyze past and proforma financial statements	Payback, return on investment
Economist	Analyze supply and demand	Where marginal revenue equals marginal cost

Financial costs are important when you are setting price, but you should consider other marketing factors: the firm's operating philosophy and the image it wishes to convey, the competitive situation, other external factors, the target market the company is pursuing, customer price expectations, product factors, promotional strategies employed, and distribution channels used. Price/quality trade-offs may exist or be perceived by target markets. (Some customers feel that because a product is more expensive, it is a better product—this may or may not be true.)

Pricing is not a unidimensional variable. For many products, the price is a package composed of several elements. Consider the real estate market. Consumers contemplating buying homes must understand list price, interest rates, closing costs, various mortgage options, taxes, insurance, and so forth. In other business situations, the price is affected by finance charges, delivery expense, trade discounts, consumer price incentives, and/or service fees. The bottom line is that price setting is not something to be taken lightly. Like other strategic aspects of the marketing plan, careful research is vital in this area.

Although marketers seldom think of pricing as a major part of a segmentation study, this is not always the case. The Cordis Corporation develops, manufactures, and markets products for the diagnostic coronary and peripheral markets, supplying some 65% of all coronary catheters used worldwide.[13] In a recent segmentation research project, cardiologists and other physicians were queried about their preferences for various features and pricing levels for a proposed new medical device.

Ideally, pricing strategy should be based on an in-depth analysis of your company's marketing situation. Specifically, a firm will take one of four directions:

- *Beat their price:* This strategy depends on high volume, because low price implies operating on low margins.

- *Meet their price:* This competitive pricing strategy recognizes market forces. In this instance, the firm competes on some nonprice issues in an attempt to differentiate itself from the other firms. This can include having a better product, an improved image or reputation, offering post-sale servicing, etc.

- *Do not compete on price:* If a higher priced strategy is being used, the firm must provide additional benefits to their customers or convince them that they are purchasing "top quality." High prices may be justified where there is limited competition, high costs associated with new product development, exclusive products offered, or limited consumer resistance.

- *Retreat due to price:* In some circumstances, the firm may not have the economies of scale or other operating efficiencies to compete profitably in a market situation. In this case, the recommended strategy might be to cut your losses and get out of that market, so you can allocate those resources toward more attractive market opportunities.

Distribution Strategy

As an integral part of the marketing mix, channels of distribution (an often neglected controllable) need to be periodically examined. A marketing channel is an exchange pathway through which goods are moved, flowing from the production point to intermediaries, and finally to the ultimate consumers. A channel might include a manufacturer, one or more wholesalers or brokers and retailers, although shorter channels are evident in many business situations (for example, mail order or the airlines' SkyMall program).

Although marketing channel decisions tend to be well entrenched (it is a relatively fixed marketing variable), present strategies should be analyzed to determine whether they are the most efficient ones possible. Sometimes minor changes such as using a new supplier can have a favorable impact on a company's distribution program. Some distribution strategy options for the firm include

- *Long versus short channels.* A long channel uses several intermediaries to handle storage, sorting, transportation, promotion, and related functions. The other extreme is the short channel, which implies a direct relationship. An example of this is the customer who buys direct from a factory outlet.

- *Wide versus narrow channels.* If the objective is to get the product into as many outlets as possible, a wide-channel strategy is employed. Building an extensive distribution network is necessary if you use mass marketing tactics. Narrower channels recognize the value of market segmentation. One example of this channel strategy might be to establish an exclusive product in selected "fine stores."

- *Push versus pull strategies.* If the product is promoted to other channel members (manufacturers to wholesalers to retailers, for example), a push strategy is used. If the end-user is targeted directly, as grocery product manufacturers promote their goods to consumers, then a pull strategy exists.

- *Imitate versus innovate.* Traditional channels of distribution are the obvious, safe, and uncreative approach. Many times it is the way to go. However, if a new or modified channel can be found, a competitive edge may arise.

These strategies are polar extremes. Not everything in life and in marketing is black or white; varying degrees of grays also occur. Therefore, a channel may be shorter or longer, wider or narrower. Combinations of push and pull, and imitation and innovation may also be required. Additionally, several of these channel strategy options may be happening simultaneously (for example, short, narrow channels).

Segmentation Strategy Management

Rather than taking a bits-and-pieces approach to strategy formation, think of the gestalt (holistic) approach to segmentation-based marketing decision making. Use profiles of selected target markets to predict and understand your customers' purchasing behavior. Furthermore, such insights are essential for developing realistic and responsive segment-specific strategies to maximize marketing performance (for example, sales and profits). A company specializing in home improvement such as The Home Depot can benefit by knowing its customers inside and out and offering them a marketing program that best satisfies their needs (Exhibit 12-5).

EXHIBIT 12-5: SEGMENTING THE HOME IMPROVEMENT MARKET

Segment-> Variables	Contractors	Project Do-It Themselvers	Minor Repairs and Remodeling
User Situation	Professionals, work-for-hire	Major home projects such as building decks or room additions	Small repair jobs/home improvements (such as painting or redecorating)
User Profile	Carpenters, contractors, electricians, painters, plumbers	Male homeowners	Baby boomers and women
Knowledge	Experts in their trades	Comfortable with tools and materials	Know little about home improvements
Motive	Earning a living	Enjoyment/hobby	Economic/self-satisfaction
Marketing Strategies	Quality goods, advance orders, separate checkout areas, easy credit access, professional discounts	Product depth/breadth, expert advice, how-to demonstrations, interactive computers with product information, value pricing	Tool rentals, friendly service, workshops for novices, use women in advertising, low prices

SUMMARY

The segmentation study is complete—prospective target markets have surfaced. Methodological issues are behind you; segmentation strategy takes center stage. By understanding customer behavior, choosing the right user segments, and designing unique positioning strategies, your firm can carve a profitable niche in the highly competitive global marketplace of the 1990s.

Sound segmentation strategy originates from researching customer needs and your internal (corporate) and external (industry) marketing environments. The proper mix of the 4 Ps leads to market success. Product strategy considers the nature of the product, its life cycle, goods classifications, product policies, and differentiation. Targeted pricing is based on your firm's operating philosophy/image, competition, cost, and customer expectations. The promotional blend combines advertising, personal selling, publicity, and sales promotion to reach prime prospects efficiently and effectively. Place (distribution) decisions relate to channel length, width, focus, and innovativeness.

Successful segmentation strategy is a systematic, integrative, and synergistic process. Evaluation and control completes the market-driven cycle—this topic is the focus of the book's final chapter.

NOTES

1. Bruce D. Henderson, "The Origin of Strategy," *Harvard Business Review,* November-December 1989, pp. 139-143.

2. Ellen Neuborne, "Specialty Stores Offer '90s Growth," *USA Today,* January 19, 1993, pp. B1-B2.

3. Al Ries and Jack Trout, *Positioning: The Battle for Your Mind* (New York: McGraw-Hill Book Company, 1986), p. 2.

4. Steven A. Sinclair and Edward C. Stalling, "Perceptual Mapping: A Tool for Industrial Marketing: A Case Study," *The Journal of Business and Industrial Marketing,* Winter-Spring 1990, pp. 55-66.

5. Marvin Nesbit and Art Weinstein, "Positioning the High-Tech Product." In Harold E. Glass (ed.), *Handbook of Business Strategy Yearbook,* (Boston: Warren, Gorham, & Lamont, Inc., 1989/1990), pp. 30-1-30-8.

6. Robert E. Linneman, "How to Grow Bigger by Acting Smaller," *Journal of Food Products Marketing* (1) 1992, pp. 79-100.

7. *Niche Marketing: Identifying Opportunities with Syndicated Data* (New York: Mediamark Research Inc., 1988), pp. 2-3, 10-13.

8. "The Best Products of 1992," *Time*, January 4, 1993, p. 63.

9. The Definitions Committee of the American Marketing Association, Chicago.

10. *See Sales and Marketing Management's Sales Manager's Budget Planner*, 1991.

11. Jon Holten, "By the Book," *Express Magazine* (Memphis: Federal Express Corporation), Spring 1993, pp. 8-12.

12. *BehaviorBank Database-A Metromail Product* (Chicago: R. R. Donnelley & Sons, Winter 1993).

13. *Cordis Annual Report* (Miami Lakes, Fla.: Cordis Corporation, 1990), p. 1.

13

ENHANCING SEGMENTATION'S VALUE

**The business executive is by profession a decision maker.
Uncertainty is his opponent. Overcoming it is his mission.**

—John McDonald, 1955

The market segmentation study has been conducted, findings specified, and strategies developed. Is your work complete at this juncture? Almost, but not quite. Two important areas must still be addressed. First, there is the implementation and evaluation of the current action plan. Second, and more importantly, is the creation of a long-term, internal marketing environment conducive to maximizing the value of customer analysis.

IMPLEMENTATION AND CONTROL

Bringing "life" to the segmentation analysis is the function of implementation. No longer are you concerned with "what ifs." As Nike says, you "just do it." Successful implementation of prescribed marketing strategy requires the talents of many professionals. Marketing analysts, researchers, planners, strategists, advertising and public relations personnel, the sales team, consultants, and marketing managers must all work in concert to accomplish corporate objectives. Additionally, the marketing department must interface with corporate management to ensure that strategic thrusts are compatible with organizational policies and values. Assuming all systems are go, a "master implementation switch" is turned on, and plans now become actions.

The Target Market Strategy Worksheet (Segmentation Skillbuilder 13) provides a summary model for identifying key strategic issues and capitalizing on them. An in-depth strategic plan is the recommended next step. You want to produce a consistent, information-backed document with synergism created among all of its components. Such a project can be readily implemented and the performance results monitored.

MANAGERIAL GUIDELINES FOR SEGMENTATION STUDIES

Segmentation can reward your firm with some or all of these riches—new customers, better customers (a segment of the market desired), more satisfied customers (designing products more responsive to their needs), increased sales, the identification of potentially profitable marketing opportunities, and improved market share. This process takes considerable time and effort, however. Successful customer analysis requires well-conceived research and planning, and strategies formulated based on the study's findings and monitored for performance. The purpose of the following managerial guidelines is to provide direction for segmentation's role in your company's marketing plan.

SEGMENTATION SKILLBUILDER 13: TARGET MARKET STRATEGY WORKSHEET

Segment Name/Brief Description:

Opportunities:

1.

2.

3.

Threats:

1.

2.

3.

Goals: Marketing Financial

Overall Marketing Strategy:

Marketing Mix Strategies:	Present Strategy	Recommended Strategies	Potential Impact
Product			
Promotion			
Pricing			
Distribution			

Marketing Mix Tactics:	Present Strategy	Recommended Strategies	Potential Impact
Product			
Promotion			
Pricing			
Distribution			

Evaluation/Control Measures:

_____

_____

_____

Segmentation is a planning tool, but it is also the foundation on which successful overall marketing strategies are built. The following eight guidelines will assist you in managing the market segmentation function in your organization (see Segmentation Action List 13).

Segmentation Action List 13: Managerial Guidelines

1. Are you integrating segmentation with other marketing management activities?

2. How involved are you in the segmentation project?

3. Do you have realistic expectations about the value of market segmentation in your organization?

4. Are you listening to the segmentation results?

5. Does your company "dare to be different"?

6. How often do you request market updates and projections?

7. Do you get professional assistance when necessary?

8. Are you treating segmentation analysis as an investment?

1. *Integrate segmentation with other marketing management activities.* Market segmentation is not an activity that should be undertaken in isolation. Segmentation findings should be incorporated into your company's marketing plan, as are product descriptions, product specifications, and promotional tactics. The judicious use of demographic, psychographic, and other segmentation techniques identifies your market niche; management must wholeheartedly support a marketing redirection, if applicable. In addition, all levels of the organization need to be involved in marketing the company, as well as its products. Segmentation also requires constancy and consistency to work effectively. It is not a "one-time deal" but rather a continuing strategic process.[1]

2. *Get involved in the project.* Ideally, the project manager should work closely with researchers, strategists, and consultants on the study. This approach provides practical information to answer today's hard-hitting questions. Furthermore, it precludes possible misunderstandings at a

later date. Frequent meetings and regular, two-way communication between management and the project team leads to better quality segmentation studies.

3. *Be realistic in your expectations.* The prudent manager sets reasonable goals. Segmentation analysis cannot overcome inherent marketing or managerial deficiencies. Used properly, however, such analysis can be a basis on which effective customer-related decisions can be made, which can positively impact the bottom line. Costs and potential benefits must be weighed, with short- and long-term paybacks evaluated. Exercise patience in assessing segmentation's value. Unlike an advertising blitz that may bring immediate results, the segmentation project may bridge several weeks or months from the conception, research, and analysis to the strategy implementation phase.

Also, other marketing elements greatly influence customer behavior, making the reconciliation of the study's findings and ultimate product usage more difficult. Hence, the need for coordination of marketing efforts is critical.

4. *Listen to the results.* Research should be welcomed as a learning opportunity. It provides another chance to probe deeply into the market in which your firm competes. Some information output may be new; other findings will build on or refine the existing knowledge pool. The research should be acted on as circumstances dictate. The use of such insight can provide the competitive edge necessary to survive and prosper in emerging or established markets.

5. *Dare to be different.* Although segmentation studies can provide fresh perspectives on a situation, in most cases, the means of translating findings into strategy is not crystal clear. Strategists should look at the findings from various angles, adding business judgment and the "creative concept" into their marketing planning scenarios. Going out on a limb entails some risk; however, innovators are frequently leaders. One automobile dealer checked car radio preset buttons of vehicles brought in for service to assess customers' listening preferences. The company proceeded to buy advertising spots on the more popular stations. Sometimes, the bold new approach helps secure a favorable market position, while the follower gets lost in the pack.

6. *Request frequent updates and projections.* The global marketing environment of the 1990s is constantly evolving. Segmentation studies should not be thought of as one-shot efforts. Staying current with relevant market conditions is a means of detecting changing trends and is helpful for current and future marketing planning.

7. *Get professional assistance when necessary.* Segmentation analysis is not something that can be learned overnight. It is advisable to consult with experts to assist in research design, obtaining data, interpreting the findings, and strategy development, as applicable. Consultants can analyze situations objectively and are more efficient for short-term projects than hiring additional staff.

8. *Treat segmentation analysis as an investment.* Management should recognize that market segmentation is a beginning, not an ending point. The completed study sets in motion a series of recommended marketing activities contributing to a customer-centered marketing plan.

A LOOK AHEAD: SEGMENTATION IN THE YEAR 2000

Although it is always difficult to make business predictions, six segmentation prognostications for the year 2000 are offered in this section. These are not meant to be earth-shattering revelations; rather, they are extensions of what is happening today and likely to occur tomorrow. The look into the marketing crystal ball reveals the following scenario.

Marketing to the Twenty-First Century Consumer

The major geodemographic and lifestyle trends that have emerged in the 1990s will accelerate. Consumer marketers will have to recognize the minority majority (the importance of African-Americans, Asians, and Hispanics), the aging population (rapid growth of the old-old segment), women as wage earners and prime decision-makers, environmentalism, and the importance of the household over the family as the key buying center (this due to divorces and one-parent families, the large single population, POSSLQs/live-togethers, and gay consumers). In her recent visionary article, Judith Waldrop cites 21 consumer trends that businesses should start tracking now to prepare for the year 2000.[2]

The Dawn of Micro/Niche Marketing

Mass marketing, for all intents and purposes, is dead. Although target marketing has been in full force for several decades, a new approach—precision target marketing—has taken over. In this era of micromarketing, niche identification, harvesting, and dominance is the key strategy. By focusing on ever-smaller yet profitable market segments, stronger company-customer relationships transpire. With technological products, users can practically invent markets for companies—customers become customizers.[3]

Tapping Computer Technology

Companies will exploit the expanding powers of computerization for segmentation. This includes an enlarged role for database marketing, desktop demographics, and online research services. Because few markets are growing rapidly, companies such as Waldenbooks, Liz Claiborne, Hyatt Hotels, and Prodigy (see Case 4 in Part 4) are calling on database information to hold on to the customers that they have. Rather than spending 50 cents a person to reach a general audience, today's advertisers will spend twice that for someone whose demographic, socioeconomic, lifestyle, and usage profile indicates they're predisposed to making a specific purchase.[4]

Segmentation and Global Strategy

Profitable strategic marketing plans extend beyond domestic borders. Aggressive companies pursue business opportunities across the globe. The EC, Asia, and Latin American markets offer intriguing possibilities for a wide range of products and services. Anything Left Handed is a London-based retailer that sells worldwide via its mail order catalog (which reads backward). The shop sells more than 200 products for southpaws, including scissors, kitchen tools, corkscrews, and boomerangs.[5] New segmentation services like Japan VALS are likely to spring up in many foreign markets.

233

Importance of Private-Sector Segmentation Providers

Companies that sell geodemographic, lifestyle, and product usage segmentation services on a custom or syndicated basis will become even more important research sources in the years ahead. Although the U.S. Census Bureau substantially enhanced its 1990 Census program capabilities by offering more data, media formats, and reports, this upward trend is likely to be checked. Budget-conscious politicians have preliminarily voted to slash the $23 million planning budget for the 2000 Census by 65% ($8 million would remain).[6] The result of this $15 million cut could be the use of samples instead of a census, the abandonment of the long form, a reduction in the short form (and replacement with a postcard?), and a significant loss of valuable secondary data.

The demographic vendors and marketing research companies could pick up most of this slack, if need be. The research community has greatly upgraded its data banks, technologies, and service offerings and is poised to satisfy the information needs of its demanding business clients.

Acceptance of Segmentation by Organizations

Market segmentation will continue to gain prominence in the next few years as more consumer and industrial companies, large and small, acknowledge the importance of this marketing activity. The turmoil that gripped GM, IBM, Sears, American Express, and other corporate giants is more than a matter of size or business cycles. Goliaths (and Davids) falter when arrogance and complacency makes them lose touch with their customers.[7]

Segmentation's role in the marketing plan will increase significantly as the world enters a new century. Expect more training, research, and publications in this area. Firms in all industries (including nonprofit organizations) are discovering the power of this strategic marketing tool for attracting and keeping customers in competitive markets. How about you?

NOTES

1. Steven M. Struhl, *Market Segmentation: An Introduction and Review* (Chicago: American Marketing Association, 1992), p. 8.

2. Judith Waldrop, "You'll Know It's the 21st Century When . . .," *American Demographics*, December 1990, pp. 23-27.

3. Regis McKenna, "Marketing in an Age of Diversity," *Harvard Business Review*, September-October 1988, pp. 88-95.

4. Carol Dannhauser, "The Era of Micro Marketing," *Adweek* (Superbrands Supplement), 1992, pp. 24, 26, 28.

5. Milton F. Shapiro, "Communique," *Sky Magazine* (Delta Airlines), July 1993, p. 18.

6. Mike McNamee, "Postcards from the Census," *Business Week*, July 12, 1993, p. 36.

7. John Greenwald, "Are America's Corporate Giants a Dying Breed?" *Time*, December 28, 1992, p. 28.

PART FOUR

STRATEGY CASES

SEGMENTATION CASES: AN OVERVIEW AND FRAMEWORK FOR ANALYSIS

The following case studies provide in-depth examples of how segmentation analysis and strategy was used successfully by organizations in diverse industries. The cases are Hot Shot to Japan (a liquor product), Metro-Dade's Greynolds Park, Over 50/Mature Consumers, Prodigy Online Computing Service, and Trophy Shops and Specialty Retailing.

By reviewing these cases, you can learn more about:

- *The types of planning and research that goes into segmentation analysis*

- *The market factors with which these organizations must contend*

- *Market-based decisions made by management, marketing initiatives resulting from the study, and how market performance was enhanced*

End-of-case questions give you an opportunity to further analyze the impact of segmentation techniques.

Think about competitive differentiation and how the focal organization can take maximum advantage of market opportunities. You may also want to consult some of the accompanying suggested readings to gain further insights on these marketing situations.

CASE 1   INTERNATIONAL SEGMENTATION: HOT SHOT TO JAPAN*

Glenmore Distilleries Company, a family controlled distiller for more than 120 years, produces and markets more than 100 different brands of quality alcoholic beverages. As of June 30, 1990, Glenmore was the sixth-largest U.S. spirits company, with annual sales of $374 million. As part of its global expansion strategy for the 1990s, Glenmore is seeking international market expansion for its nonbourbon product line. Management is considering entering the Japanese market with Hot Shot, a tropical schnapps liquor.

CURRENT SITUATION

In August 1991, Glenmore was acquired by United Distillers, the spirits company of Guiness PLC, a conglomerate. The parent company also features the Guiness brewery (Guiness Stout), a publishing division (as in the Guiness Book of World Records among other titles), hotel chains, and numerous other multinational business ventures. At the time of the acquisition, United Distillers was the most profitable spirits business in the world. Major competitors include Grand Metropolitan/IDV, Moet Hennessy, Allied Lyons/Hiram Walker, and Seagram. Guiness, listed on the London Stock Exchange, is the second largest worldwide beverage company after Coca-Cola, in terms of profits.

At the end of January 1993, United Distillers Glenmore sold a number of brands from its portfolio, Hot Shot being one of those. Hot Shot is now owned by David Sherman Corporation, St. Louis, Missouri. This case study focuses on how Hot Shot could be marketed successfully in Japan.

*This case was prepared by Dr. Art Weinstein, William Spellman, and Mireille Birt. The authors thank Renee E. Cooper, Director of Corporate Communications, Glenmore Distilleries Company, Louisville, KY and
Dr. Warren J. Keegan, Pace University, New York, NY for several good ideas on improving the case.
   1. Much of the material on Japanese drinking habits is adapted from George Fields, *From Bonsai to Levis* (New York: Macmillan, 1983), 128-131, 209.

THE HOT SHOT PRODUCT

Hot Shot was developed by Glenmore in 1986. It is priced in the $10 to $12 range in the United States. The beverage's main ingredients are sugar and vodka, which are combined with oranges, tangerines, grapes, pineapples, and avocados. Hot Shot is currently sold in a variety of sizes domestically: 1 liter, 750 ml, 375 ml, 200 ml, and 50 ml. The bottle designed for Hot Shot is simple, similar to the shape of a Miller beer bottle or wine bottle. The label was designed to be the attraction to Hot Shot. Pictured on the silver foil label are the various fruits the liquor contains with the words "Hot Shot" printed on the top two edges.

JAPAN: A MARKET ANALYSIS

Japan appears to offer good potential for product diversification. Hence, Hot Shot has an opportunity to enter the country's alcoholic beverage market. Based on a study of social customs, economic trends, and market situation, Hot Shot can favorably penetrate the Japanese market via the sound use of segmentation strategy and the development of an appropriate marketing mix.

Sociocultural Analysis

One factor that has not changed with time is the traditional Japanese ideal of group emphasis at the expense of the individual. Group affiliations in Japan are important, because the Japanese attempt to interpret everything in terms of such factors as family interrelationships, personal patronage, and recommendation. Within the employment structure of Japan, relationships between employer and employee are considered lasting and meaningful. The company stresses the importance of teamwork and group effort on all projects. Hence, a sense of family and belonging is given to the workplace through group emphasis. This relatedness has a pervasive influence on Japanese lifestyles. The Japanese love group activities of all sorts, such as the school or company field day or the association outing. Male groups from work habitually stop at a bar on the way home for a bit of relaxation, and parties are characterized by group drinking and group games.

Drinking is a social act and therefore carries certain social customs.[1] Hence, alcoholic beverages are consumed straight out of the bottle, which is offered to you by your drinking partner and vice versa. This custom is known as *sashitsu sasaretsu,* which describes the exchanging of the sake cups, and the custom has been extended to other alcoholic beverages.

Japanese culture abhors impurity. The Japanese value water for its purity, and its influence pervades various Japanese art forms. Water is considered to be natural and does not disturb the essence of whatever it is added to; therefore, water is often added to the most popular alcoholic beverage (whiskey). Living in a racially homogeneous society, Japanese have trouble with the concept of a mixed drink and invariably consider drinks that are mixed to be impure.

Drinking is no longer considered the domain of the male. There is really no social convention in Japan that frowns upon women drinking, and as in many other countries, the courting ritual often takes the form of the young woman and man sharing a drink. Research has shown that normally young women were reluctant to deviate from the drinking pattern of their boyfriends. This finding implies a desire to share with their male companions, and this is the very essence of sake drinking.

Consumer buying habits within Japan are based on social customs. Ordinarily, Japanese customers would purchase what is known as a "key bottle" from the bar. The bottle, with the customer's name written on it, would be kept until his next visit to that establishment. This saves the customer money and helps the establishment keep him as a regular patron. This custom also ensures that there is no radical break in the way alcoholic drinks are consumed.

Besides whiskey, beer, sake, and bourbon, the Japanese also drink *shochu*— a distilled drink made from potatoes. Popular in the southern island of Kyuushu, shochu resembles vodka in its clarity but has a low-class image. It is mainly consumed straight or with water. Shochu fits well into the traditional drinking pattern; this and its low price are probably the reasons for its popularity.

Consumption patterns show a continuing increase in bourbon sales in Japan. Imports of alcoholic beverages are approximately twice as large as exports. Japan is the world's largest importer of U.S. alcoholic beverages, and that market grew 12.9% to 33.2 million gallons in 1990.

Economic Analysis

Japan's population exceeds 122 million. In economic terms, Japan now possesses close to one-tenth of the global GNP with less than one-fortieth of the world population. Japan spends more than 1.5% of its GNP on eating and drinking establishments. Disposable income is considered to be at its highest level in the country's history. Hence, consumption patterns and changing lifestyles in Japan have changed not only what the Japanese are drinking but also where and how they drink it.

The Japanese economy has recently been in the doldrums following the late 1980s-early 1990s boom. Its growth was based on an unprecedented export of industrial products and an aggressive trade policy. Japan is the second largest free-market economic power behind the United States. It is one of the largest producers of motor vehicles, steel, and high-technology manufactured goods. The Japanese government retains strong control over the economy through constant consultation with businesses and authorities. The recently weak yen has forced the government to raise interest rates. However, this paves the way for U.S. companies, because the cost of overseas business will drop with the stronger dollar.

However, it is believed that the Japanese economy will continue to prosper for three reasons:

- The drop in the savings rate, shifts in the public-private cooperative economy and other changes will not come about quickly.

- Technological innovation and other conditions will provide greater advantages for Japan.

- Japan has the ability to adapt to its objectives and policies.

Unfortunately, several legal barriers and tariffs exist that hamper U.S. firms from trying to crack Japanese markets. Any U.S. corporation doing business directly in Japan should be aware of basic Japanese tax considerations, including general taxation of foreign corporations, scope and rates, capital gains, and Japanese transfer pricing rules.

In 1990, the United States and Japan reached an interim agreement on bilateral economic reforms to reduce Japan's persistent $50 billion trade surplus with the United States. Japan made concessions in six key areas: pricing mechanisms, the distribution system, savings and investments, land policy, exclusionary business practices, and company groupings. This is representative of Japan's effort to make its economy compatible with the world economy.

At year-end 1990, Japan accounted for a third of the total U.S. alcoholic beverage exports. Many researchers feel this number will become even greater in the future. Exhibit C1-1 summarizes top export markets for U.S. alcoholic beverages. An American schnapps product may be successful in Japan, given the fact that young Japanese have strong desires for Western styles and continued high alcohol consumption is expected.

Exhibit C1-1: Top Export Markets for U.S. Alcoholic Beverages, 1990 (in Thousands of Dollars)

Destination	Distilled Total	Wine & Spirits	Malt Brandy	Beverages
Japan	204,366	121,488	32,217	50,661
Canada	84,961	20,269	27,686	37,006
United Kingdom	37,095	11,090	21,532	4,473
Germany	27,740	23,474	3,028	1,238
Australia	24,586	23,260	526	800
Mexico	15,396	3,743	2,413	9,240
Netherlands	14,021	6,050	1,833	6,138
France	13,861	8,709	3,711	1,441
Hong Kong	13,573	1,457	1,692	10,424
Taiwan	9,798	784	2,138	6,876
Subtotal	445,397	220,324	96,776	128,297
Others	139,000	52,222	37,038	49,740
World	584,397	272,546	133,814	178,037

Source: U.S. Department of Commerce, Bureau of the Census.

The adjustment within Japan's liquor tax system (Liquor Industrial Association Law) has made imported spirits more affordable. Now that the liquor tax system—which in some cases added as much as 220% to liquor prices—has been revamped, imports of premium liquor have escalated. Also, more Japanese are buying imported products and drinking them *zah roku* (on the rocks). This could help to promote the sale of Hot Shot.

The transportation and distribution network within Japan is targeted toward Tokyo, the capital of Japan. On the island of Honshu there are three major international airports and five major ports. Most products, imports and exports, pass through these structures. Because roadway transportation is expensive, most products are shipped to Japan and then forwarded to their destinations by train.

MANAGERIAL CONCERNS AND APPROACHES

Based on the research to date, management is contemplating a number of key marketing factors impacting Hot Shot's entry into Japan. Here's the major issues (some resolved, others requiring further attention) and a proposed marketing plan.

Target market selection and positioning are critical international success factors. Hot Shot can succeed because the Japanese are fascinated with American tradition, history, and culture. Alcohol desire for those aged 20 to 35 is also westernized. For example, in Japan, a chain of bars named Jesse James are "Old West" in appearance and music, with only bourbon being served. Considering that bourbon is quite popular in Japan, the marketing goal is to give Hot Shot the same highly regarded image; therefore, these bars can be the primary target to begin serving this alcoholic beverage. The new entry should seek the usual premium, sophisticated young adult consumers, male and female, aged 20 to 35 (the American Hot Shot drinker profile). Specifically, young business people and college students in the United States have found Hot Shot attractive.

Cultural and product adaptations must also be evaluated. Test marketing will determine whether Hot Shot needs to be modified to Japanese tastes; however, preliminary research indicates that major product adaptation is not necessary. Hot Shot has the image of being fruity, pure, and natural. These characteristics correspond well with the Japanese preference for alcohol. Shochu and bourbon—the competitors within the existing market—can be used as a tool to gain familiarity with Hot Shot. In contrast to the United States, Hot Shot should be promoted for taste, the flavor enhanced when poured on the rocks.

Another consideration is the Hot Shot name, which does not translate into Japanese. The name can be changed to "Hota Shota," which is pronounceable for one speaking Japanese but has no literal translation, or a new brand name can be created. Therefore, through marketing and promotional strategies, a new image can be created for Hot Shot. Due to the alteration in the brand name, the labeling and package design will have to be changed for the Japanese market.

International Segmentation:
Hot Shot to Japan

The Japanese culture dictates the purchase of a large bottle of alcohol at a bar to pass around to friends. This means increased distribution of the one liter and 750-ml bottles. Perhaps even larger sizes should be introduced. On the other hand, Hot Shot can be marketed as a product for individuals and go against cultural norms (be a trendsetter) to gain attention. By doing this, increased distribution of the 200-ml and 50-ml bottles would be possible.

The product can be introduced using either a price skimming or penetration strategy; however, a skimming strategy is probably desirable. This is because the brand can be positioned as a high-status drink; the Japanese are likely to view this American product favorably.

Major promotional efforts should focus on the bars themselves (using posters, table folders, and drink sampling). The legal minimum drinking age in Japan is 20. Media regulations for liquor advertising in Japan are summarized in Exhibit C1-2. Billboard and television advertising should be used. Other supporting media, promotional budget allocations, and ad themes need to be determined.

EXHIBIT C1-2: MEDIA REGULATIONS IN JAPAN FOR LIQUOR ADVERTISING

Medium	Regulations
Television	Permitted with creative and timing restrictions; not permitted during breaks or after programs targeting children and teenagers. Actors under 20 are not permitted to appear in commercials.
Radio	Same as television.
Press	Permitted, avoiding magazines where more than 50% of readers are under 20 years old.
Cinema	Permitted.
Outdoor	All advertisements must include information explaining that consumption of alcohol by those who are under 20 years is prohibited. (Typeface must be large enough to identify.)

All codes are voluntary. Most advertising carries the statement that drinking is not allowed for people under 20 years.

The following is a proposed distribution strategy. The product can be transported to Japan by boat. Ocean freight is a more economical option than air transportation. Initial distribution would begin in Tokyo, Osaka, and

Nagoya, then spread throughout the country if results are favorable. During this time, relationships with a reputable Japanese distribution partner should be established. Having the Japanese distribute the product is advantageous in circumventing cultural and trade barriers.

END-OF-CASE QUESTIONS

1. Critique the proposed marketing strategy for introducing Hot Shot in Japan.

2. What problems will Hot Shot likely face in establishing a foothold in the Japanese market? How can these be resolved?

3. Based on the Japan VALS typology (Chapter 10), which VALS segments should be targeted by Hot Shot? What strategic changes are necessary to market effectively to these segments?

SUGGESTED READINGS

Fields, George. *From Bonsai to Levis* (New York: Macmillan, 1983).

Kanamori, Hisao. "Japan to Prosper into the 21st Century," *Tokyo Business Today*, June 1991, pp. 24-28.

Kume, Juji. "The Changing Alcoholic Beverages Industry in Japan," *Business Japan*, August 1987, pp. 55-59.

Morgan, James C. and Jeffrey Morgan. *Cracking the Japanese Market* (New York: The Free Press, 1991).

Pepper, Anne G. "Bottoms Up: New Drinking Patterns in the 1990s," *Business Japan*, August 1989, pp. 41-44.

Solo, Sally. "Japan's New Imports," *Fortune*, November 6, 1989, p. 12.

CASE

PUBLIC SECTOR SEGMENTATION: METRO-DADE'S GREYNOLDS PARK*

The Metropolitan Dade County Park and Recreation Department (Metro-Dade) in the Greater Miami, Florida, area excels in planning and redevelopment efforts. The department, a national gold medal award winner for excellence in park and recreation management, is a strong advocate of the marketing concept. Metro-Dade has found marketing research to be useful for measuring public perceptions and satisfaction levels with existing facilities, services, and programming, as well as assessing the demand for expanded and new amenities.

A recent project by this South Florida agency illustrates its research-based approach and strong user-orientation. Greynolds Park is a regional nature-based facility in North Miami Beach, Florida. The major problem Metro-Dade sought to investigate was how Greynolds Park should be redeveloped to meet the needs of its service area.

OBJECTIVES OF THE STUDY

The primary research issue was to determine the public's preference about the direction of future improvements at Greynolds (whether to increase or decrease the park's focus on nature and add more passive or active recreational opportunities). Specifically, several marketing/segmentation objectives guided the analysis:

- To geographically define the park's service area
- To develop a demographic profile of area users and potential users

*This case was written by Art Weinstein. It is based on the "Greynolds Park Market Study" prepared for the Metro-Dade Parks and Recreation Department by Pro-Mark Services, Miami, 1988. The author thanks Kevin Asher, Supervisor, Planning Section, for his instrumental and invaluable role as project director. Also, the writer acknowledges the research contributions provided by his associates, Marvin Nesbit and Joel B. McEachern, in the study.

- To learn about visitation patterns (such as frequency of usage), user motivation, likely usage of existing and proposed recreational opportunities, and nonuser constraints to visitation

- To assess visitor satisfaction, understand recreational interests/needs of the community, and determine the best methods for promoting the park

THE RESEARCH PROJECT

The data collection for Greynolds Park consisted of four separate, yet related initiatives. A toll booth survey was first conducted to establish the relevant service area for the park. This study showed that 60% of park visitors lived less than 3.5 miles from the park, 30% of the users resided 3.5 to 6 miles away, with the remaining 10% of the park goers outside of this prime geographic area.

Census-based geodemographic data about neighborhoods can assist planners in facility design issues (deciding whether a park should add playgrounds or shuffleboard courts). Demographic and socioeconomic data and cluster-based lifestyle information were purchased from Claritas. These reports provided keen insights into the composition of the market and consumers' leisure and recreational habits.

The six PRIZM clusters found in the primary service area are shown in Exhibit C2-1. Note the extremely high concentration (17 times the national average) of "Gray Power" and the "New Melting Pot" in this area. The secondary service area was also led by these groups with indexes of 992 and 1254, respectively. Other strong clusters in the secondary area included "Levittown, USA" (339), and "Single City Blues" (221).

Group	Sub Group	Nickname	Description	% Composition	Index
1	5	Furs & Station Wagons	New money, well educated, moved and mobile professionals and managers. Double income, married couples, 2+ cars, big spenders, big producers	4.4	138
			Diverse recreational interests, frequent many activities, particularly status conscious sports. Active orientation, fitness/conditioning important		
5	23	New Beginnings	Predominantly 18—34 singles and divorced individuals, prechild with employment concentrated in lower-level service and clerical occupations	6.9	159
			Few recreational interests, infrequent participation, seek solitary/small group activities and spectator sports		
4	27	Levittown, USA	Aging couples, postchild, comfortable middle class, high employment and double incomes	5.7	188
			Diverse recreational interests, participate heavily in large group activities and spectator sports		
4	39	Gray Power	Sunbelt retirement, affluent childless married couples living in mixed multiunit condos, nonsalaried incomes	48.9	1664
			Few recreational interests, participation limited by health not money, passive orientation, seek social activities with unrelated individuals		
6	3	New Melting Pot	Hispanic immigrant influx, dense urban middle class duplexes and houses. Includes extended family groups and first-time homeowner, clerical and service occupations	15.4	1703
			Few recreational interests, light participation, seek social activities with related individuals		
6	14	Emergent Minorities	Mostly black and Hispanic with high concentration of children in many single parent households. Low education and income, struggle for emergence from poverty	1.3	75
			Extremely few recreational interests, occasional participation, enjoy spectator sports		

253

**Public Sector Segmentation:
Metro-Dade's Greynolds Park**

Although the lifestyle clusters were informative, the heart of the Greynolds Park study was the primary research conducted. Three focus groups consisting of a mix of golfers, nature-lovers, and general recreationists (picnickers and bike riders) were conducted to learn about users' needs and wants. Each focus group varied by degree of park usage. Heavy users visited the park at least once a month; occasional users visited at least once a year, but less than once a month; and nonusers did not visit the park during the past 12-month period. This approach yielded important general and segment-specific findings. For example:

- All three user groups felt that Greynolds should remain resource-based (nature-oriented, passive recreation preferred), perceived the park favorably but thought it was underused, and stated that promotion was inadequate.

- Heavy users were interested in Greynold's role in the community, were primarily single-purpose users, and most concerned about the deterioration of the park and patron safety.

- Occasional users viewed the park as a backdrop for an event and sought varied educational opportunities.

- Nonusers had limited awareness of park features, desired new facilities, and liked special events.

Building on the focus group implications, a six-page survey instrument was then mailed to 2,000 service area residents (279 usable questionnaires were received). Although this response rate was a little disappointing, several intervening factors applied: the length of the survey, the large elderly population, and a lack of prenotification and follow-up procedures due to time and budget pressures. Despite these shortcomings, however, the survey provided extremely valuable and representative findings. Based on the quantitative analysis, a usage segmentation profile is shown in Exhibit C2-2.

→ **Market segment description/size:**

Heavy users (HU)	16%
Occasional users (OU)	51%
Nonusers (NU)	33%

→ **Recreational activities/interests:**

Current activity participation (top three)

HU: walk/jog, golf, playground

OU: concerts/events, picnics, bird watching/trails

Interest in existing offerings (top three)

HU: nature trails, picnics, concerts

OU: picnics, nature trails, naturalist tours

NU: concerts, picnics, nature trails

Interest in proposed offerings (top five)

HU: plant shows, marked nature trails, food festivals, canoe rentals, recreation center

OU: marked nature trails, food festivals, nature center, arts/crafts shows, plant shows

NU: food festivals, plant shows, arts/crafts shows, marked nature trails, canoe rentals

255

→ **A profile of major user type segments:**

Nature-lovers (30%)—57% female, 80% no children, 45% professionals/managers

General recreationists (28%)—68% female, 63% under 45, 52% have children

Golfers (17%)—81% male, 66% are over 65, 71% are retired

→ **Nonuser profile:**

63% women, 70% are 45 and over

In summary, the research indicated that the redevelopment of Greynolds should accent the natural beauty of the park. Five key recommendations emerged from this multiphase research investigation:

- The development of a nature-based, mixed-use facility to house a nature center, country store, and/or recreation center

- The improvement of existing facilities (for example, picnic tables, shelters, and rest areas)

- The need for public information materials (such as handouts, signage, advertising, and publicity)

- The creation of revenue-generating opportunities for the park (such as sporting concessions, fishing pier/dock, and giftshop)
- The need for special events programming such as concerts, plant shows, and arts and crafts activities

BUILDING A MARKETING-ORIENTED PARKS AGENCY

Although the need for a user orientation is evident, the diffusion process by parks managers throughout the United States has been relatively slow in taking shape. This is due to budget constraints, lack of marketing training, and attention to operations activities at the expense of marketing activities. A short distance away, the Broward County Parks district (the Greater Fort Lauderdale-Hollywood area), conducts virtually no consumer research. Instead, the district focuses its marketing attention on the development of promotional materials. The park managers feel that their planners *know* what residents seek in a park. This is a dangerous position to take. However, because of the newness of their facilities, this strategy has not come back to haunt them yet.

In contrast, Metro-Dade found that traditional market research tools and segmentation strategies prove valuable in developing visitor-oriented facilities and programming. Richard Kraus and Lawrence Allen commented on the changing role of market research in park and recreation planning:

> In the past, many leisure-service managers operated on the basis of personal conviction, subjective judgments, or rule-of-thumb appraisals. Today, there is a critical need for full documentation of program values and outcomes, and for systematic use of empirical data in all recreation and park planning and decision-making processes.

Market segmentation research can measure visitor usage of park programs, find enduring market opportunities, and monitor levels of satisfaction for key service offerings. Although progressive park marketers remain in the minority today, a transition toward customer-oriented thinking has occurred during the past decade. Successful leisure marketers of the 1990s do not necessarily need to be skilled marketing research practitioners. However, they should be sufficiently knowledgeable about the varied research procedures to know when specific techniques are needed. Additionally, they should be skilled in contracting for and managing firms brought in to assist in the market research/segmentation study.

END-OF-CASE QUESTIONS

1. As a marketing planner for Greynolds Park, discuss appropriate strategies for reaching "Gray Power" and "New Melting Pot" consumers (review the PRIZM discussion in Chapter 6).

2. Which market segments should Greynolds target based on usage categories (heavy, occasional, or nonusers) and user type (nature-lovers, general recreationists, and golfers)?

3. Based on the facts presented in this case study, how should parks management proceed in redeveloping Greynolds Park?

4. What types of segmentation research methods and analytical approaches should the leisure service organization use to segment markets? Should this market research conducted in-house or by outside firms?

SUGGESTED READINGS

Crompton, John , "Selecting Target Markets—A Key to Effective Marketing," *Journal of Park and Recreation Administration*, 1, 1983, pp. 7-25.

Kotler, Philip, and Alan R. Andreasen, *Strategic Marketing for Nonprofit Organizations*, 3rd Edition (Englewood Cliffs, N.J.: Prentice-Hall, 1987).

Kraus, Richard, and Lawrence Allen, *Research and Evaluation in Recreation, Parks and Leisure Studies* (Columbus, Ohio: Publishing Horizons, 1987).

Weinstein, Art, "Analyzing Market Opportunities in Service Organizations: A Leisure Services Case," in Michael Levy and Dhruv Grewal (eds.), *Academy of Marketing Science Proceedings*, Miami Beach, May 26-29, 1993, pp. 430-433.

CASE 3

ATTITUDINAL SEGMENTATION: OVER 50/MATURE CONSUMERS*

A marketer's dream, one might think when considering the mature market. Possessed of high assets and incomes, it conjures up a fantasy of someone's grandmother sitting on a pile of gold bullion. The mature population (43% of all households) controls 51% of all discretionary income in the United States, on a per capita basis. Census figures show that the median net worth of households aged 50 to 65 is $68,749 ($73,471 for households over 65). These net worth figures are approximately twice that for all U.S. households. Although those over 50 are overconsumers of healthcare and medicines, they also buy 41% of all cars sold in the U.S. and take 46% of all vacation and pleasure trips.

Unfortunately, after initial runs at mature consumers, many marketers dismiss them as difficult to identify and reach. Although marketers have been segmenting mature consumers for more than 30 years, their segmentation strategies have almost uniformly been based on demographic characteristics, such as age or income.

Demographics alone have not been successful because they are oversimplistic. Five-year-old children around the country, relatively unformed by life, share many of the same lifestyle characteristics. People over 50, though, have had diverse life experiences and are not as homogeneous. Devising a marketing strategy, for example, based on the idea that all persons aged 50 to 60 yearn to go on a cruise doesn't reflect reality. To propose that all women aged over 70 delight in spending their days baking cookies for grandchildren is laughable. Mass marketing won't work with this highly heterogeneous group.

*This case was prepared by Carol M. Morgan and Doran J. Levy, Ph.D., Strategic Directions Group, Inc., Minneapolis, MN. Data is from the 50+(R) studies. Copyright ©1993 Carol M. Morgan and Doran J. Levy.

The secret to reaching the mature market includes both segmenting the market and taking into account attitudes and motivations that differ not only by segment, but by specific goods or services. In pursuing this elusive market, Strategic Directions Group, Inc., a Minneapolis-based marketing consulting firm, first completed a national motivational segmentation study on people aged 50 or more in 1989. In 1992, the study was expanded, surveying an additional 3,000 persons aged over 50. Each of them provided more than 1,000 pieces of information.

The 50+ studies differed from other research because the mature population was segmented based on attitudes and motivations, not on demographics or lifestyles. The attitudinal information was then combined with additional data from the study on a wide range of topics, including travel, investments, physiology and health, lifestyle, purchasing patterns, residence, demographics, media usage, and activities. The 50+ study was also unique because it segmented the respondents using three separate strategies. These segmentations focus on attitudes toward retirement and financial planning, food, and health.

The study revealed four Self segments, four Health segments, and three Food segments. Exploring only some of the products in the study (hundreds were tested) yielded key segment differences in product consumption. By understanding the psychological dynamics of the 50+ segments, marketers of specific products/services can plan better appeals to reach their prime prospects.

THE SELF SEGMENTS

In identifying the attitudes of those over 50 toward themselves and social and financial issues, respondents were asked to sort 60 attitude statements on such topics as finances, retirement, appearance, activities, and housing. Statements included: "I wish I could move to a safer neighborhood," "Plastic surgery is something I would consider to keep looking younger," and "I have to admit most of my investments are conservative."

Types of Self Segments

Using the Marketer® segmentation system, four Self segments were found: the Upbeat Enjoyers (22%), the Insecure (29%), the Threatened Actives (21%), and the Financial Positives (28%).

Upbeat Enjoyers feel they have become more attractive with age and are optimistic about their futures. They always want to "work at something." With a median annual pretax household income of $37,112, Upbeat Enjoyers have the second highest incomes of the four Self segments.

The Insecure, for whom financial security is a major concern, are most interested in receiving senior travel discounts. This segment feels that the best years of their lives are over and that they have become less attractive with age. The Insecure have by far the lowest household incomes, a median of $11,001.

The Threatened Actives accept themselves as they are and have a positive outlook on life, although they are concerned about being crime victims. This segment wants to continue working. They prefer to shop where they can get age-related discounts. Their median income is $19,491, the second lowest of the Self segments.

The Financial Positives are financially secure and consider themselves to be successful people ready to enjoy life. They believe it is important to look as young as possible. When shopping, the Financial Positives look for value. The wealthiest of the four segments, this group has a median income of $37,222.

Differences in Purchasing Behavior: The Upbeat Enjoyers Versus the Financial Positives

In 1990, mature consumers bought 41% of new cars. Although about a quarter of Upbeat Enjoyers and Financial Positives plan to purchase a new car within the next two years, the type of car they purchase may differ. Financial Positives usually buy American automobiles. Twenty-five percent of Upbeat Enjoyers say their next cars will be foreign. This compares to 16% foreign car ownership and 17% purchase intent among the over 50 population (see Exhibit C3-1).

Exhibit C3-1: Targeting Foreign Car Buyers

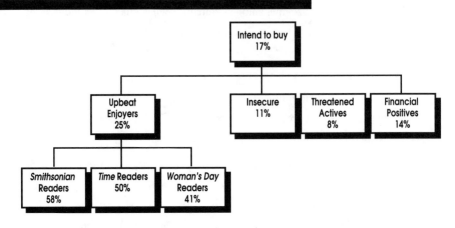

Although both are affluent segments, Upbeat Enjoyers and Financial Positives differ significantly in their consumption of cosmetics. Financial Positives are overconsumers of skin and hair products and cosmetics. This group wants to look as young as possible and is most receptive to plastic surgery. Upbeat Enjoyers believe that they have become more attractive with age and are "sexier than ever." Changing their appearance through the use of rejuvenating creams is of little interest to them. Only one in five women are night cream users, versus one in three for Financial Positives (see Exhibit C3-2 for further details on cosmetic usage by segment).

Exhibit C3-2: Which Cosmetics Do You Use Regularly?

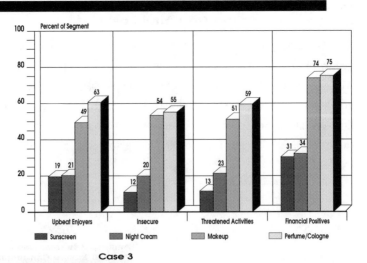

Case 3

The Upbeat Enjoyers want to participate in the good life, but in contrast to the Financial Positives, they rely more heavily on credit to do so. Twenty-six percent of Upbeat Enjoyers use an American Express card at least once a week (17% for Financial Positives). Fewer Upbeat Enjoyers (60%) pay off their Visa balances in full each month compared to the Financial Positives (74%).

THE HEALTH SEGMENTS

In identifying the needs and attitudes of those over 50 toward health-related trends and issues, respondents were asked to sort 50 attitude statements regarding drug use, illness, doctors and hospitals, and healthy eating and exercise. The statements included: "At this time of my life, I don't think I can do any more than I am doing to stay healthy" and "I think it is important for older people to have their hearing checked occasionally." Four Health segments were discovered: the Proactives (40%), the Faithful Patients (22%), the Optimists (20%), and the Disillusioned (18%).

The *Proactive* segment is committed to exercise and good nutrition, trust their doctors, and are careful to take an entire prescription. They seek out a great deal of information about how to stay in good health. Proactives believe they have adequate medical insurance. Because they believe in having their hearing tested regularly, it's not surprising that 16% of those over 65 wear a hearing aid (this compares with 11% of Faithful Patients and 6% of Optimists).

Although the *Faithful Patients* are aware that they should eat well and exercise to stay healthy, they do not believe they are doing so. Instead, they rely on doctors and medications. Faithful Patients, the youngest Health segment, look to religion during times of poor health. One in three females in this group takes painkillers regularly, compared to 22% of the mature population.

The wealthiest of the four Health segments, *Optimists* feel that they almost never get sick and take medicine only when it is absolutely necessary. They feel quite strongly that the United States does not need guaranteed healthcare, and they are the only segment that doesn't believe that HMOs are a good idea.

The poorest of the Health segments, the *Disillusioned* strongly believe that their insurance is inadequate and are adamant that the United States should have guaranteed healthcare. This group is the least trusting of doctors. They actively seek out information about how to stay healthy and are careful to eat a balanced diet.

The female Disillusioned are the heaviest consumers of antacids (37% versus 22% for the overall mature market).

FOOD SEGMENTS

In identifying the needs and attitudes of those over 50 toward food trends and issues, respondents were asked to sort 50 attitude statements regarding food and eating. The statements included: "I'm willing to pay more for easy-to-prepare foods," "I am trying to cut down on the amount of salt I consume," and "Eating at restaurants is too expensive." Three food segments were found: the Nutrition Concerned (46%), the Fast & Healthy (38%), and the Traditional Couponers (16%).

Eating regular meals and not skipping meals is of great importance to only the *Nutrition Concerned*, who believe that how you feel is influenced by what you eat. More than the other two Food segments, they admit that they are swayed by advertising. This group has the highest median household income.

Only the *Fast & Healthy* are interested in foods packaged for the microwave and in individual or smaller servings. This segment tries to eat foods that are good for them. They prefer meeting friends at a restaurant rather than at home. This group has the lowest median household income of the three Food segments.

The *Traditional Couponers* believe they are using more coupons for discounts and increasing their reliance on favorite brands. With little interest in healthy eating, this group uses more convenience foods and cooks fewer meals. They favor restaurants that offer special discounts to people over a certain age.

Companies which produce, distribute, and market foodstuffs should consider how each of the 50+ Food segments represents both a current trend and a future opportunity. For example, companies that are packaging and branding fresh fruits and vegetables should be aware of the Nutrition Concerned. They are the only segment that is committed to cooking from scratch. Exhibit C3-3 illustrates how the segments differ based on usage of four categories of vegetables.

EXHIBIT C3-3: VEGETABLE CONSUMPTION

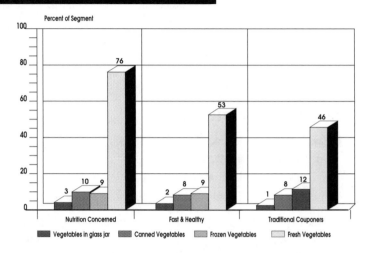

Percent of Segment

	Vegetables in glass jar	Canned Vegetables	Frozen Vegetables	Fresh Vegetables

Nutrition Concerned: 3, 10, 9, 76
Fast & Healthy: 2, 8, 9, 53
Traditional Couponers: 1, 8, 12, 46

265

Marketers of low-fat convenience foods can tout the nutritional benefits of their products to the Fast & Healthy. They also want single portions that can be microwaved—31% eat a frozen dinner once a week or more (in contrast, less than 7% of the other two Food segments do).

MARKETING IMPLICATIONS
AND CONCLUDING REMARKS

The 50+ segments are quite useful for developing promotional strategies. Network television, for example, is viewed most heavily by the Insecure, the Faithful Patients, and the Fast & Healthy. Other segments (for example, the Financial Positives and Upbeat Enjoyers) are active magazine readers. Whereas *Family Circle* is an excellent way to reach female Upbeat Enjoyers, males in this segment prefer *National Geographic.*

Attitudinal information can be correlated with behaviors and demographics to build direct marketing applications and improve targeting. In Food segments, the Traditional Couponers spend dramatically more than the other two segments on direct marketing. Although they represent just 16% of the mature population, if a list were compiled limited to males between 50 and 55 with incomes under $50,000, the percentage of Traditional Couponers in that population would increase to 39%.

Attitudinal Segmentation:
Over 50/Mature Consumers

In every respect, from how they feel about themselves to their views on food and health, the 50+ segments define mature consumers far more clearly than would a mere examination of behaviors or demographic characteristics. Information from segmentation studies based on attitudes can be used to create products and services, target direct mail campaigns, devise effective advertising, and succeed in one-on-one selling efforts.

END-OF-CASE QUESTIONS

1. Based on what you read about the Self segments, how might the Upbeat Enjoyers and Financial Positives differ with respect to travel and shopping at department stores? How would you target the Insecure and the Threatened Actives for these product categories?

2. Which of the four Health segments—the Proactives, the Faithful Patients, the Optimists, or the Disillusioned—is likely to be the heaviest user of vitamins? How about the lightest user of vitamins? Why?

3. Discuss appropriate advertising media and promotional appeals that could be used by fast food or sit-down restaurants to best serve the 50+ Food segments—the Nutrition Concerned, the Fast & Healthy, and the Traditional Couponers.

SUGGESTED READINGS

Morgan, Carol M., and Doran J. Levy. *Segmenting the Mature Market* (Chicago: Probus Publishing, 1993).

Ostroff, Jeff. *Successful Marketing to the 50+ Consumer* (Englewood Cliffs, N.J.: Prentice Hall, 1989).

CASE   HIGH-TECH SERVICE SEGMENTATION:
PRODIGY ONLINE COMPUTING SERVICE*

When Prodigy was introduced, online services were still a novelty and primarily the province of only the most computer literate. The early services targeted the "computer crowd" and not the general public.

In those early days, Prodigy also thought that those with computers and modems were the most appropriate audience for their new product. One clearly identifiable segment were the personal computer (PC) user group members around the country. These groups are easy to identify; there is even a national organization of user groups. Prodigy gave away software with a month's free membership in the service to these PC user group members to generate trials. Later, the service asked for the regular price from those interested in remaining with Prodigy.

However, there were a couple of things Prodigy hadn't counted on. In 1988, the telecommunications field was still in its infancy. Modems were expensive and slow. The people who did own modems were mostly sophisticated online services users and devotees of private bulletin board systems and specialized networks of computer users. To this target market, and to the columnists in the trade press, Prodigy looked like "the Fisher-Price toy of online services."

Prodigy also misjudged the direction and likely growth of the home computer market. As Prodigy planned its nationwide rollout, industry indicators pointed to "the year of the home computer." Computer hardware vendors, including IBM and Apple, came out with new models, targeted directly at the home computer market. What nobody predicted was that 1989 would find a nervous buying public shying away from major "luxury" purchases like home computers.

*This case was prepared by Dr. William J. McDonald, Assistant Professor of Marketing and International Business, Hofstra University, Hempstead, NY.

As a result, Prodigy flopped. The main reason was a poor match between the needs of the targeted market and Prodigy's offered services. Although Prodigy had found an easily identifiable market, it couldn't conquer it. In retrospect, the outcome is understandable, if not obvious. The members of the computer crowd targeted by Prodigy were accustomed to the sophisticated online services like CompuServe, Delphi, and Genie, not to a visual and extremely user-friendly environment like Prodigy. The older services ran all sessions on their main computers; users talked to one another as a group experience. Thus, they could talk to the others who were "there" with them at their keyboard. In contrast, Prodigy was a more solitary experience. The other services also offered vast repositories of programs to download, which Prodigy didn't. A "macho factor" also operated: Those who had mastered the sophisticated services had a certain superiority complex, feeling a sense of accomplishment for having mastered telecommunication software vagaries and a complex series of commands. To this market segment, Prodigy was too easy.

Some six or eight years ago, PCs—both at home and in the workplace—were the province of "experts." Today, computers have been democratized; they are everywhere and used by almost everyone. Legions of secretaries have gleefully abandoned the typewriter in favor of word processing on their PCs. Attorneys who once slogged through musty law books are doing their research electronically with a few keystrokes. Physicians maintain their patients' records (and billing and insurance information) with computers. Architects and automobile designers use computer-assisted design (CAD) programs; farmers track their harvests and livestock on PCs; accountants have abandoned their green eyeshades and green ledger sheets for spreadsheets. There is no area of American endeavor that's not been touched by computerization and made simpler by the ubiquitous PC.

However, until recently, most home PCs were there for business reasons; their owners either worked at home or routinely brought work home from the office. Most of those home PCs had a single "owner"—men working at work. Other family members were largely excluded for a number of reasons. First, they didn't know how to use PCs and the "owner" didn't want to spare the time and energy to teach them. Second, not many of them were really interested in designing databases or using spreadsheets—the common business applications available for PCs. Most word processors were hard to learn. Games for PCs were slow to be developed and expensive. With the emergence of more user-friendly software and operating environments, PC use expanded, but still only the "owner" was using the PC on a regular basis. Prodigy helped changed that with its easy access and use. In a way, it was a revolution, if only in terms of putting the power of the PC in the hands of everyone.

Today, a significant percentage of new computer purchases are for home use. It's probably not that consumers feel any richer than they did in late 1989; it's more likely that a home computer is perceived as a useful, if not necessary, tool and less as a luxury. Another major factor is that computers are a lot less expensive now.

PRODIGY'S ONLINE SERVICES

Prodigy currently has well over 1.5 million subscribers, with 2 million expected by the middle of 1993 (see Exhibit C4-1). CompuServe, the closest competitor in the online derby, has fewer than a million members (960,000). Today, the Prodigy service is accessible with a local call by 95% of the households in the United States. As Exhibit C4-2 shows, the company has nearly half of the $500-million annual market for consumer online information services.

Exhibit C4-1: Prodigy Subscriber Levels

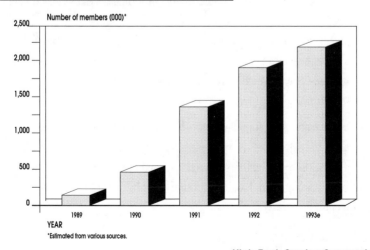

Number of members (000)*

YEAR
*Estimated from various sources.

High-Tech Service Segmentation:
Prodigy Online Computing Service

EXHIBIT C4-2: 1992 ONLINE COMPUTING SERVICES' MARKET SUBSCRIBER SHARES*

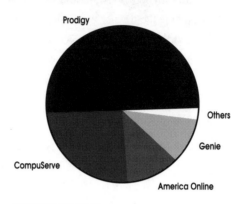

*Estimated from various sources.

An online shopping mall provides customers with a wide range of products at prices that are usually about the same as retail outlets. The malls are open around the clock, seven days a week. For example, Comp-u-Store Online is a powerful and useful shopping club that is available on several online services, including Prodigy, CompuServe, and America Online. Included in Comp-u-Store's product list of 250,000 items are books and magazines, home electronics, and automobile accessories. Prodigy offers a graphical user interface, making it easy for new computer shoppers to get started.

Online shopping services: Using online shopping services can be simple and effective. Prodigy can put consumers in touch with name brand clothing at Spiegel, for instance. Executives can even obtain attaché cases. From their modems, users can stock their offices with everything from paper clips to fax machines. Sears, which is available through Prodigy, offers a wide a selection of items online.

Online travel planning: Prodigy can help to minimize the hassles of business travel to cities like New York. Prodigy's guide to New York includes information on nightlife, attractions, events, shopping, the weather, the lottery, dining, and lodging. Prodigy's Mobil Travel Guide lists restaurants by cuisine.

Online banking: About 15 banks offer home banking through Prodigy. Prodigy enables customers to pay bills, receive statements, transfer funds, and open accounts. However, major banks have had spotty results in encouraging customers to bank electronically. Four factors are changing that:

- Automated teller machines and Touchtone telephone services provided by many banks have educated consumers.

- As the prices of PCs have dropped, more customers have them and can now link up with banks.

- As more banks merge or fail, there will be fewer branches and longer lines.

- New software and computer services make electronic banking cheaper and easier.

Online investing: More than 3,000 mutual funds can be researched thanks to Prodigy. However, even though 25% of all U.S. households have money in funds, few turn to PCs to manage the funds. The American Association of Individual Investors has found that 64% of its 110,000 members own computers, but only about 40% do any investment analysis with them. Just one-third of that group use the computers for fund investing.

A PROFILE OF PRODIGY MEMBERS

Today, Prodigy is aimed at the many millions of people who have not tried, or stayed with, present online services and not at the million or fewer serious information customers who are regular users of electronic information and understand personal computing and have made an effort to master communications software, online searching, electronic mail, and online user groups. Most of Prodigy's list of computing information menus point the user to advertisements for various products. Although the ads have useful product information, they do not take advantage of the medium. A few brief reports on major PC industry stories and announcements of forthcoming major product releases are contained in Prodigy's news service. Prodigy's simple messaging system on its PC Bulletin Board may suit many of its users, turning user groups into one of its successes.

Initially, Prodigy took a big risk by selling the product through the consumer market rather than through software vendors. However, as retailers and computer makers have promoted the machines, as pricing has come down, and as consumers have become more familiar with computers through their jobs, the home computer market opened up. Prodigy's main selling point is its ease of use and value. Prodigy offers numerous services, including news, weather, sports, and financial and business news (updated throughout the day), an online encyclopedia, banking, and stock quotes, among others.

According to Prodigy's research, if you're a new Prodigy member, the chances are good that you've just purchased your first home computer. There's only a 20% chance that you even know about other online services. (In 1990, there was a 40% chance that you would.)

On an average Prodigy day, there are 500,000 "sessions." (A session lasts from sign-on to sign-off on a single ID.) On that same average day, somewhere between 20 and 30% of Prodigy members will sign on at least once.

Some 60% of Prodigy users are adult males, 30% are adult females, and 10% are children under 18 years old. Some 72% are married, with about 17% single (assume that percentage includes children) and 10% are divorced. Some 10% of Prodigy members are over 55. These numbers seem to bear out Prodigy's orientation and initiative as a family service.

Prodigy touts attractive demographics of its audience—whose average household income is $70,000—to advertisers. The major obstacle to Prodigy's growth remains consumers' hesitancy to buy a home computer.

PRODIGY INSTALLS A NEW PROGRAM

Karen and Brad Perkins seem like ideal customers for an online information service. They're suburban knowledge workers: She's a patent lawyer; he heads a high-tech startup firm. Both have an insatiable appetite for all kinds of information, and they log on to check stock quotes, get science news, and consult an electronic encyclopedia when their six-year-old son blurts out a tough question.

But customers such as the Perkinses have been a vexing problem for Prodigy. Why? Prodigy says the $12.95 that the Perkinses pay each month doesn't cover the costs of delivering service to them. So Prodigy counts on advertising revenues for goods and services sold on, as well as commissions from those transactions, to make up the shortfall. But even though Prodigy vendors sell everything from airline tickets to designer jeans, the Perkinses haven't bought a thing in the nine months since signing up. Says Karen: "I'm sure I'm on their bad-consumer list."

Expanded Menu

With so many "bad" consumers among its members, Prodigy is revamping its business model. Prodigy is losing money. By contrast, number two CompuServe, a unit of H&R Block Inc., has been profitable since 1981. To meet its own deadline of profitability by the "early 1990s," Prodigy must change its ways.

A new Prodigy is emerging. It has unveiled a slew of new features. Instead of simply charging one low price for the basic service and hoping to make up the difference with ads and commissions, Prodigy is adding extra-cost options similar to a cable-TV company's premium channels. New premium service include action games for kids and the ability to download public domain software. Also, for an extra fee, customers have the option of using 9600 baud modems to speed up Prodigy's on-screen graphics, which many consumers say change too slowly.

Cartoon Clothes

In addition to boosting revenue, the new premium services may help fend off growing competition. Rivals such as Sierra Network, which specializes in games, and America Online Inc., which caters to specific markets, are carving profitable niches. They have gotten unintended help from Prodigy, which has spent about $50 million in advertising and promotions since 1990 to get ordinary consumers to log on.

Still, Prodigy hasn't turned enough people into electronic shoppers. One reason: Prodigy displays cartoon-like graphics, not photographic images of merchandise. That's not a problem if you're selling a mutual fund, but "people won't buy a designer dress this way," says Jerry Schillinger, business development manager for Spiegel Inc., one online merchant.

In time, new technology should "open up the market" for interactive home shopping, says David Waks, Prodigy's director of business development. Waks is testing new ways to enhance Prodigy with photos, video, and sound. One possibility, he says, is to transmit the service to television sets rather than to

PCs, using interactive cable systems. Another idea is to mail members CD-ROM disks that can store handsome electronic catalogs. But neither technology will be in widespread use anytime soon, Waks notes.

In the meantime, Prodigy is eliminating many of its online merchandisers. Instead of having dozens of retailers doing a little business, says Geoffrey Moore, Prodigy's director of market programs, "it's better for us to have a smaller number of happy retailers." Spiegel says it's staying because it's content with the business it does selling sheets, towels, and such. Among merchants that have already left are Contact Lens Supply, Sharon Luggage, and Buick, which had offered brochures. In general, says Moore, successful Prodigy merchants sell known entities such as magazine subscriptions or compact disks.

Message Mania

Each day, Prodigy's members now send out about 65,000 private electronic mail notes and post an average of 80,000 messages to bulletin boards. Members have unlimited access to bulletin boards dealing with every topic from cooking tips to the TV show "Northern Exposure."

To reduce its telecommunications costs, Prodigy is encouraging subscribers to write and edit their messages and memos before logging on. Previously you had to be online while you wrote. If enough members cooperate, Prodigy may be able to put off further expansion of its already massive, nationwide network. Big capital projects are getting harder to fund because IBM and Sears have been cutting their annual investments in Prodigy since 1990.

CAN GTE OUTDO PRODIGY?

Years ago, Connie Edwards was walking through a town fair near her home in the Los Angeles suburb of Cerritos when she was approached by representatives from her telephone company. GTE Corporation asked her if she wanted to try a new interactive information service that would be delivered to her home via cable television. "At first, I wasn't sure what it was about," says Edwards, a healthcare technician. But the service costs just $10 a month, so she and her husband, a high school teacher, decided to splurge. Since then, the Edwards and their two teenagers have been using Main Street about 8 to 10 hours every week.

As one of two test-market towns, Cerritos has helped prepare GTE for its rollout of the country's first cable-delivered information service. The launch marks the opening round in a battle for what promises to be a multibillion-dollar industry by the end of the decade. GTE is the first company to hook up with cable, which provides faster transmission than phone lines and is installed in six times as many U.S. homes as PCs with modems. "The mass market values services like Prodigy," says Thomas A. Grieb, general manager of Main Street, "but it doesn't want to use computers."

Big Plans

GTE is about to begin its first commercial tryout of Main Street, in San Diego. Consumers who sign up will use a remote-control device to browse through electronic encyclopedias, take practice SAT exams, play interactive games, shop for gifts, scan the news 24 hours a day, and invest in stocks via brokers Quick & Reilly. By 1997, GTE wants to launch Main Street in the top 20 U.S. media markets and grab 20% of the 60 million households with cable.

Despite such predictions, GTE doesn't truly know what sort of information services consumers want. In focus groups, families such as the Edwards almost always say education is their top priority. But GTE's own monitoring of its 400 test-market families in Cerritos and Newton, Massachusetts, shows that subscribers spend most of their time on Main Street playing such games as Sweethearts, in which viewers' use their remote controls to guess when couples are lying about their relationship. Men favor QBI, which lets viewers predict whether a quarterback in a real NFL game will pass or run.

Main Street, however, may not be the most efficient way to play such games. Because fully two-way cable is still mostly in the testing phase at Tele-Communications Inc., Time Warner, and other cable giants, Main Street users must supplement their cable service by plugging a telephone line into the back of a box provided by GTE. That way, instructions punched into the remote control can be transmitted to GTE's network of computers. If there's a phone call, a message flashes on the screen, giving Main Street users the option of interrupting their session to take the call.

No Mall?

GTE's most serious rival is plainly Prodigy. In early December 1992, Prodigy announced that it will begin conducting tests on cable by mid-1993, using technology from X-Press, a division of Liberty Media Company, a leading home-shopping programmer.

But both Prodigy and GTE need to convince consumers that shopping via cable is better than ordering from catalogs or going to the mall. Because the monthly fees that consumers pay don't nearly cover the cost of providing the services, GTE also relies heavily on ad revenues and commissions from shopping transactions. And the Edwards "haven't used the shopping much," on Main Street, says Connie. If too many customers turn out to be like the Edwards, Main Street will just be a new and exciting way for GTE to lose money.

SEGMENTING THE ONLINE SERVICES MARKET

In marketing, the *diffusion process* refers to the way an idea is communicated to potential adopters. Mass media advertising to the target market and direct mail create awareness and provide information sources during the introductory stage. Evaluation also depends on word-of-mouth, as the consumer weighs the benefits of the service versus its cost. Testimonials help establish credibility. During the adoption period, consumers look for information to relieve post-purchase anxiety and, therefore, look again to the mass media for confirmation or to company sales representatives for assurance.

Consumer segmentations take place along demographic, lifestyle, and benefit criteria, with these resulting segments: risk takers; innovators and opinion leaders (others listen to and respect their judgment about products); educated people able to use the services fully to indicate potential to others; family-oriented types who allow their children to use the PCs at home; those used to drawing information from new, unusual sources; those who don't view computers as "big brother in 1984;" people who exhibit a degree of trust in banks (won't lose my money and privacy will be protected); and, those able to afford such services.

Several consumer needs are being satisfied by online services:

- Prestige—first on your block with the newest in electronic gadgetry

- Convenience—everything available at your fingertips; do not have to leave your living room to shop

- Instant gratification—information available when you want it, rather than when a facility is open

- Novelty/excitement—being part of a new craze sweeping the country

- Efficiency—one-stop shopping

- Ease of use—just press the buttons

- Timeliness—advantage of "real time" information (useful, for example, when customers are buying stocks)

Promotional strategy focuses on the service and its perceived benefits, the target market characteristics, and the appropriate media. These strategies develop the benefits of convenience, value for the money, excitement, ease of use, and innovation without risk. The services do not want to suffer from a "gadget" image. Unfortunately, print media messages can be copy-heavy when explaining product features. Advertisers should see beyond narrow vehicles such as computer magazines and find a wider target audience by using more general publications such as *Fortune* or *Time.*

END-OF-CASE QUESTIONS

1. Given the benefits of hindsight, how would you have introduced Prodigy in 1988? What services would you have offered and how would you have segmented the market?

2. In today's market, what additional market segments should Prodigy consider targeting to expand its subscriber base? And what services will it need to offer to appeal to those new market segments?

3. Most households in the United States don't own a PC. What additional market segments could Prodigy attract if it was offered through the cable television industry's lines? How would Prodigy have to change its services to appeal to the needs of that new market segment(s)?

4. Some industry experts argue that future households will be offered a vast array of entertainment and information service through local cable and telephone lines. Some discuss the emergence of 500 channels with movies, information, shopping, and other services in an interactive marketplace between households and service providers. What is the most appropriate place for Prodigy in this scenario? What services should it offer and to what market segment(s)?

SUGGESTED READINGS

This case makes extensive use of the following references:

"Can GTE Outdo Prodigy?" *Business Week*, December 28, 1992, p. 42D.

"Hot New PC Serves," *Fortune,* November 2, 1992, pp. 108-114.

Kane, Pamela. *Prodigy Made Easy*, Second Edition (Berkeley, Calif.: Osborne McGraw-Hill, 1993).

"Prodigy Installs a New Program," *Business Week*, September 14, 1992, pp. 96-97.

Schepp, Brad and Debra Shepp. *The Complete Guide to CompuServe* (Berkeley, Calif.: Osborne McGraw-Hill, 1990).

CASE SMALL BUSINESS SEGMENTATION:
TROPHY SHOPS AND
SPECIALTY RETAILING*

One of the most critical strategic decisions small business owners/managers face is determining the type of customers they should pursue. Typically, small retailers do not have a "game plan" for conducting effective market segmentation and selecting the right target markets. This fundamental marketing strategy is too often left to chance—based solely on an entrepreneur's "gut feel" or at best, a cursory analysis of a particular market.

Specialty retailers, due to the uniqueness of their business situations, require even more of a customer-oriented focus than do traditional retailers. Specialty retailers can be defined as relatively uncommon businesses that satisfy specific customer needs. Examples include retailers who sell baseball cards, skateboards, musical instruments, or rare books. Typically not found in neighborhood shopping centers, specialty retailers appeal to a limited customer base and emphasize product depth over breadth. This case provides a practical illustration of how one type of specialty retailer, trophy shops (referred to in its industry as recognition retailers) can benefit from market segmentation techniques.

BACKGROUND

In addition to trophies, most recognition retailers feature plaques, engravings, small gifts, and related products. Specialty retailers can use market segmentation analysis to better understand their customers and market. First, recognize that different types of customers buy different types of products

*Much of the material in this case is adapted from Weinstein, Art, "How Specialty Retailers Can Use Market Segmentation Techniques to Increase Sales: The Case of the Recognition Retailer," in Gwen Fontenot (ed.), *Proceedings of the Small Business Institute Directors' Association National Conference*, Washington, D.C. (February 16-19, 1989), pp. 206-209.

(such as trophies, plaques, and pen sets). Second, consider that a retailer's product assortment must be carefully merchandised to maximize profitability. As an example, an industry expert noted that there are over 15,000 advertising specialties available. Obviously, it only makes sense to handle goods and services that are most in demand.

Segmentation Strategies

The trophy shop has two basic strategic choices: to segment the market or use an undifferentiated marketing strategy. Based on a two-county telephone survey of 12 recognition retailers in South Florida, the consensus was that entrepreneurs generally felt that everyone was a likely customer (the mass marketing approach), rather than targeting those who were the most likely customers to buy. Progressive trophy shops and specialty retailers, however, are effective segmenters.

The recognition retailer that separately targets corporations, schools, professional associations, and small businesses is employing a differentiation approach. Under a concentration segmentation approach, the trophy shop may be interested in serving a single market—for example, the corporate market. Concentrated marketing is less expensive than differentiated marketing and may be the appropriate choice for a new business or a growing firm with limited resources. One Miami-based trophy retailer targeted sailing and yachting clubs, a segment largely ignored by major competitors. By actively pursuing this market niche and placing advertising in boating magazines, this retailer prospered.

Sometimes it pays to break the market down to the finest detail—often to the individual customer level. This strategy might be appropriate for firms specializing in customized and relatively expensive products. Faced with a smaller market, a targeted marketing program is designed to appeal to the few, but key prospects. For specialty/recognition retailers to effectively incorporate market segmentation techniques into their marketing plan, a four-step approach can be used (see Exhibit C5-1).

EXHIBIT C5-1: THE FOUR-STEP MARKET SEGMENTATION PROCESS

1. *Define the relevant market.* The market definition should reflect the firm's primary geographic trade area, its product focus (such as awards, trophies, or ad specialties), and major customer orientation (such as sales-oriented companies, schools, and associations).

2. *Determine appropriate dimensions to use in segmenting markets.* Segmenting dimensions or bases are methods/variables used to divide the total market into smaller and more manageable parts of the market that can be targeted effectively and cost efficiently. Physical dimensions include geographic and demographic bases, whereas appropriate behavioral dimensions for the recognition retailer include product usage by customer, product/product line, and situation/occasion—and to a lesser extent— psychographics and benefits. These are discussed in the next section.

3. *Gather the necessary information.* Marketing information for making segmentation decisions is available from a variety of sources. Among these include customer files, published sources (such as census reports, trade journals, and newspapers), mailing lists, trade associations, Small Business Development Centers, universities, marketing research firms and consultants, chambers of commerce, governmental agencies, or via in-house custom designed marketing surveys. Research objectives, needs, and budget will dictate which sources are most appropriate for the small trophy shop or specialty retailer.

4. *Analyze and evaluate the information.* Once the data has been collected, it is important to be able to make sense out of the research. Numbers alone are meaningless unless they provide practical information to help make better business decisions.

After the data has been gathered and analyzed, it is essential to translate the findings into action—marketing strategy and implementation.

SEGMENTATION BASES FOR THE RECOGNITION RETAILER

There are a number of useful ways specialty retailers can segment their markets. The following overview discusses some of the more important options.

Geographics

Geography is one of the simplest and most effective means for segmenting a market. Because recognition retailers' products are specialty goods, customer trade areas are larger than traditional neighborhood retailers. Specific views of geographic market definition vary by entrepreneur. One small retailer defined his trade area as the local community; another retailer just a few miles away stated that as an exporter, his market was worldwide. Regardless of chosen scope, a geographic analysis of the trade area is the recommended first step. A careful analysis of the population and industrial base within this targeted area should be undertaken and reviewed periodically. Such geographic measures as census tracts and zip codes can be studied to better understand local market conditions.

Demographics

This segmentation base comprises consumer and business demographics. These variables should be studied in conjunction with the geographic boundaries specified. Consumer demographics include basic population statistics of an area such as the number of people, the number of households, age and income distribution, racial and religious backgrounds, education levels, occupations, and so on. This data can provide valuable insights into a community and assist the trophy retailer in offering desirable products. Some areas for opportunity that can be spotted through consumer demographics might be school and church activities, team sporting events, and civic and community clubs.

Often more important, however, to the recognition retailer are business demographics. This set of data can reveal how many companies are located in an area, the types of companies (insurance agencies, banks, and so on), the number of employees in the company, and so forth. This information can be of tremendous value to the trophy retailer. For example, sales-oriented companies and incentive-driven firms are more likely to have a need for these products. Similarly, larger companies have a greater need for recognition products than do smaller firms. An understanding of basic consumer and business demographics in the geographic market can provide a huge edge over competitors who have not invested the time and effort into scientifically learning about their market.

Product Usage

One of the best ways for segmenting markets is through analyzing past and expected purchasing behavior (product usage). This can be done in three ways. First, through examining customer files (good recordkeeping is essential), marketers can find out a great deal about their customers. The 80/20 rule means that approximately 80% of the firm's sales come from about 20% of its customers. Analyze customer files to learn which customers are the best ones, the heavy users; those that are dependable, regular customers; those that are infrequent customers; and inactive customers. An ABCD coding system can be established, assigning an A to the heavy user, B to the average user, C to the light user, and D to the former customer. Of course, one other customer category exists: the nonuser. This approach enables the firm to target various user groups to improve marketing performance. For example, type A customers may be contacted monthly, whereas D customers might be followed up annually.

The second product usage dimension examines product profitability. Again, the 80/20 rule is important here. Research has shown that typically 80% of a firm's sales come from only 20% of the firm's products. Products (engraved pens or ribbons) and product lines (such as laminations or trophies) should be tracked to determine fast sellers. Slow-moving items waste valuable selling space and should be cut back or eliminated. The ABCD classification approach can again be used to analyze product movement.

The final product usage alternative considers the purchase situation or occasion. By identifying the use for the product, often it is possible to effectively target key markets. Some examples include these:

- Various managers in large companies can be targeted. Recognition products are often needed by personnel managers as retirement gestures, sales managers for top-performing salespeople, and marketing managers as promotional incentives (ad specialties).

- Organizations and clubs may need recognition products for monthly meetings, acknowledging member service, and related situations.

- Sporting organizations have a regular need for trophies.

Once an understanding exists of who is in the market and what and when they need products, it is relatively easy to target select customer groups. In fact, in many cases it is easier for the specialty retailer to target its market, because customer needs are more apparent than in many other industries.

Other Behavioral Bases

The recognition retailer can use other dimensions to target its market. These include psychographics (personality traits and lifestyles) and benefit segmentation. However, because of the complexity of using these higher-level segmentation techniques, it is recommended that the specialty retailer only consider these approaches once the firm has a thorough understanding of geographic, demographic, and product usage analysis and has successfully implemented the results.

As you can see, there are many alternatives to consider in segmenting specialty retail markets. It is desirable to use various techniques to get the best possible understanding of potential market segments. Next, the most desirable segment or segments can be targeted, and a unique marketing positioning strategy developed to meet the needs of these customer groups.

THE VALUE OF MARKET RESEARCH FOR SPECIALTY RETAILERS

Most recognition and specialty retailers do little or no market research. However, market research and segmentation techniques can reward the small business with some or all of the following riches—new customers, better customers (a segment of the market desired), more satisfied customers (because products offered are responsive to customer needs), increased sales, the identification of potentially profitable opportunities, and improved market share. It is not an overnight process, but through systematically researching and segmenting a market, marketers can be better prepared for attracting and keeping customers in competitive markets, for years to come. Exhibit C5-2 demonstrates how one trophy shop used market research techniques effectively to build a small business.

END-OF-CASE QUESTIONS

1. How should the trophy shop apply market scope factors and geographic market measures to define markets?

2. Based on distance and/or drive time, what is an appropriate primary trade area (PTA) and secondary trade area (STA) for this type of small retailer?

3. How should consumer and business demographics be used to segment this market?

4. Product usage analysis was discussed in detail in the case. How could psychographics, benefits, or other behavioral segmentation dimensions be used by the specialty retailer?

Pete's Trophies is a small retailer located approximately 30 miles south of Miami. The store's most important product lines based on sales are plaques, trophies, ribbons, and pen sets. In starting this business seven years ago, the shop's owners, Peter and Jane Haslam, realized that it was critical for them to understand their market.

To do this required a lot of market research. First, they visited more than 20 trophy and awards retailers in different cities across the United States (a most unusual vacation) to see how others were operating their businesses. A number of these retailers were quite helpful in sharing information. Next, an in-depth investigation into the local area was undertaken. The Haslams learned that there was only one local competitor (a sporting goods store) that farmed out most of its recognition business. Additionally, many local organizations were traveling to Miami to obtain trophies, plaques, and related products. Numerous conversations with large and small businesses, individuals, and community leaders confirmed their hunch that there might be a need for a full-service recognition retailer in the area. Several potential customers provided informal purchase commitments and referral sources for additional business. The final step in assessing the feasibility of this venture was to conduct a market test. The Haslams rented an engraving machine and participated in a local art show. The demand for key chains, initialized jewelry, and luggage tags was very encouraging.

285

Pete's Trophies was now a reality. However, the need for further market research and the development of a strong marketing program was now a major priority. The key to segmenting this market was understanding the needs of the major awards purchasers in their immediate area (they defined their market as customers within a 10-mile radius of their shop). The Haslams had good success marketing their products to four of the largest local organizations (a public utility, the military base, the National Parks Department, and the State Agricultural Center) and to the two largest sporting groups in the area (the Soccer Club and Little League teams).

A comprehensive, yet well-focused marketing strategy was effective in reaching their target markets. This included such promotional strategies as Yellow Pages advertising, billboards, and direct mail. Additionally, new business was generated through the owners' active involvement in the local Chamber of Commerce. Although Pete's Trophies and many of its customers were recently devastated by Hurricane Andrew, its loyal core of satisfied clients and positive image is helping them regain its place in the small business community.

**Note: Some names and events in this example have been changed.

SUGGESTED READINGS

Berman, Barry. "The Changing U.S. Consumer: Implications for Retailing Strategies," *Retail Strategist* (A Semiannual Report for Top Management from KPMG Peat Marwick and the Hofstra University School of Business, No. 1, 1991), pp. 16-23.

Ebel, Richard G. "Specialty Advertising for Small Business," *Management Aids* #4.021 (Fort Worth, Tex.: U.S. Small Business Administration, 1987).

Forseter, Murray. *"The Allure of Specialty Stores,"* Chain Store Age, October 1987, p. 5.

"How Niche Retailing Can Lead to More Market Share," *Stores,* September 1986, pp. 59-60.

Nesbit, Marvin, and Art Weinstein. "How to Size Up Your Customers," *American Demographics,* July 1986, pp. 34-37.

Rauch, Richard A. "Retailing's Dinosaurs: Department Stores and Supermarkets," *Business Horizons,* September-October 1991, pp. 21-25.

Schwarz, Joe. "The Evolution of Retailing," *American Demographics,* December 1986, pp. 30-33, 36-37.

PART FIVE

APPENDIXES OF

RESOURCES

APPENDIX | Major Sources of Demographic/Marketing Information

The following list of key references are helpful for gathering information needed for segmentation studies. The lists are arranged alphabetically under categories. Generally, these sources are readily available for review at your local public or academic library. Recommend that your company purchase publications that marketing staff consult frequently. Also, this list is by no means complete, because research sources can vary considerably by industry and market. It does, however, represent a good starting point—a general reference directory for marketers. The appendix is organized into three parts: consumer demographics, business demographics, and secondary sources.

I. CONSUMER DEMOGRAPHICS

American Demographics. This lively, authoritative monthly magazine is the leading source for demographic information relevant to consumer change and marketing insights. This journal gives you the essential facts, figures, forecasts, and analysis for identifying and segmenting markets. It features articles on age, education, geography, income, lifestyles, subcultures, trends, spending, and timely consumer topics.

CACI's Sourcebooks. CACI Marketing Systems publishes reference books of selected census data, updates, and forecasts for every zip code and county in the United States (*Sourcebook of ZIP Code Demographics* and *Sourcebook of County Demographics*). These desktop guides are easy to use and provide logical and streamlined profiles of 1990 census demographics; they are also available on CD-ROM. *The ZIP Code Mapbook of Metropolitan Areas* displays 320 maps in an 11" x 17" format.

Census of Population and Housing 1990. This resource offers detailed data on the U.S. population for predefined geographical areas. Census content includes basic population and housing items, as well as social and economic characteristics. Many specialized reports are available. Census products are disseminated in several forms: printed reports, computer tapes, microfiche, online information systems (CENDATA), CD-ROM, and floppy diskettes. The TIGER mapping system provides a handy complement to 1990 Census products.

County and City Data Book. This source is an all-purpose database for all U.S. counties and large cities (population over 25,000). Statistics on population, housing, race, education, marital status, income, employment, occupation, crime, and economic sectors are provided. Available on CD-ROM.

Editor and Publisher Market Guide. This annual reference combines 1990 census data with updated surveys for U.S. and Canadian markets. Local population, household, income, retail sales, newspaper circulation, and related data (and estimates) are featured.

Rand McNally Commercial Atlas and Marketing Guide. Besides being one of the largest books in print, this annual atlas includes traditional area maps, and data on population, economics, communications, and transportation. Canadian statistics are also included.

Sales and Marketing Management's Special Publications. This monthly magazine aimed at sales and marketing professionals offers reference guides such as *The Survey of Buying Power, Survey of Media Markets,* and *The Sales Manager's Budget Planners.* These publications feature population estimates, household data, age distributions, and retail sales information. *S&MM's* special issues are particularly helpful for evaluating existing or new markets, analyzing sales territories, measuring market potential, and related marketing decisions.

State and Metropolitan Area Data Book. This government publication reports—via tables, charts, and maps—data on U.S. MSAs. The largest part of the reference is arranged by city, and in that section each city is usually divided by suburbs, central city, and MSA. Includes business and government statistics as well as demographics.

Statistical Abstracts. The *U.S. Statistical Abstract* is a logical starting place for many market researchers. This annual reference summarizes and indexes consumer data from the important U.S. government publications. Most states have their own statistical abstracts filled with similar demographic information.

Statistical Handbooks. A series of four targeted publications on *Aging Americans, the American Family, U.S. Hispanics, and Women in America*. In addition to a unique demographic focus for each, these books also address political, social, cultural, and economic issues.

The Numbers News, a monthly newsletter by *American Demographics*, provides market trends and current data releases from government agencies, consumer surveys, and other marketing resources.

Other Good Sources of Consumer Demographics. Business reference librarians were impressed with two new publications from SRDS, the *Lifestyle Market Analyst* and the *Lifestyle ZIP Code Analyst*. Claritas' *National Encyclopedia of Residential Zip Code Demography (REZIDE)*, Donnelley's *Market Profile Analysis*, Woods and Poole's *State Profiles*, and the *Zip Code Sale Information Guide* are also worth consulting.

II. BUSINESS DEMOGRAPHICS

Business Census Reports. These publications consist of the following series of individualized Census reports: *Retail Trade, Wholesale Trade, Services, Construction, Manufacturing, Mineral Industries, and Transportation*. These national or state economic reports provide statistics on different kinds of establishments, sales and employment size, and payroll by designated geographic areas and SIC codes. The business censuses are taken every fifth year in years ending in a two or seven (such as 1992 or 1997). In addition to the basic data collected, a number of special subject reports are included detailing specific industries or market related facts. Now available on CD-ROM.

County Business Patterns. A Census Bureau publication organized by county and prepared on an individual state basis, this important reference provides data by SIC code and major industry group. Among the information provided include the number of establishments, number of employees, number of establishments by employment size, the number of large establishments, and payroll for states and counties.

Through this source, the industrial marketer can readily identify the number of prospects in a market, determine whether the market is dominated by large or small firms, and estimate market share for a given industry and geographic area. Available on CD-ROM.

Dun's Census of American Business. Do you know how large the national market is for your product? Or where to find the greatest concentration of prospects for it? How about where to locate branches, outlets, and service centers? This source can answer these questions and more. Information includes sales volume, employee size, industry classification, SIC code, and other pertinent data.

Other Good Sources of Business Demographics. You might also check *Markets of the U.S. for Business Planners* by Thomas Conroy and *Manufacturing USA,* a Gale publication. Many state and local/county government agencies provide business demographic information. In addition, don't neglect consumer (Donnelley's *Market Profile Analysis*) or secondary sources (such as *The U.S. Industrial Outlook*). These and many other nontraditional sources contain some business demographics, even though that is not their primary purpose.

III. SECONDARY SOURCES

Business Indexes. Some of the major library indexes that you can use to access trade-related articles are *Predicasts F&S, Business Periodicals, Wall Street Journal, New York Times, American Statistical,* Business Index, and Magazine Index. Many of these are now available for use on a computer.

Computerized Databases. The latest and greatest entrant into the research "arena," online databases are becoming more prevalent as a means of finding published information. There are now dozens of useful databases for marketing applications. Examples include Dialog, ABI Inform, Trade and Industry, the Predicasts' series, Nexis/Lexis, and UMI's Newspaper Abstracts. See the Gale *Directory of Databases* for further information.

Directories. Trade directories are one of the best sources for market and customer information. Literally hundreds of specialized directories are available, and they can be of tremendous value to companies seeking marketing information. Some of the most widely used directories include *The Encyclopedia of Associations; National Trade and Professional Associations of the United States; Findex Directory of Market Research Reports, Studies, and Surveys; Thomas Register of American Manufacturers* (available on CD-ROM); *MacRAE's Blue Book; Ward's Business Directory of U.S. Firms;* state industrial directories; and Standard and Poor's and Dun and Bradstreet's directories. Don't know where to look? Consider Gale's *Directory of Directories.* It is an annotated guide to business and industrial directories, professional and scientific rosters, and other lists and guides of all kinds.

Statistical Sources. A variety of useful statistical sources provide descriptive information about markets. Some sources provide statistics only, such as *Predicasts Forecasts.* Other sources, such as *The U.S. Industrial Outlook* and *Standard and Poor's Industry Surveys,* supplement statistical data with important narrative summaries. U.S. Department of Commerce publications are a good source to tap.

Trade Journals. Some of the best sources for market information are trade journals. These industry-specific publications contain a wealth of information, and one or more trade journals typically exist for virtually every major market or industry. To locate trade journals, a variety of sources can be consulted. Some of these include *Ulrich's International Periodicals Directory, Standard Rate and Data Service—Business Publications Rates and Data, Bacon's Publicity Checker, Writer's Market,* and the *Gale Directory of Publications and Broadcast Media.*

Trade Journals (Special Issues). Three of the best sources of trade information that is published infrequently are *Harfax Guide to Industry Special Issues, Special Issues Index by Greenwood Press,* and *Ulrich's Irregular Serials and Annuals.*

APPENDIX B

COMPANIES PROVIDING SEGMENTATION SERVICES

There are hundreds of full-service and specialized marketing research companies and consulting firms offering many types of market segmentation services for all types of businesses and industries. This appendix lists the segmentation services provided by major companies in the field. Two sources of information were used in compiling this reference: direct correspondence with companies and *American Demographic's 1993 Directory of Marketing Information Companies.**

This directory consists of more than 40 companies and is divided into eight sections:

1. Leading U.S. demographic companies

2. Other U.S. demographic companies

3. Canadian demographic companies

4. Geodemographic mapping and products

5. Demographic/mapping software

6. Lifestyle/psychographic analysis

7. Usage segmentation

8. Statistical segmentation services

Most of these firms are well established; others are relative newcomers, quickly building a reputation. Shop around carefully before you decide which company to use in your next segmentation project.

---

*Adapted and reprinted with permission ©*American Demographics*, 1993. Subscription information available from 800/828-1133.

1. LEADING U.S. DEMOGRAPHIC COMPANIES

CACI Marketing Systems

1100 N. Glebe Road
Arlington, VA 22201
800/292-CACI Fax: 703/243-6272

"Discover America" 1990 Census Reports; Demographic Snapshots,
1980-1990 Census Comparison Reports; *Sourcebook of Zip Code
Demographics; Zip Code Mapbook of Metropolitan Areas;* CD-ROM,
diskettes, magnetic tape; ACORN geodemographic system.

Claritas/NPDC

201 North Union Street
Alexandria, VA 22314
800/284-4868 or 703/683-8300

PRIZM lifestyle segmentation; small-area demographic data; COMPASS
PC-based market analysis and mapping system; MAX3D online market
analysis system; LifeP$YCLE life insurance usage segmentation; Market
Audit survey of financial product use.

Donnelley Marketing Information Systems

70 Seaview Avenue,
P.O. Box 10250
Stamford, CT 06904
800/866-2255 Fax: 203/353-7276

1990 and historical census data, current year estimates, and five-year
projections; ClusterPLUS lifestyle system; Demographics On-Call
consumer and business reports; full-color computer plotted maps;
industry directories; other services include geocoding, thematic mapping,
ZIP+4 coding, and mailing lists.

Market Statistics

633 Third Avenue
New York, NY 10017
212/984-2292 Fax: 212/983-1588

Updates demographic, economic, retail trade, and business-to-business
data; PC mapping software packages; DART (Data Analysis and Reporting
Tool); *Demographics USA-County and Zip Code Editions;* publishes *Survey
of Buying Power.*

National Decision Systems/Equifax

539 Encinitas Blvd
Encinitas, CA 92024
800/866-6510 Fax: 619/944-9543

1990 census demographics and geography; demographic updates and projections; Business-Facts marketing database; Micro-Vision Zip+4 system; linkages with MRI, Simmons, NPD/Crest, and other services; free full-color data catalog.

Urban Decision Systems

2040 Armacost Avenue
Los Angeles, CA 90025
800/633-9568 Fax: 310/826-0933

Demographic reports, maps, graphs, publications, and diskettes; more than 40 different reports and custom reports; Zip Code book; MarketBase customized marketing databases; Data and Maps On Call; site location packages; Demographic Reference Guide.

297

2. OTHER U.S. DEMOGRAPHIC COMPANIES

The Burns Group

Box 8834
Red Bank, NJ 07701
908/741-0888
[Demographic consultants]

Center for Continuing Study of the California Economy

610 University Avenue
Palo Alto, CA 94301
415/321-8550
[California population statistics and trends]

Decision Demographics

1875 Connecticut Avenue, NW, Suite 520
Washington, DC 20009
202/462-9400
[Custom demographics]

NPA Data Services

1424 16th Street, NW, Suite 700
Washington DC 20036
202/265-7685
[Historical data and projections, 1967-2020]

TargeTrends Associates, Inc.

71 West Trail
Stamford, CT 06903
203/968-8763
[Geodemographic promotion and household/zip targeting]

TGE Demographics

95 Brown Road, Suite 126,
Cornell Business and Technology Park
Ithica, NY 14850
607/257-2337
[Demographic trends, projections, and mapping software]

Woods & Poole Economics

1794 Columbia Road, NW
Washington, DC 20009
202/332-7111
[Long-range projections for counties and metro areas]

3. CANADIAN DEMOGRAPHIC COMPANIES

Blackburn Marketing Services

1 St. Clair Avenue East, Suite 901
Toronto, Ontario M4T 2V7
416/923-7944
[Full service Canadian demographics]

Canadian Market Analysis Centre

3430 Mansfield Road
Falls Church, VA 22041
703/824-0200
[Canadian demographics for postal codes, site reports and maps, geodemographic database, and custom projects]

Compusearch

330 Front St. W., Suite 1100
Toronto, Ontario MV5 3B7
416/348-9180

[Full range of Canadian demographic and business data, demographic forecasts, CONQUEST/Canada, LIFESTYLES clustering system, and PRIZM-Canada]

4. GEODEMOGRAPHIC MAPPING AND PRODUCTS

AMERICA.dbf

100 Galen Street
Watertown, MA 02172
617/964-1572
[Map sets on CD-ROM, census data, and TIGER file processing]

DataMap, Inc.

7525 Mitchell Road, Suite 300
Eden Prairie, MN 55344-1958
800/533-7742
[Demographics, mapping, and software for market research]

Geographic Data Technology, Inc.

13 Dartmouth College Highway
Lyme, NH 03768-9713
800/331-7881
[Cartographic databases based on 1990 Census geography]

GeoSystems

227 Granite Run Drive, Suite 100
Lancaster, PA 17601
800/637-3006
[Computer mapping and GIS software]

Intelligent Charting, Inc.

600 International Drive
Mt. Olive, NJ 07828
201/691-7000
[Customized maps, reports, and analyses and geocoding]

Urban Science Applications, Inc.

200 Renaissance Center, Suite 1200
Detroit, MI 48243
313/259-1362
[Geodemographic market analysis systems and consulting]

Western Economic Research

8155 Van Nuys Blvd., Suite 100
Panorama City, CA 91402
818/787-6277
[Maps and reports for California and the western states]

5. DEMOGRAPHIC/MAPPING SOFTWARE

ESRI

380 New York Street
Redlands, CA 92373
909/793-2853 ext. 1375
[Desktop geographic exploration system and GIS software]

GEOVISION, Inc.

5680 Peachtree Parkway
Norcross, GA 30092
404/448-8224
[Statistical mapping software]

LPC

4343 Commerce Court, Suite 500
Lisle, IL 60532-3618
708/505-0572
[Geodemographic and lifestyle software and services]

MapInfo

200 Broadway
Troy, NY 12180
800/327-8627
[Desktop mapping software]

Sammamish Data Systems

1813 130th Ave., N.E., Suite 216
Bellevue, Washington 98005
206/867-1485
[Census data integrated software packages, mapping,
TIGER file processing]

Scan/US, Inc.

2040 Armacost Avenue
Los Angeles, CA 90025
310/826-0933
[Software and data products for geographic analysis]

Strategic Mapping, Inc.

3135 Kifer Road
Santa Clara, CA 95051
408/970-9600
[Atlas family of personal computer software systems]

Tetrad Computer Applications

3873 Airport Way, Box 9754
Bellingham, WA 98227-9754
800/663-1334
[PCensus Desktop Demographics (software/database)]

WorldTech Systems, Inc.

21 Altarinda Road
Orinda, CA 94563
510/254-0900
[Desktop mapping software system]

6. LIFESTYLE/PSYCHOGRAPHIC ANALYSIS

ACG Research Solutions

Chromalloy Plaza, Suite 1750
120 South Central
St. Louis, MO 63105
[Attitude and image segmentation studies]

Langer Associates, Inc.

19 West 44th Street, Suite 1601
New York, NY 10036
212/391-0357
[Qualitative studies of marketing and lifestyle issues]

Sorkin-Enenstein Research Service, Inc. (SERS)

500 North Dearborn Street
Chicago, IL 60610
312/828-0702
[Consumer lifestyle segmentation]

SRI International

333 Ravenswood Avenue
Menlo Park, CA 94025
415/859-3882
[VALS 2]

Strategic Directions Group, Inc.

Suite 311, Textile Building
119 N. Fourth Street
Minneapolis, MN 55401
612/341-4244
[Q-Sort psychographics and over-50 market]

Yankelovich, Inc.

8 Wright Street
Westport, CT 06880
203/227-2700
[The Monitor]

7. USAGE SEGMENTATION

Mediamark Research Inc.

708 Third Avenue
New York, NY 10017
212/476-0249
[Custom research and user/nonuser profiles]

Nielsen Marketing Research

Nielsen Plaza
Northbrook, IL 60062
708/498-6300
[The Nielsen Household Panel provides insights on consumer purchase behavior]

Simmons Market Research Bureau

420 Lexington Avenue
New York, NY 10170
212/916-8900
[Information on media habits, lifestyle, and usage and knowledge of more than 4,000 brands in 800+ categories]

8. STATISTICAL SEGMENTATION SERVICES

The Burke Institute

50 E. Rivercenter Blvd.
Covington, KY 41011
800/543-8635 ext. 6135
[Market structure analysis and custom projects]

SDR, Inc.

2251 Perimeter Park Drive
Atlanta, GA 30341
404/451-5096
[Segmentation consulting and software—specialize in multivariate procedures]

APPENDIX   YOUR SEGMENTATION BOOKSHELF

Ambry, Margaret. *Consumer Power: How Americans Spend Their Money*. Ithica, N.Y.: New Strategist Publications, 1991.

Ambry, Margaret. *The Almanac of Consumer Markets: A Demographic Guide to Finding Today's Complex and Hard-to-Reach Customers*. Ithica, N.Y.: American Demographics Press, 1990.

Baker, Sunny, and Baker, Kim. *Market Mapping: How to Use Revolutionary New Software to Find, Analyze, and Keep Customers*. New York: McGraw-Hill, 1993.

Barabba, Vincent P., and Zaltman, Gerald. *Hearing the Voice of the Market: Competitive Advantage Through Creative Use of Market Information*. Cambridge, Mass.: Harvard Business School Press, 1991.

Berrigan, John A., and Finkbeiner, Carol T. *Segmentation Marketing: New Methods for Capturing Business Markets*. New York: HarperCollins, 1992.

Bonoma, Thomas V., and Shapiro, Benson P. *Segmenting the Industrial Market*. Lexington, Mass.: Lexington Books, 1983.

Crispell, Diane (ed.). *The Insider's Guide to Demographic Know-How: How to Find, Analyze, and Use Information About Your Customers*, Third Edition. Ithica, N.Y.: American Demographics Press, 1993.

Day, George S. *Market Driven Strategy: Processes for Creating Value*. New York: The Free Press, 1990.

Francese, Peter F., and Piirto, Rebecca. *Capturing Customers: How to Target the Hottest Markets of the '90s*. Ithica, N.Y.: American Demographics Press, 1990.

Haley, Russell I. *Developing Effective Communications Strategy: A Benefit Segmentation Approach*. New York: Wiley, 1985.

Hughes, Arthur M. *The Complete Database Marketer: Tapping Your Customer Base to Maximize Sales and Increase Profits.* Chicago: Probus Publishing Company, 1991.

Lazer, William. *Handbook of Demographics for Marketing and Advertising: Sources and Trends on the U.S. Consumer.* Lexington, Mass.: Lexington Books, 1987.

Linneman, Robert, and Stanton, John L. *Making Niche Marketing Work: How to Grow Bigger by Acting Smaller.* New York: McGraw-Hill, 1991.

McKenna, Shawn. *The Complete Guide to Regional Marketing.* Homewood, Ill.: Business One Irwin, 1992.

Michman, Ronald D. *Lifestyle Market Segmentation.* New York: Praeger, 1991.

Morgan, Carol M., and Levy, Doran J. *Segmenting the Mature Market: Identifying, Targeting and Reaching America's Diverse, Booming Senior Markets.* Chicago: Probus Publishing Company, 1993.

Niche Marketing: Identifying Opportunity Markets with Syndicated Consumer Research. New York: Mediamark Research, 1988.

Ostroff, Jeff. *Successful Marketing to the 50+ Consumer: How to Capture One of the Biggest & Fastest Growing Markets in America.* Englewood Cliffs, N.J.: Prentice Hall, 1989.

Piirto, Rebecca. *Beyond Mind Games: The Marketing Power of Psychographics.* Ithica, N.Y.: American Demographics Press, 1991.

Pinson, Linda, and Jinnett, Jerry. *Researching and Reaching Your Target Market.* Fullerton, Calif.: Out of Your Mind . . . and Into the Marketplace, 1988.

Popcorn, Faith. *The Popcorn Report.* New York: Doubleday, 1991.

Ries, Al, and Trout, Jack. *Marketing Warfare.* New York: McGraw-Hill, 1986.

Scotton, Donald W., and Zallocco, Ronald L., editors. *Readings in Market Segmentation.* Chicago: American Marketing Association, 1980.

Settle, Robert B., and Alreck, Pamela L. *Why They Buy: American Consumers Inside and Out.* New York: John Wiley & Sons, 1986.

Struhl, Steven M. *Market Segmentation: An Introduction and Review.* Chicago: American Marketing Association, 1992.

Swenson, Chester A. *Selling to a Segmented Market: The Lifestyle Approach.* New York: Quorum Books, 1990.

Vavra, Terry G. *After-Marketing: How to Keep Customers for Life Through Relationship Marketing.* Homewood, Ill.: Business One Irwin, 1992.

von Hippel, Eric. *The Sources of Innovation.* New York: Oxford University Press, 1988.

Weiss, Michael J. *The Clustering of America: A Vivid Portrait of the Nation's 40 Neighborhood Types—Their Values, Lifestyles, and Eccentricities.* New York: Tilden Press, 1988.

Zandl, Irma, and Leonard, Richard. *Targeting the Trendsetting Consumer: How to Market Your Product or Service to Influential Buyers.* Homewood, Ill.: Business One Irwin, 1992.

SUBJECT INDEX